# Walk the Lines

Born in the Midlands in 1971, Mark Mason moved to London when he was 20. Over the next 13 years he sold Christmas cards in Harrods, made radio programmes for the BBC and busked outside Eric Clapton gigs at the Royal Albert Hall. He also published three novels, several books of non-fiction, and wrote for publications as diverse as *The Spectator* and *FourFourTwo*. He continues to do some of these things, though has now defected to Suffolk, where he lives with his partner and son.

Praise for *Walk the Lines*

Mark Mason

# WALK
# THE LINES

To Veronica,
Best wishes,
Mark Mason

arrow books

Published by Arrow Books 2013

4 6 8 10 9 7 5

First published in Great Britain in 2011 by Random House Books
Random House, 20 Vauxhall Bridge Road,
London SW1V 2SA

www.randomhouse.co.uk

Addresses for companies within The Random House Group Limited can be
found at: www.randomhouse.co.uk/offices.htm

The Random House Group Limited Reg. No. 954009

A CIP catalogue record for this book
is available from the British Library

ISBN 9780099557937

Typeset by Palimpsest Book Production Ltd, Falkirk, Stirlingshire

Penguin Random House is committed to a sustainable future for
our business, our readers and our planet. This book is made from
Forest Stewardship Council® certified paper.

Printed and bound in Great Britain by Clays Ltd, St Ives plc

For Barney

# Contents

# Introduction

It seems almost ungrateful. An entire Tube network, waiting patiently and obediently for the chance to serve, for the honour of whisking me speedily off to any part of London my heart desires – and I'm shunning it. I'm insisting on going by foot. The whole way. Every one of the 11 lines, all 269 stations, God knows how many miles. In fact, forget 'ungrateful': it's positively perverse.

But the Tube needn't feel slighted. It's because of the Tube that the idea occurred to me in the first place. Without its multi-coloured tendrils spreading eagerly over the map, London would still be defying me. For years I've dreamed of the ultimate walk, the one that would comprehensively capture the capital. It's commonly agreed that Shanks's Pony is the vehicle of choice for anyone seeking to truly understand any great city, be it London, Paris, New York, wherever. (This is one of the reasons Los Angeles can never really be called a city: you have to drive everywhere.) But once you've lived in London for any length of time – it was my home for 13 years – you're kind of walked out. Not in the sense that you've done enough of it. The opposite, in fact: you can't *get* enough of it.

When you first move to London, necessity acts as your sat-nav. You walk to flat viewings, to job interviews, and then, with any luck, to your job. You walk to the shops, to the cinema, to parties. You walk purely to learn the city's layout. It becomes a habit. But like any habit it can gain the upper hand, start to control you rather than you controlling it. At some point (it may take years) you realise you're an addict. Simple, honest right-into-Haymarket-left-into-Jermyn-Street isn't enough any more. You need the hard stuff. You need your Sackville Street (the longest London street without any turnings off it), your Knightsbridge (only street name with six consecutive consonants), your Haunch of Venison Yard (just a great name, though making the pilgrimage is particularly hardcore as it doesn't lead anywhere). A fascination with London powers not just your imagination but also your feet. The mind bone's connected to the heel bone.

Once you've caught the bug, you feel an urge to plan your walks, be it thematically, geographically or by some other means. There must be a *raison d'être* to your ramble. The first time I did it was one summer's day about ten years ago, when I happened to remember a house in East Finchley where a friend of a friend had put me up once. It was only for a couple of weeks, between leaving one flatshare and finding another. No sooner had the memory appeared than a mental triangle formed, linking the two flats with the house. As the flats were in Wapping and Kentish Town it was a very bizarre triangle, with two ultra-acute angles and one monstrously obtuse one, but no matter. I looked out of the window. Nice weather. Itchy feet. It was screaming out to be done: walk the triangle.

Even before my shoes were on, the plan had expanded. Obviously I should walk to the East Finchley starting point (I then lived in Marylebone). And if those three places could be linked, the first of my London abodes, then why not all the others? There'd been nine in total, which the more geometrically savvy of you will realise resulted in me walking a nonagon, beginning and ending at my flat. As most of the abodes were scattered across the Islington–King's Cross area it was a nonagon that made the triangle look normal, a shape resembling a collapsed wedding marquee with only one pole left standing and several guests still seated at their tables.

Other walks followed: the route of the London Marathon; Lord's to the Oval; the boundary of the Congestion Charge Zone. Each time, needless to say, my partner's response was the same, and consisted of just one word: '*Why?*' It's the sort of attitude that always has men turning wearily to their friends, emitting a fatalistic sigh and saying, 'They just don't get it, do they?' Yet I can see Jo's point, which is that my walks don't *have* a point. Not one that's immediately obvious, anyway. There's always the 'because it's there' argument. But the route between Kettering's eight largest newsagents is there, and I don't want to walk that. No offence to Kettering, but I'm sure even its most vigorous defender will admit it's no London.

So that's the answer, isn't it? Not 'because it's there' but 'because it's London'. Samuel Johnson called the city 'the school for studying life'.[1] He's certainly right, but I think there's something else fuelling the need to walk it (a need I still regularly indulge even though home is now a village in Suffolk). It's not just about studying, about observing or noting. It's about owning. About claiming the city's greatness, or at least some small part of it, for yourself. That's why there has to be an order to the walk, some logic, a set of rules. It's almost as though those rules are a religious service, and by following them you achieve a bond with London.

It follows, therefore, that the more extreme the rules, the stronger the bond. There's an obvious conclusion to this, which is to take 'extreme' to the extreme, and walk every street in London. That's what a character in Geoff Nicholson's novel *Bleeding London* does. It appeals to the completist in me, but there are two problems. The first is the practical one mentioned by the character himself: it takes so bloody long. Several years, in fact, doing nothing else for seven days a week. Even if you could spare the time, though, there'd still be the other problem: it's *too* complete. There's no method to it, no construction, no art. Walking every one of London's streets would be like reading a whole dictionary but never forming a sentence. It would be the trainspotter definition of 'complete', like those Bob Dylan fans who write out all the lyrics to every one of his songs in the belief that it counts as some sort of achievement.

But if 'all of London' doesn't count as 'all of London', then what does? For years I sought the answer, dreamed of

---

1. You were afraid that was going to be a different quote, weren't you? Don't worry. When a man is tired of hearing that when a man is tired of London he's tired of life, it's entirely understandable.

some magical formula that would square the circle: a walk that took in the whole city, but without taking in the whole city. Surely there had to be a sequence, an equation, some sort of document that, were I only to follow it, would allow me to say 'London, you are mine'.

It would be nice, having mentioned the phrase 'square the circle', to tell you that it happened on the Circle Line. But actually it was the Bakerloo. Specifically, the bit between Embankment and Charing Cross. There I sat, gazing up at the line map opposite, and remembered a claim I'd recently heard: that the shortest distance between any two stations on the whole Tube network is not, as most websites and books will tell you, that between Covent Garden and Leicester Square, but the brief hop my train was doing now. As it turns out this is mistaken; distance between station entrances above ground doesn't, of course, equate to distance below ground. But still, let's say that Embankment to Charing Cross is 300 yards: if you were to make the journey on a standard Zone 1 single ticket, it would cost you the equivalent of £23 per mile. Not even the most money-grabbing usurer would expect any return business at those prices, which is why London Underground have taken to erecting signs at many stations in the centre of town indicating the pedestrian route to other nearby stations. For a lot of journeys it's not only cheaper but also simpler and quicker to walk.

Quite right too, I thought. Might help with a few waistlines. That American family I'd just spotted at Waterloo, for instance. Then I caught sight of my reflection in the carriage window. OK, I'm no Mr Creosote, but which of us couldn't do with shedding a few pounds? Why hadn't I walked today's journey? Waterloo to Baker Street wouldn't have done me any harm in the trimness department.

By now my gaze had switched to the Tube map itself, the small one they display in carriages, depicting Zone 1 and a bit of Zone 2. I traced the Bakerloo Line as far as it went (Kilburn Park), and imagined walking it. Then I imagined the rest of the line, up to . . . Harrow and Wealdstone, wasn't it? At this point something fantastical happened: my mind drew in the rest of the map, each line snaking out from its central section like flowers shot in time-lapse. And there it was, the solution to my problem: walk the Tube system. Overground.

In the very instant the idea occurred, I heard two distinct sounds. The first was of my own footsteps rhythmically pounding the streets (and roads, and lanes, and alleys . . .). The second was the faint but unmistakable sound of Jo asking, '*Why?*' I already knew why. This was my way of covering the city. This was my route into, and out of, and over and through, London. It was geographically exhaustive, but in a very ordered, very logical way. The idea was – and I feel a little stupid using this word, but only a little – beautiful.

The Tube does this to people. It has achieved a special place in London's collective imagination. Originally a servant to the city, it has in some respects become its master. Rather than time-lapse flowers, in fact, the plant the system most closely resembles is ivy, gradually establishing a stranglehold over a stately home. Where once the Tube was a mere mode of transport, it now dictates not just property prices but also where that property gets built in the first place, *and* how that property is viewed: flatshare adverts boast their location in Zone 2 rather than Zone 3. London has put the Tube train before the horse; so much so that the Underground gets referenced in all sorts of weird contexts. Cricket commentators talk of a batsman's near-miss as 'playing down the Metropolitan when the ball went down the Jubilee'. Meanwhile, at the other end of the latter line, a health study illustrated lower life expectancy in the east of the capital by saying that if you travelled from Westminster to Canning Town, you lost approximately one year per stop.

The system is also the inspiration for at least two other challenges, though unlike mine these involve actually using the Tube as a means of transport. There's visiting all the stations in one day (current world record: 16 hours, 44 minutes and 16 seconds), while in the Circle Line pub crawl – often now done for charity – you have to exit at each of the 27 stations and have a drink at the nearest pub. This is based on the old – some of us would say 'proper' – Circle Line, namely the one that actually formed a circle. None of this 'lasso-like extension out to Hammersmith' nonsense.

Having said that, what makes the pub crawl especially satisfying is that the old line wasn't a perfect circle after all. Look at the map and you'll see it narrows at the eastern end, forming the shape of (oh, the elegance of it) a beer bottle on its side. And herein lies one of the reasons I found the 'walk the lines' idea so beautiful: it would involve a map. In fact, given that I'd need an *A to Z* to find the shortest routes between all the stations, it would involve two maps. It would involve – and even writing the words now produces a frisson of a tingle – *cross-referencing between maps*.

At Baker Street station I paused on my way out and examined the full-sized Tube map in the ticket hall. A thing of beauty in itself, and like any thing of beauty a source of inspiration. 'Putting yourself on the map' might be an obvious joke here, but that's what it's all about. Even respectable cartographers do it: look at the Ordnance Survey map of the Isle of Wight, just above the village of Blackgang, and you'll see that the artist has subtly included his own name (Bill) in the short marks denoting the cliffs. Walking the lines – all of them, every last inch of the way – would be my own method of putting myself on the map.

Besides this, of course, the journey would be a structure on which to hang my education about London, both its history and its present. There are bits I know, but lots more I don't. Sherlock Holmes may have said 'it is a hobby of mine to have an exact knowledge of London', but his namesake and contemporary[2] Oliver Wendell Holmes knew better, pointing out that 'no person can be said to know London. The most that anyone can claim is that he knows something of it.' Fulham, for example. I've never got to grips with Fulham. Been there a handful of times, but beyond a vague sense that it's just past Chelsea and was once Hugh Grant territory, I know, as the Spanish waiter used to say, nothing.

After a while, it seems to me, every Londoner – whether

---

2. Possibly even relation. What, you don't believe a fictional character could be related to a real one? I refer you to *On Her Majesty's Secret Service*, in which we learn that James Bond might have been descended from Sir Thomas Bond, after whom the famous London street is named.

born in the city or not – hardens in their partiality. You get to know the area you live in, and you still feel comfortable in the areas you *used* to live in, but there are huge chunks of the place you never go to, indeed never want to go to. Something quite parochial appears in you. It always reminds me of the Rabbi Lionel Blue joke about the Jewish guy marooned on a desert island for several years. His rescuers find that he's built two synagogues. 'We can understand you building one,' they say. 'But why did you need a second?' 'Simple,' he replies. 'That's the synagogue I go to. And that's the synagogue I don't go to.' Every Londoner, or one-time Londoner, needs parts of the city they don't feel comfortable in, almost as though that gives greater validity to the areas where they do feel at home. As I stood there in Baker Street station, I looked forward to challenging that instinct in myself. Like Sherlock just up the road, I was going to learn at least something about *every* part of the capital.

What's more, as I looked at the ends of the lines and saw suburban names like 'Amersham' and 'Epping', I remembered that the London Underground extends way beyond what any normal person – that is, anyone other than a local government planner – would reasonably define as London. This would be another question that the project could help resolve: what exactly *is* London? In my more fundamentalist moments I define the city as the City, arguing that anywhere outside the old Roman wall is an imposter. Other equally arbitrary definitions float in and out of favour: the area bordered by the mainline railway stations (Victoria, Liverpool Street, Euston and so on) . . . the 0207 telephone code area . . . a six-mile radius around Charing Cross (the area London cabbies learn for the Knowledge). A century ago Ford Madox Ford observed that 'London begins where tree trunks commence to be black'. What's the answer now?

As I stepped out onto Baker Street I knew I'd found my task. This would be my very own urban odyssey, my horizontal Everest. Eleven lines, one by one.[3] In each case I'd walk from one end to the other, station by station, travelling into the heart of the greatest city in the world, then back out again. Not that this was about finding London's heart. Or not just about that, anyway. This was about finding its soul.

Preparations for something like this are pretty minimal. A Tube map, an *A to Z*, some other maps to cover the bits the *A to Z* doesn't . . . and that's about it. Oh, and some proper footwear. The most comfortable my feet had ever been was while training for a marathon several years back, so I decided to go for the same make of trainers, ASICS.[4]

And so there I was. Have maps, have shoes, will travel. I was going to do it. I was going to walk the lines.

---

3. None of this London Overground or DLR nonsense: they're not part of the Tube. The purist in me even resents their presence on the map. Though the realist knows we can't expect tourists to be psychic.

4. Which, I discovered while being fitted, stands for 'Anima Sana In Corpore Sano', a variation on the Latin phrase meaning 'a healthy mind in a healthy body'. The project was educational before it had even begun.

# I

# Victoria Line

## Drawing a bead

Brixton Tube station, 11.30 on a Wednesday morning. The end of the line. Or, as far as my feet are concerned, the start of it.

There are a number of reasons for choosing the Victoria Line as my maiden voyage. At 13 miles it's a decent length (the Waterloo and City is a mere 1.5 – don't know how it's got the cheek to call itself a line at all), but walkable in a day, so it can act as a sighter, allow me to draw a bead on the beast that is the London Underground. All but one of its stations connect with other Tube lines or mainline services, giving that feeling of linkage, of tying up London, that's at the heart of the project. And while it starts in a place I know relatively well (Jo used to live in Brixton), it ends in Tottenham and Walthamstow, places I barely know at all, making this literally a journey into the unknown. One of the few things I do know about Walthamstow is that it nearly gave part of its name to the line. Hoping to ape the success of 'Bakerloo' (Baker Street to Waterloo), Tube bosses toyed with 'Walvic' (Walthamstow to Victoria) as well as 'Viking' (Victoria to King's Cross) before plumping, rather boringly you have to say, for what must surely be the commonest place name in the world.[1]

Having said I know Brixton, I'm surprised to find that in the few years since I've been here it's changed noticeably. At least the bit outside the station has. A wise man once commented that no one ever arranged to meet anyone outside Brixton station twice. An entrance *that* narrow trying to cope with *that* many passengers, with several bus stops *that* nearby, made the arrival of each train look like an emergency evacuation. But not only has the entrance now been widened, the area around it has also lost the air of intimidation that used to hang over it, even at this time on a weekday morning. The phone box-like 'iPlus Point', which would surely once have been a vandal magnet, works perfectly. The touch-screen options include 'Local History', where you learn about race riots and 'Guns of Brixton' by The Clash. 'Since then,' the text adds quickly, 'things have got calmer.' And you know what? It really feels like they have.

The air of relaxed tolerance threatens to spill over into cliché, however, when a Frenchman and his boyfriend emerge from the Tube and start unpacking their folding bicycles, so I decide to start walking. But for a moment or two the feet won't obey. This puzzles me, until I realise what's going on. The journey of a thousand miles, we're

---

1. No such timidity for the creators of *EastEnders*: inhabitants of Walthamstow and Stratford, they combined the two to make Walford.

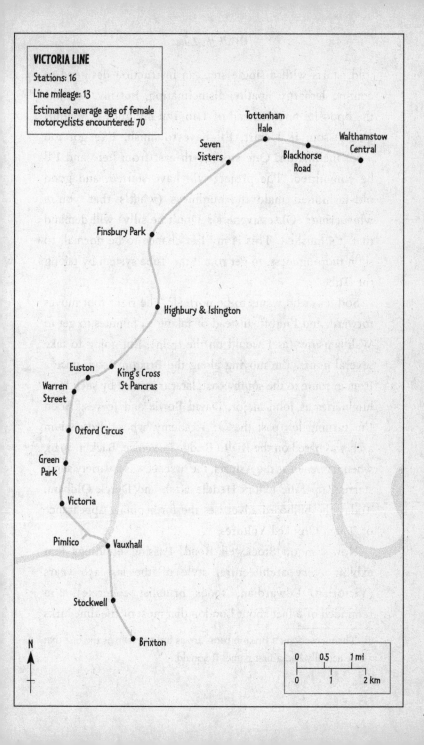

**VICTORIA LINE**

Stations: 16

Line mileage: 13

Estimated average age of female
motorcyclists encountered: 70

Tottenham
Hale

Seven
Sisters

Walthamstow
Central

Blackhorse
Road

Finsbury Park

Highbury & Islington

Euston

King's Cross
St Pancras

Warren
Street

Oxford Circus

Green
Park

Victoria

Pimlico

Vauxhall

Stockwell

Brixton

N

| 0 | 0.5 | 1 mi |
| 0 | 1 | 2 km |

told, starts with a single step, an instruction designed to counter lethargy, apathy, disinclination. But my worry is the opposite one. Instead of Lao Tzu my guru is Magnus Magnusson: if I start, I'll have to finish. I've got too *much* inclination. One step north-east from here and I'll be committed. The project will have started, and good old-fashioned male thoroughness (what's that you're whispering? 'Obsessiveness'? Don't be silly) will demand that it's finished. This is my last chance to be normal, to shun thoroughness, to get round the Tube system by taking the Tube.

Sod it – who wants to be normal? The right foot moves forward, and I'm off. Instead of taking 34 minutes to get to Walthamstow (as I would on the train), I'm going to take several hours. I'm moving along the Brixton Road, once a Roman route to the south coast, later traversed by such local luminaries as John Major, David Bowie and Jeeves.[2] Soon I'm turning left past the O2 Academy, whose proscenium arch was based on the Rialto Bridge in Venice. Back in 1929, when it opened as the Astoria, the first act was a variety show starring operatic tenors Heddle Nash and Derek Oldham. Today the billboard advertises the forthcoming appearance of Them Crooked Vultures.

Now I'm on Stockwell Road. Passing buildings that exhibit every architectural style of the last 150 years (Victorian, Edwardian, 1960s brutalist concrete), I'm reminded of a fact about London that most of the time lurks

---

2. The manservant's Brixton roots are as little-known as the fact that he actually had a first name: Reginald.

dimly in the depths of your consciousness without ever really surfacing. Namely that the city isn't a city, it's a collection of villages. Go back further than those 150 years and you'd find a place called Brixton and a place called Stockwell, with this road linking them. It's hard to believe as you walk past a shop selling T-shirts saying 'American Gangster' and 'Got Swagger Like Me?', but all this really was once fields. Brixton Windmill still stands a mile or so south of here, physical proof that the landscape was open enough to let the sails turn. Then along came the railways, and suburban expansion, and all the new houses blocked the wind. As if to really rub the mill's nose in it, Brixton became home to the first UK street lit by electricity, which in 1880 adopted the name that Eddy Grant made famous a century later: Electric Avenue. The windmill gets the last laugh, though: it's soon to reopen, powered by electricity.

The blackboard outside Brixton Cycles informs the world that Albert Einstein thought of the theory of relativity while riding his bike. Further along towards Stockwell appear the restaurants that have given this area the nickname 'Little Portugal'. The Portuguese population here is the largest outside the mother country, though today's *sardinhas assadas* are being consumed a little sombrely, owing to last night's exit from the World Cup. (This would have been bad enough in itself – but at the hands of *Spain?*) Soon I'm approaching Stockwell Tube station itself. 'Two down,' says a voice in my head. 'Two hundred and sixty-seven to go.' Then I realise this would be true only if I were visiting each station just the once. But many are served by several lines. Stockwell itself, for instance, will be revisited on my Northern Line walk. I tell the voice in my head to shut up.[3]

Nipping into the ticket hall, I look for the plaque marking Stockwell's place in Underground history, namely that it was one end of the first-ever Tube line. 'What?!' you shriek, preparing to hurl this book into the nearest waste receptacle. 'Everyone knows that the first line was between Paddington and Farringdon Steet in 1863!' Well, yes, that was the first line. But lots of it was overground, with only 'cut and cover' tunnels giving it a subterranean veneer (if indeed a veneer can go under something). The first proper 'tube' railway – i.e. with no surface disruption, cut completely underground, à la *Great Escape* – was the City and South London Railway, opened in 1890. The sign marking the centenary of this date isn't, however, immediately apparent.

'Do you know where the plaque is?' I ask the guard at the ticket barrier.

'Eh?'

Maybe my assumption that Stockwell had only a limited role in Tube history was mistaken. Maybe there are dozens of plaques – albeit very well-hidden ones – and the guard needs more specific instructions. 'The one about this being

---

3. The exact number of stations depends on which source you consult. Some count the two Edgware Roads as one, and indeed the two Hammersmiths. Some even arrive at 270 by separating the two Paddingtons (they're at opposite ends of the mainline station). I'm saying 269 because to my mind the Edgware Roads and Hammersmiths are distinct in a way that the Paddingtons aren't.

on the first Tube line. The first proper Tube line, I mean.'

A blank look, a shake of the head. He works here for a living and he doesn't know it was part of the first-ever proper Tube line.

'It was in the 1800s,' I explain. 'Stockwell was one end of the line. The other was somewhere up in the City, I think.'

Another shake. 'Sorry, sir. No idea.'

'Oh, well, not to worry.' I'm turning to leave when I notice the plaque. It's directly behind the guard, about two feet above the spot where he stands day in, day out. To give him his due, once it's pointed out he does actually show some interest. Together we read that the City and South London Railway went up through Kennington and Borough, finishing at King William Street (very handy for the Bank of England). It formed the basis of what was to become the Northern Line, but we shouldn't hold that against it.

As I step back out into the sunshine, I think of the Victoria Line drivers far beneath me. (The line's depth varies between 65 and 85 feet.) Opened in the late 1960s, the Victoria was the first line to employ the Automatic Train Operation system, whereby the train, reading coded signals transmitted through the track, drives itself. Another innovation was the hump-backed design of the line's stations. These allow the trains to store gravitational energy as they pull in, then release it as they pull out, making their operation quicker and more efficient. Today, as I think of those trains, and their role in inspiring my steps across London, they seem like diffident sherpas, willing to show me the way but only if they themselves stay hidden.

Over the road to Stockwell Memorial Park, a modest triangle whose capacity to deliver peace is compromised somewhat by the several lanes of Clapham Road and South Lambeth Road traffic thundering past. Nonetheless a brightly painted mural does what it can to lift the spirits by depicting people with local connections. There's Vincent van Gogh, who lived for a year in nearby Hackford Road. There's the 'taking aim' image used in the opening credits of every Bond film, in tribute to the actor born in what he calls 'Saint Ockwell', Roger Moore. There's Violette Szabo, who went over to France during the Second World War to act as a secret agent and bomb Nazi bridges. Executed by the Germans in 1945, she became the first woman ever to earn the George Cross. The mural originally showed her with a pistol pointing at her head, which even in Stockwell was seen as insensitive, so it was repainted. The latest addition to the mural would have raised the pistol's cringe-factor even further: it's of Jean Charles de Menezes, controversially shot at Stockwell station in 2005. Perhaps in future years two other local residents might find their way on to the brickwork: Will Self, whom you might expect, given the area's boho-grunge coolness, and Joanna Lumley, whom perhaps you wouldn't. She lives in Albert Square (the real one, though wouldn't it be good to see her in Walford's?), and according to one local blogger is often to be seen buying cat food in the Nine Elms Sainsbury's.[4]

From here my trek continues up South Lambeth Road. The streetscape is still messy, an architectural pick 'n' mix that

---

4. One of the capital's few remaining retail apostrophes. Harrods stopped using theirs in 1921, Selfridges in 1940.

reminds you of the shelf in a second-hand bookshop where they put all the random, dusty old books that don't fit anywhere else, but once again London's rural past is hidden just beneath the surface. Tradescant Road, on the right, marks the site of the noted botanical garden lovingly constructed by the seventeeth-century naturalist (and gardener to Charles I) John Tradescant. The street itself is pretty inoffensive, and to claim that no attractive patch of greenery should ever be developed would be to reject the existence of cities at all. But still, marking Tradescant's achievement by sticking a road over it and giving that road his name reminds me eerily of the line from *Jeffrey Bernard is Unwell*: 'My father designed the entrance to the Strand Palace Hotel, which was so brilliant it's now in the Victoria and Albert Museum. In any other country it would still be outside the Strand Palace Hotel.'

Stockwell is fading now, morphing into the area that gives its name to the third station on the Victoria Line. That name originated with Falkes de Breauté, a thirteenth-century sidekick of King John, to whom the monarch awarded the Manorship of Luton. Falkes later increased his property portfolio, by marriage this time, when he gained the rights to an area just south of the Thames. With the sort of disregard for spelling you only got in the Middle Ages he built Faulke's Hall, which became Vauxhall. Six hundred years later the Vauxhall Motor Company started here (on the site where Ms Lumley now buys her cat food), and to this day Vauxhall cars bear de Breauté's griffin as their emblem. By 1905 the company had become so successful that it had to move out of London. The site of its new premises? Luton. The griffin had flown back home.

Vauxhall as a name travelled even further, though only by mistake. A Russian delegation visiting London in 1840 to learn about the city's successful new railways (those were the days) were shown the London and South Western Railway's terminus at Vauxhall. Believing the name to be the general word for that sort of building they copied it, which is why the Russian word for a train station is 'вокзал', pronounced 'vokzal'. Nowadays Vauxhall station is hemmed in on every side by major roads, making the going for pedestrians round here cumbersome-to-suicidal. Most people hop straight on a Tube, or take a bus from the state-of-the-art station next door, powered by photoelectric cells on two huge ramps leading pointlessly into the sky. The last time this many double-deckers stood beneath ramps this big, Evil Knievel was involved.

On the other side of the railway arches from the bus station stands the pleasant(ish) park known as Spring Gardens, in tribute to an early title for the attraction that for 200 years defined this area: Vauxhall Pleasure Gardens. Dating from the 1660s, this 12-acre site became *the* place to come in order to commune with nature and be fed and entertained, a sort of Center Parcs of its day. Some of the music played there was composed by Handel, who since 1712 had lived in London, and of whom there was a statue in the gardens during his lifetime.[5]

In 1837 the gardens received some unfortunate publicity

---

5.  An even greater honour was Handel's burial in Westminster Abbey, though the fact that he himself requested this in his will does take some of the shine off.

when they were the launch site for the first-ever fatal parachute jump. Hot-air balloon displays had long been held here, but on this occasion the basket contained one Robert Cocking. You'd think with a name like that he'd have tried to lead as quiet a life as possible, but no, Mr C. decided that the successful parachute jumps already made by other people hadn't been successful enough. He wanted to prove the superiority of his new 'improved' design, so after taking off from Vauxhall and rising to 5,000 feet he jumped out somewhere over Lee, between Lewisham and Blackheath. Whatever his improvements were, they didn't stop him arriving at Burnt Ash Farm somewhat sooner than he'd expected, and in the afterlife a very short time later.

My route now lies across Vauxhall Bridge. But before leaving South London I pause, and realise that the bridge itself, with the train station next to it, is bringing the whole of my walk so far into focus. It was the bridge's arrival in 1816 that opened up the whole of this area, turning Vauxhall and Stockwell and Brixton from settlements in their own right to parts of this ever-expanding thing called 'London'. Even though the bridge was tolled – a penny for pedestrians, 6d for a score of cattle – nothing could put the brakes on suburban sprawl once the railways arrived, and Vauxhall Bridge became the first to carry a tram over the Thames. This section of the Victoria Line wouldn't open until 1971 (the rest predating it by a couple of years), but nevertheless, as I stand here now, contemplating the lead that the line is giving me, things are starting to make sense.

\*　\*　\*

It just says 'Government Offices' in the *A to Z*. A small blue square nestling against the south-east corner of the bridge, as though it was an outpost of the Department of Paperclips. But we all know exactly whose offices these are: MI6. It's hard to see why the *A to Z* is so coy; the Intelligence Service even advertises jobs in *The Times* now. The head of the service is still called 'C', in tribute to the first incumbent, Mansfield Cumming, whose Christian name gave Ian Fleming the 'M' for his fictional equivalent. Though when the producers of *Die Another Day* tried filming the building – reputedly as deep below ground as it is high above – they were banned. Eventually Foreign Secretary Robin Cook relented, saying that 'after all Bond has done for Britain, it was the least we could do for Bond'.[6]

Looking back from halfway over the bridge, what holds my attention today isn't the razor wire or the security cameras, but a gated arch just below the building, from which a tiny trickle of water emerges and runs down the shingle and sand into the Thames. This is one of London's *other* rivers, the underground minnows that make their way unobtrusively through the suburbs in order to feed their more famous cousin. The Effra, in this case, which has followed me from Brixton. On the north bank, just west of the bridge, you can see the outfall of the Tyburn. Further down the river's south bank, towards Westminster, is Alembic House, whose penthouse flat is owned by Jeffrey Archer – who, when you

---

6. In the film the headquarters has its own Tube stop, Vauxhall Cross, supposedly a disused stop on the Piccadilly Line. Which in reality, and like many London cabbies, never comes south of the river.

ask for directions to the bathroom, reportedly says, 'Past the Picasso and left at the Matisse,' as if that will make you like him.

Once over the bridge I'm into Pimlico, which even though it was on the 'correct' side of the river remained undeveloped until the early nineteenth century because the land was so marshy. Even when the buildings did go up the area remained unfashionable, and when the goodly Reverend Gerard Olivier moved here in 1912 it was to convert the residents of the 'slums'. Things were different by 1989, both for Pimlico and the vicar's son Laurence, whose ashes were that year interred in Poets' Corner just up the road at Westminster Abbey.

Bessborough Street curves round to reveal Pimlico station, the fourth of my walk, and the only one on the line not to connect with other Underground or mainline services. Knowing this makes me feel sorry for it, but I wipe away my tears and carry on towards the area's grandest square, St George's. At the far end of the square, in Pimlico Gardens, is a statue of William Huskisson MP, who would no doubt like to be remembered for his stunning parliamentary oratory, but is actually famous as the first person in Britain ever to be killed by a train, when George Stephenson's *Rocket* hit him on the opening day of the Liverpool to Manchester railway in 1830.

Virtually every one of Belgrave Road's white stucco mansions is now a backpacker-level hotel. The slightly grubby feel is heightened by the phone boxes full of tarts' cards. British Telecom's struggle to rid their London street furniture of these adverts has been going on for almost as long as superpowers have been trying to conquer Afghanistan, and with similar degrees of success. The cards reappear as quickly as they're removed; one even tries to cash in on World Cup and Wimbledon fever with 'Match Fit? Let's play *my* game!' I notice that all of these small business ventures use mobile rather than landline numbers. That must *really* wind BT up.

Past the Passport Office, outside which groups of people wait in the glazed hopelessness known only to those who are about to deal with a British civil servant, and then I'm bearing down on the back entrance of the transport hub that combines trains, coaches, buses and Tubes in one almighty temple to Travel known simply as Victoria. The teeming mass of humanity sucks you in like a spider too near the plughole in an emptying bath, and before you know it you're heading through the retail mall towards the main concourse. From here you can access the busiest Underground station on the network.[7] Of course that's not on my agenda today, but I do allow myself a small detour over to platform 8. If you ever want a sense of peace at Victoria, this is the place to come. Not because it's especially quiet, but rather because a plaque at the ticket barrier commemorates the arrival of the station's most famous (though nameless) visitor. At 8.32 p.m. on 10 November 1920, this was the end of the journey from Dover for the train carrying the Unknown Warrior.

Outside, on the pedestrian island between Vauxhall Bridge Road and Victoria Street, stands Little Ben, a replica of the famous clock tower just down the road. The thing is 30 feet

---

7. Around 80 million passengers each year. I'll have to wait until the Central Line for the least busy station.

tall and I've walked past it hundreds of times; yet only in my advance reading for today's walk did I learn of its existence. Gazing up at its hands I feel guilty for what I said about the guard at Stockwell.

We're now in the land where phone numbers begin 0207 222, the prefix dating from the days when telephone dials bore letters on each digit. The inspiration for Westminster's code was 'ABBey'. Working my way round to Lower Grosvenor Place, I find myself outside the Queen's garden wall, looking along it to the junction where the road becomes Hobart Place. It was here, in 1823, that London saw its last-ever burial of a suicide at a crossroads. This was how they punished you back then if you took the ultimate decision.[8]

Heading along the wall the other way brings me to the Royal Mews shop, part of the programme whereby the Firm are opening up their most famous home. The souvenirs are as obvious as you'd expect – teddy bears, tea towels, DVDs – though occasionally a touch of subtlety is allowed, for instance the girls' pink T-shirts saying nothing but 'Pussy cat, pussy cat, where have you been?' The textbook about British monarchs is refreshingly modern in its openness, even going so far as to mention that Edward I 'preferred the Queen's brother to the Queen'.

---

8. Had the *Daily Mail* been around they'd no doubt have cited the lack of repeat offending, though this victim – Abel Griffiths – was spared what a report of the time called 'the disgusting part of the ceremony of throwing lime over the body and driving a stake through it', which was how the authorities used to do it before they went soft.

Back out into the sunshine. On the other side of the road is a huge wooden hoarding disguising some building works. The boards spread right across several four-storey frontages and out over the pavement, forming a tunnel through which pedestrians can pass. It's all painted dark green, and studded with artificial shrubbery. 'I have no idea what that is,' says an American tourist to her friend, 'but I love it.' She turns her back on London's premier tourist attraction to take a photo of what is essentially some posh scaffolding. But then even the royals themselves have never been completely sold on the palace. In Victoria's time the drains used to stink the whole place out, and as recently as the 1990s Prince Philip complained that his quarters were so far from the kitchen that his food was cold by the time it arrived.

Right at the moment, though, my thoughts have turned to the only other man we know (for sure) to have shared the Queen's bedroom. When Michael Fagan ended up sitting on Her Majesty's mattress one early March morning in 1982, it wasn't part of a stunt, let alone a mission of murder. He hadn't planned to break in at all. He was going through a difficult period in his life, and had been out walking all night when, sometime in the pre-dawn hours, he found himself heading along the Mall towards the Palace. 'What would happen,' he asked himself, 'if I just kept going?' Security guard in the wrong place, wall a touch too easy to scale, and there he was, strolling the corridors. Standing here, I know how he felt – not about popping in for pillow talk with the Queen, just about how hypnotic it can be to keep walking in a straight line. My straight line isn't *quite* as literal as Fagan's, though it looks it on the Tube map thanks to the sublime insight by cartographer Harry Beck that the lines don't have to be geographically accurate. But still, the knowledge that this light blue streak is guiding me unveeringly across London gives me a sense of power, as though I'm laying waste to the city with a Zorro-like swish.

The traffic lights on the far side of the Palace conveniently turn red just as I want to cross, halting a woman who's seventy if she's a day, sitting astride a huge 1970s Suzuki motorbike, cigarette hanging vertically from her bottom lip. Once across, I turn to see her roar away. The back of her denim jacket says 'The Clash'.

Into Green Park, which has been royal since the days of Charles II. He took his daily constitutional here, hence the name Constitution Hill.[9] Another mark he left here was the absence of flowers. His wife Catherine discovered he'd picked some to give to another woman, and, less than happy about it, ordered that every last flower in the park be ripped out. To this day there are no formal flowerbeds there. Then up the hill towards Piccadilly, from which you could see the hills of Wimbledon in the nineteenth century, as well as the Crystal Palace at Sydenham.

After walking for six and a half miles, and two and a half hours, I reach Green Park station. The Queen travelled here by Tube on 7 March 1969, the day she officially opened the

---

9. It couldn't have been the other meaning when you think about it, as we famously don't have one, or at least not one that's written down.

Victoria Line. Her ticket cost 5d. The pointlessness of her one-stop journey from Victoria was further exacerbated by the fact that she lived halfway along it. At least she was spared the horrors that had confronted the workmen near here as they cut the tunnel for the line: they accidentally ploughed into a centuries-old plague pit.

As a resolute above-ground traveller, of course, none of these thoughts concern me today. Instead, a left turn into Dover Street takes me officially into the neighbourhood that according to the writer Sydney Smith 'enclosed more intelligence and ability, to say nothing of wealth and beauty, than the world had ever collected in such a space before'. This is very possibly true, although we should remember that Mayfair got its name from an annual fair (guess which month it was held in) that had to be banned in 1764 for being too rowdy. On the right is the entrance to Brown's Hotel, opened by James Brown.[10] I say the entrance to Brown's. What I actually mean is *one* of the entrances to Brown's: a corridor runs right through to Albemarle Street on the other side. This was handy for Michael Portillo during the 1995 Tory leadership election, when he was being followed by journalists desperate to know his plans. Getting his driver to drop him at the Dover Street door, he would hurry along the corridor and out on to Albemarle Street, where he'd hail a cab and go merrily on his way. Inspired by his example, I cut through the hotel myself.

Bond Street, the capital's *plus chic* shopping strip, is also a

---

10. No, not that one; we're talking 1837 here, making this the oldest five-star hotel in London. It's one of the few that still feels like one.

revision exercise for one of the most important London lessons: look up. Three floors above Loro Piana at number 153 (clothes, accessories, doorman waiting to sneer at you for not being rich enough) are four Henry Moore sculptures from the 1950s. Realising that no one in London *does* look up, Moore bemoaned the lack of an audience for the pieces and tried, unsuccessfully, to buy them back.

Down at street level, the bench on which life-sized statues of Churchill and Roosevelt are seated is, as usual, attracting tourists who want to squeeze between the great allies and have their photo taken, as though they were Stalin at Yalta. The woman there now is of a certain age, dressed to the nines (dare I say the nine-and-a-halves?), sporting expensive sunglasses and white hair that's been not so much styled as launched. She's gazing fondly into FDR's face; surely an American. Looking about for her husband, or whoever's taking the picture, I realise she's actually on her own. With a final grin, and a pat of the Presidential knee, she stands up and heads into a nearby jeweller's.

Into Conduit Street, so-called because it was where a water supply from the Tyburn ran, left up Regent Street, which marks the boundary with Soho (the hunting cry for a hare – if a stag broke cover it was 'tayho'), and I'm at my next station, Oxford Circus. After the relative peace of Mayfair, it's a bit like stepping out of a particularly under-used library into the World Who-Can-Get-In-Each-Other's-Way-The-Most Contest. The qualifying stages, that is. Before they've whittled it down from the initial three million.

It's the old quandary, of course. You can't love a city

for being so good that people want to come from all over the globe to see it, then moan when people come from all over the globe to see it. It's just that I wish some of them would observe some sort of pavement etiquette. What would happen if you drove your car in the manner of an Oxford Street pedestrian? Stop suddenly to chat and admire the view; pull out without warning across the path of an overtaking vehicle; execute a perfect one-eighty into the face of oncoming traffic? Forget points on your licence, you'd be scratching the days on your cell wall. And yet the two-legged versions of these four-wheeled crimes are seen as not just acceptable but, given the evidence before me today, compulsory.

At least Oxford Circus shows that London can learn from the rest of the world. Boris Johnson was so impressed with Tokyo's diagonal pedestrian crossings that he introduced one here. And so it is that I can walk straight from the crossroads' south-west corner to its north-east one, arriving in the shadow of Topshop, the planet's largest fashion store. I think about its number of changing rooms (200), its number of coat hangers (200,000), the way Topshop calls this store a 'region' in itself (it outsells all their outlets in the Midlands combined), and I remember the first-ever description of this city. It was by the Roman historian Tacitus, referring to the year AD 60. He called Londinium 'a place filled with traders and a celebrated centre of commerce'.

North of Oxford Street and things are quietening again. The Langham looks as elegant as ever, which is only fitting for the first London hotel to serve afternoon tea. It's gone three o'clock now, and I'm not untempted, but decide that rushing such a British institution would be unseemly.[11] So instead I grab a quick sandwich from a café on Great Portland Street, and continue up through Fitzrovia.

It was Charles FitzRoy himself – 1st Baron Southampton to the likes of you and me – who laid out much of the area in the eighteenth century. Ironically Warren Street, which in the mid-twentieth century was the home of London's second-hand car market, now lies a few yards inside the Congestion Charge Zone, ensuring that it remains a dull backwater where vehicles on the nearby Euston Road can be heard but not seen, their engines roaring like the ghosts of yesteryear's Triumphs and Jags.

After Warren Street station comes the trek down the main road towards Euston. Deep beneath my feet the Victoria Line tunnel is snaking in a most curious way. Or rather the Victoria Line *tunnels* are. Looking at the Tube map it's easy to forget that each coloured line represents one tunnel for each direction of travel. At Euston station, the southbound tunnel briefly rises up from below the northbound so that it's on the same level as the Northern Line, allowing passengers to achieve what Tube planners call, with their customary romance, a 'cross-platform

---

11. So revered is the custom that the hotel issues its own style guide. Leave the spout pointing towards the pourer, don't raise your little finger, and it's definitely not milk in first: Victorian hostesses proved their china was high quality by showing that it didn't crack with just hot tea inside.

interchange'. By the time it reaches Warren Street, it's on its way back down again, submitting once more to the northbound's superiority.

On my right I pass the modern University College Hospital building, its huge edifice of tinted green glass seeming appropriately medical but essentially soulless. On the steps of the A&E department are three or four patients, one in a wheelchair, who have been sent outside to smoke – though whether they face greater danger from their cigarettes or the exhaust fumes of several lanes of gridlocked traffic is hard to say. Next to them a drunk in unwashed army fatigues sits slumped so far forward that his head nearly meets his knees. He's in danger of spilling his White Stripe.

Euston station appears on the left. Had its former entrance, the famous Euston Arch, still been there it could have formed a pair with the O2 Academy's in Brixton: it too was inspired by Italian architecture. As it is, the station's archlessness makes it a pair with Buckingham Palace, the home of Marble Arch until it was moved in 1851. There is still a statue of Robert Stephenson here, though, the engineer son of George Stephenson whose train did for poor William Huskisson. Across the road, guarding the crypt of St Pancras Church, are some slightly stranger-looking statues: the caryatids were made too tall for the gap they had to fit in, so several inches were lopped off their waists.

I'm now walking between Euston and King's Cross, in what amounts to a transportational black hole: on the Victoria Line King's Cross is north of Euston; on the Northern Line it's the other way round. King's Cross takes its name from a tall, much-despised monument to George IV that used to stand at the crossroads. Two centuries later it appears on the ever-amusing 'If England Had Lost the War' Tube map as 'Koenigskreuz'.[12]

I pop in to see the Harry Potter fans queuing politely to have their pictures taken with the luggage trolley that Network Rail have left sticking magically out of a wall, in tribute to the wizard's departures from Platform 9 and three quarters. It would be cruel to point out to them that J. K. Rowling has since admitted mixing up her stations, and was actually thinking of Euston when she wrote the book, so I don't. As they snap away a train arrives at an adjacent platform. One of the alighting passengers is a monk, wearing black robes and sandals, carrying an ultra-modern plastic suitcase in dayglo-green.

North-east now, up through the area of Islington known as Barnsbury. I used to live here. So, at around the same time, though in a much grander residence, did Tony Blair. (Seeing his old house on Richmond Crescent it's hard to resist a chuckle at the fact that a subsequent owner has painted the front door bright red.[13]) I saw the then Leader

12. A friend of mine once attended a Tube-themed fancy-dress party where another guest came dressed as a seven-foot prawn. 'No, can't get it,' said my friend. 'Put me out of my misery.' 'King Crustacean,' came the reply. Someone else wore a beehive hairdo: High Barnet.

13. This is the door through which a just-woken Cherie was mercilessly photographed by the press the morning after the 1997 election. Her later regret at selling the house when they moved into Downing Street – the property market was just beginning its upward thrust – is said to have fuelled her subsequent house-buying habit.

of the Opposition on Copenhagen Street once: I was trudging home from Sainsbury's laden with shopping; he was studying documents in the back of a chauffeur-driven car. Of course it's unfair to base any sort of metaphor on the incident, although with the benefit of hindsight I can see how even then this particular representative of the working classes was destined to end up on a seemingly endless and very well-remunerated tour of the world's first-class departure lounges.

The memory gives me an idea: the personal Tube line. Everyone who's lived in London, or even just visited it a few times, will have a list of places that hold special and private significance. These memories may be momentous – weddings, births, muggings – or they could be trivial, like the place you bought an ice-cream on a hot day, or slipped while running for a bus, or passed a well-known politician in the back of his car. Take, say, a dozen of these places, and imagine them on the map. Then imagine a Tube line that runs through all of them. Not through the nearest existing Tube stations: through the places themselves. It would be your very own line, messing up the neat verticals and horizontals of the real Underground map, curving crazily and haphazardly like the bee in the opening credits of *The Good Life*. Only you are allowed to ride it. In fact, only you would *want* to ride it.

Soon, as I plough on towards Highbury and Islington station, my love of order and logic and straight lines will reassert itself. It's only because the real Tube map is there, its structure so rigid and unforgiving, that this momentary rebellion has anything to rebel against. But just for a couple of minutes, as I retreat inside my head and ride the Mason Line – without even knowing where all its stops would be – it's fun. A return ticket to the past.

At a table outside the Hope and Anchor on Upper Street an unshaven man in his forties sits drinking a pint of lager and paying scant attention to his young son sitting opposite. The boy, bored and working his way through a packet of fruit pastilles, is still in school uniform. A well-dressed woman passes them, pushing a Mamas and Papas buggy containing an equally well-dressed toddler, a boy by her side of roughly the same age as the pastille-chewer but wearing a different school uniform. Balanced on top of the buggy is a punnet of ripe strawberries, which the woman eats with a white plastic fork. London has great inequalities of wealth, it's true, but very rarely are those inequalities enforced through geography. In just about every area (Belgravia's an exception), multi-million-pound houses stand just yards from 'problem' estates.

Past my eleventh station, and up on to Highbury Fields. The park is full of people enjoying the weather: playing football, walking their dogs, or, in the case of one man, combining the two by trying to get the ball (unsuccessfully) off his terrier. An Islington Council noticeboard announces that 'in 2006 the council worked with the local community to develop a vision for the park . . . The council's East Area Committee approved the Vision [their inconsistent capital] in July 2007.' New developments include 'a park furniture and materials guide', though there's no explanation as to what a park furniture and materials guide actually is. No one apart from me, it goes without saying, is reading the notice. They're too busy enjoying the park.

Several of the Georgian terraced houses facing on to Highbury Fields are for sale, most of them through the firm Hotblack Desiato. Although I've seen their boards many times before, the sheer outrageousness of the name has never really struck me before. Can there ever have been a Mr (or indeed a Mrs, Miss or Ms) Hotblack? And if so, why on earth did he shun the obvious career in adult films to set up an estate agency? When I reach the main road and see one of the firm's offices, I can't resist going inside to ask.

Half a dozen twenty-somethings sit at their desks, all but one of them on the phone. The remaining operative stares at his computer screen, moving the mouse with his right hand and holding a chocolate bar in his left. I'm just thinking about taking out my mobile and calling him when he looks up. 'Can I help you?'

'Yes, I was wondering about your firm's name. Was there really a Mr Hotblack?'

'Yeah. I've met him. Geoff.'

'Geoff Hotblack?'

'Mmm. He's quite old now.'

'And he teamed up with a Mr Desiato?'

'Yeah. Good name, isn't it? Attention-grabbing.'

I can't argue with that, standing where I am.[14]

A few doors along I pass the Highbury Barn pub. It says everything about the modern Premier League that this favoured haunt of Arsenal fans advertises 'divine wines', but the name actually comes from a barn that stood here in the When-All-This-Was-Fields era. For a hundred years, until the late nineteenth century, it was a North London version of Vauxhall Pleasure Gardens, hosting concerts, banquets and dances, as well as circus and pantomime acts. The open spaces also featured displays by Charles Green, the age's foremost hot-air balloonist, who injected spice into his ascents with gimmicks such as being accompanied by 'a lady and a leopard' (the latter so docile it sat at the former's feet – do we suspect the involvement of a syringe?), and replacing the basket with a horse and rider. Green also made flights from Vauxhall, sadly including the one that lifted Robert Cocking up where he so clearly didn't belong.

Apart from Mr Bean, famous residents of modern Highbury include Clive Anderson and Nick Hornby (who as Arsenal fans relish the club's proximity) and BBC politico Nick Robinson (who as a Manchester United fan doesn't).

---

14. The employee also reveals that the estate agent was the inspiration for the character of the same name in *The Hitchhiker's Guide to the Galaxy* by local writer Douglas Adams. 'He said he'd been struggling like mad to think of a name for this character. Then one day he saw one of our boards and couldn't believe his luck. He got home and rang the office to ask if they minded. As it happens it was Geoff himself who picked the phone up. For years afterwards people used to ask him how he'd got the nerve to steal the name of his firm from Douglas Adams's book.'

Even the area's manhole covers have a certain glamour: I notice one on Blackstock Road called the 'Rapide 40 Slideout'. Shortly afterwards, I pass a halal butcher, then an Ethiopian delicatessen, and sense that the ethnic mix is changing. This is the area – and Tube station – known as Finsbury Park.

Self-deprecating locals point out that pronounced backwards the name is 'crappy rubsniff'. In 1974 the British R&B musician Graham Bond chose the station as the venue for his suicide.[15] Today, as the evening rush hour gets under way, the surrounding area certainly feels like the point at which my trek's style quotient is to take a downward dip. At one of what feels like 300 bus stops clustered confusingly on the several main roads that congregate here, another drunk – a more lively one – holds court. Swigging from a bottle of cider, he treats anyone who wants to listen, and indeed everyone who doesn't, to a commentary on the random phenomena that pass for his thought processes. He remains seated, and there's obviously no violence in prospect. But I do cast a glance up Seven Sisters Road and think back to that morning's breakfast-table conversation with Jo.

'I'm looking forward to the end of the walk. I've never been north of Finsbury Park on foot before.'

Jo butters some toast, and eyes me carefully. 'You're looking forward to walking through Tottenham?'

'Yeah. I went to Seven Sisters Tube station to go to a match at White Hart Lane once, but I've never walked round there.'

---

15. Technically this mention should wait until chapter 8, as he threw himself under a Piccadilly rather than a Victoria Line train.

'I've driven it.'

'And?'

She applies the marmalade. 'Grim. Very grim.'

Seven Sisters Road was built in 1833 to link Holloway in the west with Tottenham in the east. The fields through which it passed included a raised knoll containing the remnants of Hornsey Wood, all the other trees having fallen victim to the need for grazing land. Londoners would come here to escape the city's grime, to indulge in boating and archery. Today this land is known as Finsbury Park, and as I walk along its eastern side, gazing through the railings at yet more sunbathers and dogwalkers, the peaceful sight helps allay my initial fears about this, the 'here be dragons' section of my journey.

The next major junction, though, marks the end of the greenery. This is Manor House, taking its name from the nineteenth-century pub that stood here (on the Manor of Brownswood) next to the toll road leading north, the modern Green Lanes. A Manor House pub survived until about a decade ago, but the building is now a Costcutter, leaving only the Tube station next door to bear the name. Not a station to delay me today – it's on the Piccadilly Line – but mention it to any London cabbie and you'll see a glint in his eye: it's the start of the first 'run' they learn for the Knowledge (here to Islington's Gibson Square).

Over the crossroads, I head eastwards along the next chunk of Seven Sisters Road. There are six lanes of traffic, lined either side with pre-war council flats. At only seven storeys they lack the capacity to depress of their post-war counterparts the tower blocks, but there are acne-like satellite dishes and the occasional boarded-up window. Jo's 'grim' echoes round my mind.

The terrain stays like this for a good 20 minutes. There's never a stretch that's absolutely devoid of trees, though, and the lawns between the blocks seem fairly well-maintained. People coming and going from the flats seem happy enough. A parade of shops appears on the left. One or two are derelict, but the Brazilian café seems lively, as does its compatriot grocery next door. The entrance to the flats above one shop bears a cheerily handwritten note: 'Please knock hard and wait for two mins, we have a few flights of stairs to come down. Thanks.'

Soon afterwards there's a brand-new residential block, each apartment's windows tinted a different colour – turquoise, orange, pink – like Elton John's sunglasses collection nailed to a wall. Then a smart Toyota-approved used-car dealership. The Merciful Bakery offers 'delicious African and Caribbean food'. One shop has been converted to the Cino Social Club, with two pool tables filling the front room and a group of Turkish elders playing cards in the back.

Under a railway bridge, the *A to Z* confirms that South Tottenham now looms large in my sights, but still there's no sign of those dragons. A sign outside the Polski Ksiegowy accountancy practice offers tax returns for £120, and 'all legal issues'. Through the open door of a minicab firm I hear an argument, and under pretext of stopping to check my notes

I take a sneaky glance inside. A large woman is using her beautiful Nigerian sing-song intonation to bellow at the female controller behind the glass partition. Every syllable is enunciated perfectly and on a different note.

'He has acc-used me be-fore of ov-er-charg-ing! I will not acc-ept this! I do not ov-er-charge!'

The controller, a tired-looking woman in her fifties, starts to say something. She gets as far as 'Look . . .'

'Airt pounds! AIRT pounds! That is the corr-ect fare for this jour-ney!'

'But . . .'

'Airt pounds! It is fair that I charge airt pounds!'

'Listen . . .'

'Airt pounds! Airt pounds! Airt pounds!' There's more of the same from both parties, but it's clear who's going to win. The Nigerian driver storms out to her car. If I were the customer I'd get my £8 ready.

As the notes come into focus before my now-unpretending eyes it strikes me that this could be the perfect place to clear up a mystery. Advance research has failed to come up with any conclusive answer. I step into the office.

'Yes, love?' says the controller. She seems glad to see a face that isn't screaming 'Airt pounds!'

'I don't suppose you happen to know why this area's called Seven Sisters, do you?'

She looks momentarily fazed, then intrigued. 'No,' she says with a smile. 'Come to think of it, I don't.'

'I've read something about there being a ring of seven trees somewhere round here. Planted by seven sisters.'

She thinks. 'Can't say I've noticed them anywhere. You could try the library.' But the directions she gives would take me too far off course. I decide to move on.

At the main junction with Tottenham High Road I see the steps up from the Tube station,[16] and remember climbing them en route to the football match. The area is just as busy today – queues at the multiple bus stops, people using the shops, workers leaving the office buildings – but there doesn't seem to be the same air of hostility in the air. 'Hardly surprising,' you say. 'There's no match on today.' But the antagonism back then wasn't from football fans. There were hardly any around: I'd arrived well before the match in order to meet a friend for a drink, and anyway the ground itself is a good 20 minutes' walk north of here. No, the problem, I realise now, was not the area – it was how I'd got here. The problem was the Tube itself. Descending underneath London's streets at Oxford Circus, I'd travelled in a sealed metal box all the way to a point directly underneath South Tottenham, then resurfaced. Now Oxford Circus is different from South Tottenham; but it's not that different. People still get on buses and buy newspapers and talk on their mobile phones and look in shop windows, and however bad the crime statistics, it's still very much odds against that on any particular day any particular individual will encounter trouble. (In fact I'd wager you're more likely to get your pocket picked at Oxford Circus than up here.) The trouble with the

---

16. *I'm Sorry I Haven't A Clue* aficionados will remember the importance of Seven Sisters in the 'Mortimer's 2nd Amendment' rules of Mornington Crescent – players have to sacrifice it in order to prise open their opponent's laterals.

Tube, though, is that by cutting out the intervening territory it creates the impression you're going somewhere *radically* different. Any sense of London as a continuum is lost.

Whereas today I've experienced that continuum, bonded with it every step of the way. By walking the road between Finsbury Park and here I've realised for the first time how these parts of the jigsaw fit together. It's like when you look at an old photo of yourself and realise for the first time how many grey hairs you've got; you never noticed them in the mirror each day because they appeared one by one. You're different from the old you, but you're still you. Now, this evening, I see that Tottenham's different from Central London – but it's still London. How curious that the thing that disguised this from me was the London Underground.

It's twenty to seven now. Across the main road, where Broad Lane forms the next stage of my eastward trek, is a small green dotted with bushes and trees, the one remaining bit of nature from the days when Henry VIII came here to hunt deer. In the middle, on a grassy mound no more than a foot or so high, some of the trees form a circle. I stop to count them . . . yep, seven. Outside one of the terraced houses on the far side of the green a man who looks exactly like Sid James is washing his car. I walk over to him.

'I don't suppose they're the seven sisters, are they?'

'Excuse me?' Given his appearance, the heavy Spanish accent comes as a surprise.

'I've heard that the name Seven Sisters came from seven trees that were planted in a circle.'

El Sid looks at the trees, then back at me. He says nothing.

'I was just wondering if you happened to know whether these were the seven trees?'

His gaze returns to the mound. I see his lips moving as he counts. 'Yes, they are seven trees.' His look suggests some confusion as to how I've given my carer the slip.

There are times when it's best simply to walk away. This is one such.[17]

Heading for Tottenham Hale now, towards the River Lee, where goods ships used to be unloaded. At first there's little evidence of any surviving mercantile spirit. Broad Lane is a major traffic route, so there are garages and tatty news-agents, but nothing more. The sign above a long-abandoned shop reads 'Electricals Ltd – Stockist of mazda and atlas lamps'; the death of the capital letter has been going on longer than I thought. Perhaps this is finally the part of Tottenham that merits Jo's 'grim'. But then, as the road curves round, a series of sights appear on the right like increasingly magical oases in a desert: a brand-new branch of Costa . . . a JD Sports . . . a Boots . . . Next (sorry: 'next' – the death continues) . . . Asda Living ('Home, Café, Books') . . . B&Q . . . This is Tottenham Hale Retail Park.

In the large central car park, shiny new Clios and Astras queue patiently for spaces. Smiling customers of all races and religions head for PC World or Comet or Halfords. One of

17. Later research confirms that this is indeed Page Green, where the original seven elms were planted. After several subsequent replantings the current circle dates from 1997, when five families each of seven sisters shared the digging duties.

the units is home to the poshest branch of Poundworld I have ever seen. Inside it's indistinguishable from a mid-range supermarket. All the lines are there – food, drink, cleaning products, garden tools . . . At the checkout a Hasidic Jew waits to buy a football and a skipping rope.

Are we all middle-class now? Over the road is Tottenham Hale Tube station, with its Stansted Express link and efficiently organised cab rank. It's the third-last stop on the Victoria Line, and like the first, Brixton, serves an area that has managed to lose its synonymity with race riots. In 1985, around the time of the riots in which PC Keith Blakelock was killed on the Broadwater Farm Estate, the local MP Bernie Grant caused outrage by saying that the police had got 'a bloody good hiding'. Just now, on Tottenham High Road, I passed a sign for the Bernie Grant Arts Centre.

Doubtless there are still alleyways in both N15 and SW9 which you'd be ill advised to visit at two o'clock on a Saturday morning. But the evidence is here, as it was at the very start of my walk in Brixton: London has changed in the last few years. The old worry that you might get into trouble for simply looking at someone the wrong way has – at least in these two parts of the city – vanished. Tottenham Hale Retail Park could have been lifted from one of the calmer suburbs of Milton Keynes.

For a while this gives me a rumbling sense of disquiet. These stores' success has been funded by a credit boom the likes of which we've never seen before. It feels somehow unreal, a superstore-shaped sticking plaster over the area's old problems. An image keeps filling my mind of Jack

Nicholson at the end of *One Flew Over the Cuckoo's Nest*, becalmed only because he's been lobotomised. Standing outside Costa, I remember the old saying about bread and circuses – is it now coffee and retail parks? Is this what London should be about? Doesn't a great city need its danger, its edge, its rawness?

Perhaps. But then that's an easy thought at seven o'clock on a gloriously sunny Wednesday evening in a secure location. Stand in that dark alleyway at two o'clock on that Saturday morning and the reality would hit you (if you'll forgive the pun) very differently. Preferring Dickens to Disney is all very well, until you come face to face with Bill Sykes. Besides, to wish that London was immune from boom-and-bust economics is to wish away the city's entire history. A few miles south of here they've turned boom and bust into an art form. 'A credit boom the likes of which we've never seen before' – who am I kidding? From the South Sea Bubble to the dot.com dream, the Square Mile has for centuries done boom and bust like nowhere else on earth. And that is simultaneously its greatest sin and its greatest achievement. Economic cycles aren't foisted on us by bankers or politicians, they're the result of ordinary people – like the ones here now in this retail park – spending too much and then having to pay it back. They're the purest expression of human desire and human fallibility. Recession following expansion is as inevitable as winter following summer. The colours in which London paints that picture are especially vivid.

Leaving the park, I see, out of the corner of my eye, a black man talking to a friend. 'They is all cheesing me off,

blood, innit?' he says. 'They is like "what you lookin' at?",
and I'm like "I is lookin' at *you*, man".'

So there's at least one representative of old Tottenham
still around. I wonder what trouble this homey from the
'hood has been causing.

'And I'm staring at them, man, and they is giving me some
*well* bad vibes. But I ain't takin' none of it, I'm standing them
down, blood, standing them *down*. And they know I'm on to
them for *real*.'

I turn to look at him. Instead of low-slung jeans and
copious jewellery I'm confronted with a uniform and a
name-badge. He's a security guard for Next.

'Ain't no way no one's lifting from *my* store, blood,' he
continues. 'I tell 'em it's only five items in the changing room
at one time. Actually it's eight, but I'm telling them five. You
feel me?'

What is London going to do now? The one thing I certainly
don't expect it to do is just stop.

The name of the road should have been a clue: Ferry Lane.
Initially it lifts me up over the railway line heading north
from Tottenham Hale station. As well as mainline trains this
carries Tube trains to their depot a few hundred yards away.
It's the only section where the Victoria Line emerges above
ground, making the line unique: as a passenger you travel
from one end to the other without seeing daylight. It strikes
me that from now on all my walks will contain sections where
my project's inspiration comes into view. The thought is a
comforting one.

Then the bridge continues over water. At first it's just the River Lee, whose houseboats lend a vaguely rustic feel but don't mark an end to the city. Soon, though, huge expanses of shimmering blue open up on either side – the reservoirs that separate Tottenham from Walthamstow. Sited amongst them, on the left, is the Paddock Community Nature Park, and although this name screams 'part of London trying to be green', the reservoirs really aren't. They really are the point at which London ends. Ducks bob lazily, a swan glides by, and two old men sit practising the ancient form of meditation known as 'fishing'. In the distance, to the south, you can see Canary Wharf. But it *is* the distance. The towers there are part of London. This isn't. The water all around me is a barrier to building. This is where the villages cease to join up. Finsbury Park morphs into Manor House morphs into Seven Sisters, but when it comes to Tottenham and Walthamstow, never the twain shall meet.

Which would elicit the approval of the writer Cyril Connolly, who said that 'no city should be so large that a man cannot walk out of it in a morning'. Warren Street to Blackhorse Road, the station whose appearance opposite an industrial estate marks a return to built-upness, has taken me just shy of four hours, making toast in Fitzrovia then a pre-lunch snifter in Walthamstow more than feasible. As I wind my way down past the Edwardian terraced villas of Blackhorse Road itself, then along the pedestrianised High Street that claims to host Europe's longest daily street market, I know that the 'Welcome to the London Borough of Waltham

Forest' sign back there was about as accurate as the ones outside 'London Luton' airport.

The market stalls are all packed away now, and only a few people dawdle along the High Street. One middle-aged man talks on his mobile: 'It'll be an hour and a half before I'm in Romford, Matilda.' Is anyone still really called Matilda? Then he adds, in a tone that is either sinister or suggestive, I can't decide which: 'If you're going to have a bath, have a bath now.'

As the final station draws near, I find my feet slowing. Not because of tiredness, although after seven and a half hours there is a certain weariness. It's because I don't want to stop walking. London has shown me things today that it only revealed because I was on foot: how its neighbourhoods fit together, how some of them are less depressing than I'd imagined, where the whole thing ends. The Victoria Line has opened up in a way that it never did when I took the Victoria Line. 'I only went out for a walk,' wrote the nineteenth-century naturalist John Reid, 'and finally concluded to stay out till sundown, for going out, I found, was really going in.' Tonight, at four minutes past eight, I think I know what he meant.

As it happens, I have to carry on past Walthamstow Central anyway. Starving as I am, the nearby kebab and burger outlets aren't quite tempting enough to entice me in. Instead I cross Hoe Street to the leafier area that styles itself 'Walthamstow Village'. It's certainly attractive – in fact it could pass for a particularly exclusive enclave of Clapham – but I'm not standing for that name. As of about half an hour ago I know that *all* of Walthamstow is a village.

In Eat 17 (parquet floor, Scandinavian minimalist lighting, pale grey walls) I reflect on the day. The Victoria Line has 13 miles of track, whereas I have walked a little under 15 miles. This gives a foot-to-wheel ratio of 1.15. But the Victoria is a very simple line, with no branches to be walked between, no big diversions away from the route. Let's say the ratio for the whole project will be nearer to 1.5. With 249 miles of track, my plates are going to cover about 375 miles. That's 14 marathons. Or a walk from London to Dumfries, with a Liverpool to Manchester hop tacked on the end.

Taking care not to splatter my *A to Z* with the gravy from my herb-encrusted pork loin and creamed mash, I put it face down on the table and gaze at the Tube map on the back cover. The lines look like pieces of string draped over the huge parcel that is London, ready to tie it up. But I know now that they're magic pieces of string. Instead of knotting their ends together, all you have to do is move your fingers – or your feet – from one end to the other. By walking from Brixton to Walthamstow I've done the light blue piece, tied up that stretch of the capital. Now it's time to choose another.

Symmetry's always attractive. This first journey was bottom left to top right. How about a spot of top left to bottom right? How about the Bakerloo?

# 2

# Bakerloo Line

## Maps are an art, not a science

Y ou wouldn't think that Sherlock Holmes and Kenneth
Williams had very much in common, apart from
their bachelor status. But there are at least two
things, and today I'm encountering them both. Later, on my
Bakerloo Line walk, I'll pass through the Baker Street/
Marylebone area that was home to both men. First, though,
I'm in Covent Garden, in a beautiful building on Long Acre
that dates from 1901, and with which both Sherlock and
Kenneth were connected. This is the map shop – no, map
emporium – known as Stanfords. Before his days of Carrying
On, Williams worked here as an apprentice draughtsman. In
*The Hound of the Baskervilles*, Holmes sends to Stanfords for
a map of Dartmoor. 'I have been to Devonshire,' he boasts
to Watson at Baker Street, despite the fact that 'my body has
remained in this armchair . . . My spirit hovered over it [the
map] all day.'

I feel like doing some hovering of my own. Specifically, I
want a map on which I can record my walks. Footsteps are
imaginary – they exist in your memory, as do the walks they
create, but nothing permanent is left, nothing you can carry

away and say, 'Look, that was what I did today.' For a while I thought of using my *A to Z*, drawing over the streets I've covered to create a lasting document that denotes the achievement. But not only does the *A to Z* not cover the whole area I'll be walking, it also splits each journey over several pages. This won't quite convey the scale of the thing. I need one big map. Brushing aside the thought that the people you usually see with big maps are shunting little swastikas around them, I've headed for Stanfords. I never need much of an excuse to do that: it is the Mecca of maps, Cartography Central.

'Unfortunately there won't be one map that's big enough,' says Piotr, the member of staff to whom I explain my request. 'You need every single street name on it, right?'

'Yes. Essentially the equivalent of the *A to Z* with all the pages stuck together. Except bigger, obviously. Out to the ends of all the Tube lines.'

He nods. 'They do single sheets that cover Central London like that. Even one for the Knowledge. But to cover an area as large as the Tube network, the scale just wouldn't work. You wouldn't be able to read the street names. You wouldn't even be able to make out the streets.' He walks over to a set of large drawers. 'There is this. The Masterplan of London series.'

*Masterplan?* I'm getting disturbing thoughts of swastikas again. As soon as Piotr takes out one of the maps, though, I'm smitten. There are nine of them, each measuring 40 inches by 30, which when arranged in a three-by-three grid cover the entire area within the M25.[1] The look is exactly the same as the *A to Z*, for the very good reason that the maps are made by the same firm.

'Have these got the ghost streets on?' I ask. The few streets that the Geographer's A to Z Map Company Ltd deliberately misname so they'll know if anyone is copying their maps without permission.

Piotr nods. 'They will do, yeah.' Not that either of us knows what they are, of course. That's sort of the whole point of keeping them secret.

We gaze at North London spread out beneath us, this being the sheet Piotr has chosen. It's no use fighting it. This set of maps has to be mine. As Piotr rolls them up at his desk, I notice some other maps he's been working on. One is clearly urban, and looks vaguely familiar, but I can't quite place it.

'Where's that?' I ask.

'Islington,' Piotr replies.

'Really?'

'Yeah.' He points at a junction. 'That's Upper Street, with Essex Road coming off it.'

'Oh, yes.' It's a nineteenth-century map, it turns out, but that's not where the confusion lies. The problem is that it's an Ordnance Survey map, not only lacking street names but also showing every road at its correct width. Only when you see one of these do you realise that the *A to Z* makes major

---

1. Even this misses out a tiny section at the end of the Metropolitan Line, but Piotr explains there's no map in the same style that will cover this. In a way I quite like the imperfection, a reminder of just how gargantuan the Tube network is.

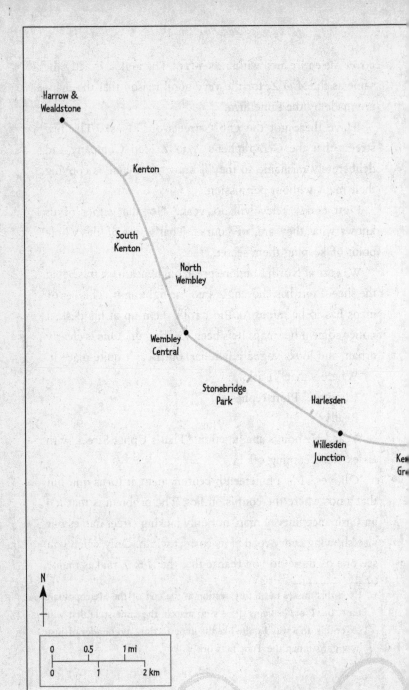

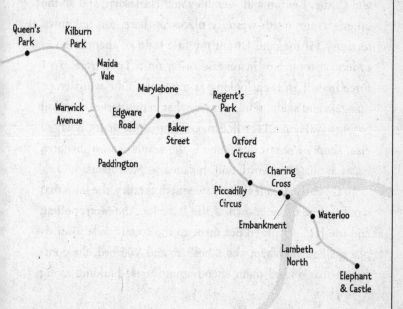

streets larger, so letting you pick them out more easily. Piotr shows me other maps, where identifying even Oxford Street takes a bit of work.

'Funny, isn't it?' I say. 'You think of maps as infallible. You assume they're telling the absolute truth.'

'Every map tells you something different, depending on what the mapmaker chooses to put on it.' He smiles. 'They're works of art, not of science.'

Have you ever tried to not look out of a train window? It's surprisingly difficult.

But as my Bakerloo Line train emerges above ground just north of Queen's Park, that's exactly what I have to do. After walking out of London on the Victoria Line, this time I've decided to walk into it, heading southbound to the Elephant and Castle. Kenton and Wembley and Harlesden, and all the other strange north-westerly places up here, are unknown territory for me, and I want my first sight of them to be in order, on foot. Not in reverse order on a Tube train. So I force myself to keep looking at my notes. One word crops up again and again, reminding me that in this part of London basing a walk on a Tube line makes more sense than anywhere else, simply because the Tube is the whole reason this area exists at all. That word, and this area, is Metroland.

In the early decades of the twentieth century, the lines that would come to be known as the Bakerloo, the Metropolitan and the Jubilee surged out through the countryside towards places like Amersham and Chesham and Watford, the companies that owned them encouraging house-building along the way to give themselves more customers. The Metropolitan Railway's marketing bods coined the name Metro-land, enticing Londoners with thoughts of a rural life within easy reach of the big bad city. Catchy name: before the end of the First World War it had found its way into a poem by the writer George R. Sims: 'Hearts are lighter, eyes are brighter, in Metroland, Metroland'.

Just one problem with this success: there was too much of it. Build enough homes in the countryside and you stop it from being the countryside. Housing estates sprang up in Neasden, Wembley, Pinner, Rickmansworth, Chorley Wood, Rayners Lane, Eastcote, Ruislip, Hillingdon . . . well, you see the problem. Sooner or later lots of little estates add up, in essence, to one big estate. Between the two World Wars, Wembley grew by 552 per cent. Harrow gained 134,480 new inhabitants, the largest increase of any local authority in Greater London. In trying to escape itself, the city had only made itself bigger.

The Bakerloo Line had its origins in the Baker Street and Waterloo Railway, whose construction began in 1898 under the leadership of businessman Whitaker Wright. In 1904, however, work came to a temporary halt when Wright was convicted of fraud at the Royal Courts of Justice. He himself came to a more permanent halt, responding to the verdict by walking into a neighbouring room and swallowing cyanide.[2] But soon the American Charles Yerkes stepped in. He had stood on Hampstead Heath looking down on the Square Mile,

---

2. If that had failed he had a revolver in his pocket.

and decided that this Tube thing was the way of the future. His Underground Electric Railways Company of London (UERL) would provide the basis for the modern system; as well as the Baker Street and Waterloo project, he took over the precursors of the Northern and Piccadilly Lines.

It was rumoured that parliamentary permission for the line up to Baker Street had been forthcoming because MPs and peers wanted a quick route to Lord's for the cricket. Whether or not that was true, on its first day in 1906 the line attracted 37,000 users, and within four months the 'Bakerloo' nickname (coined by a newspaper) had become official. In the intervening century various extensions and branches have opened, closed and been swapped with other lines, with the result that in the early afternoon of this blustery summer day my destination at the top of the Bakerloo is Harrow and Wealdstone.

All thoughts of posh public schoolboys are dispelled as I emerge from the station – Churchill's alma mater is a mile or so south of here in Harrow proper, served by Harrow-on-the-Hill station, which will be on my Metropolitan Line walk. This is Wealdstone, and to be frank, I don't like it. There are two Irish pubs, a kebab house, a minicab office, a food and wine store, an Indian restaurant, a Chinese restaurant, and a firm of solicitors. Together they form the Platonic ideal of disillusionment. By comparison, the bright red of the McDonald's sign a little way up Wealdstone High Street, which stretches away to the north, looks glamorous. Bad luck: I'm heading south.

Despite sharing my name, Masons Avenue does little to

help me feel at home. The terraced houses are dirty and badly maintained, and it's hard to see how they'd make your heart lighter or your eyes brighter. A dash of colour is provided by the plastic sign on the Sri Ayyappan Kovil temple, but as those colours are the exact same blue and yellow used by IKEA, the effect is distinctly un-Hindu. A shortcut through an industrial estate turns out, thanks to some razor wire and padlocks, not to be a shortcut after all, just a way of delaying me by ten minutes. The postcodes of the units begin HA3 – the first time the project has taken me outside 'points of the compass' territory. It's hard to argue that this is London at all. So I won't.

Kenton Recreation Ground provides a little greenery, before Kenton station appears, the second of the 25 on today's menu. Allowing myself the tiniest of detours, I reach the point where Lapstone Gardens meets Mentmore Close. The streetscape has become posher now – the houses are grand Edwardian semis, combining wooden beams, brickwork and (less understandably) pebble-dashing. The typical drive contains a German executive car and a Japanese runabout, neither of them more than five years old. But the vehicle with which this particular corner will forever be associated is a red 1970s Austin 1100. For this is where Basil Fawlty used an upended tree to give his uncooperative car 'a damn good thrashing'.

The scene feels very appropriate. There's something about this sort of suburbia that's horribly repressive, as though the occupant of each and every house is only one corporate restructuring away from a Fawlty-style meltdown. For all the outward peace, the angst-per-square-foot ratio seems dangerously high. It's only after a few more minutes that I realise why: it's because no one walks anywhere. In this respect, if no other, Kenton is like Los Angeles. I haven't seen a single non-car-encased person for ten minutes. Some of these people must use the Tube, otherwise it wouldn't be here; but obviously only in the rush hour. By and large they live in big boxes, then get into smaller boxes to drive to other big boxes. There's none of the pavement-jostling proximity to other grubby humans that makes a city a city. How can eyes be brighter if you never get close enough to *look* anyone in the eye?

A sign reminds me that this is the London Borough of Brent, a name that never had a particularly good ring to it, even before Ricky Gervais came along. The Bakerloo Line tracks run behind Windermere Avenue, and I see the occasional tantalising glimpse of a train in the gaps between houses, like the girl in the red coat in *Don't Look Now*. The trains heading south tease me with thoughts of a speedy return to London – look, here's South Kenton station now. But I can't. I've got to walk the walk.

Looking at the *A to Z*, a small brown oval containing a smaller green oval helps keep my spirits at least an inch or two off the ground. The tracks I'm following curve round to the south-east. Soon I'll be passing within about half a mile of it, this monument, this institution, this symbol of a national obsession. It took its name from the area I'm now entering, which in turn took it from someone – we don't know who, but they were Anglo-Saxon – called Wemba. The 'lea' was his clearing. So yes, football fans are right to chant it as three syllables. They really are on their way to Wemba-lea.

Since 1923 the stadium has struck terror into players, though few had as extreme a reaction as Brian Laws. Playing for Nottingham Forest in the 1989 League Cup final, he emerged from the tunnel to be confronted by the famous Wembley roar. 'The noise just hit me and I wet myself with the excitement. Luckily I was wearing white shorts.' In 1985 the early arrivals for Live Aid underestimated just how big a crowd they were going to be part of, and spread out blankets for their picnics. The famous Twin Towers have now given way to the new stadium's enormous arch, though as is the way with cities the one place it's hard to see it from is Wembley.[3] Only occasionally does the very top peek naughtily over a roof. It's a reminder of how hilly North London is.[4] No matter, I tell myself. Sooner or later the whole of the stadium will come into view. Sooner or later there'll be at least one memorable vista.

In the meantime there are more depressing miles to be slogged (only three and a bit done so far). Wembley Commercial Centre seems far too dilapidated to have a firm called 'Balloon Time' as one of its tenants, but unlike the

---

3. Have you ever tried finding the Empire State Building from three blocks away?

4. The Rhinebeck Panorama of *c.*1806 is another. A painting of the city from south-east of St Paul's, it shows the hills stretching away into the distance. The original is one of the many things worth seeing at the Museum of London.

industrial estate in Harrow it does facilitate a shortcut, so I shouldn't be too harsh. Presently North Wembley station appears and then my route takes me along Llanover Road, neither of them likely to set architects' hearts a-flutter, even if the grime were cleaned off. A middle-aged Indian businessman passes me, his dyed blond hair and trim beard giving him an unfortunate likeness to an Asian Noel Edmonds. There are more of those occasional pockets of affluence that London always seems to throw into the mix, as unexpected as they are fleeting – in this case Keswick Gardens, off to the left, a row of larger semis with healthy green hedges – but by and large the Bakerloo is still failing to impress. On the right I find that mythical beast Acacia Avenue. This one is a mere 40 yards long, with only seven houses on each side, truncated by the Tube line I'm following. Somehow this makes me feel guilty.

Soon I reach Wembley Central station, on the busy High Road that runs east–west through the area's heart. It's surrounded by shops, several of them high-street chains (T. K. Maxx is doing good business), and even a newly built apartment block that's injecting some much-needed colour. Rows of buses disgorge passengers and swallow up more. The ethnic mix is a fairly even split between black, Asian and white, much of the latter Eastern European. At last my walk has encountered a bit of life. But it still feels suburban. It still doesn't feel like London.

A side street follows the Tube line as it curves round to the south and east. I see my first-ever Sikh building gang. Then two Rastas, one of them holding a ladder as the other stands at the top clearing a blocked drainpipe. 'Alla mess,' he says, "e fulluppa shit, yeh?' Then a litter-strewn passageway leads through to the equally litter-strewn expanse of a playing field. Only when my eyes lift from the rain-sodden Argos catalogues and rusting Stella cans do I notice that this is it. This is my vista. On the far side of the field, half a mile beyond the trees and houses, looms the top half of Wembley Stadium.

If it doesn't quite take my breath away it does at least halt my steps for a moment. The arch is indeed very tall, and there's the undulation of the roof and its lattice-like metalwork to look at. But then I lower my gaze an inch, to what's between Wembley and the litter, in the middle of the park: a group of Asian lads playing cricket. England might have won the football World Cup over there at the stadium's predecessor, but that was nearly half a century ago. Twice in the last five years the big sporting story has been several miles south of here, when England won the Ashes at the Oval. I watch the lads, oblivious to the mighty Wembley as they execute off-drives and dive for catches, and think about England cricketers of recent years: Nasser Hussain, Owais Shah, Monty Panesar . . . Perhaps it's time the sporting world moved on.

Besides, as yet another quiet suburban street leads away from the park and hides the stadium once and for all,[5] this

---

5. Tokyngton Avenue, its name derived from a little-used title for this part of Brent. Surely the only other place name beginning with those four letters is Japan's capital city? The contrast couldn't be greater.

*still* isn't London. That's the trouble with icons – they're too big to go right in the middle of a city. Wembley is London's world-famous sports stadium, Heathrow is its world-famous airport, and neither of them is in London. OK, airports can't be right in the middle of cities, that'd be stupid. You can, it's true, arrive into London on the Eurostar, but even that only gets you as far as St Pancras. Central, but not the centre. Think about the ring of mainline terminals (King's Cross, Euston, Paddington and so on) and you realise that's exactly what it is: a ring surrounding a vast centre. And whatever you try to pinpoint as the exact centre just doesn't work: Oxford Circus, Piccadilly Circus, the Bank of England . . . as great as they are, they all feel like places on the way to other places. There's no one place where you can stand and say, 'This is it – I've found London.' Never stops you looking, though.

Just over two hours in now. There's Stonebridge Park station, then one of those God's Meccano arrangements that takes the several lanes of the Harrow Road over the several more lanes of the North Circular (pedestrians catered for surprisingly well, actually), then more quiet side streets. Their names tell the story of how this area has changed: Shakespeare Avenue, Milton Avenue and Shelley Road are followed by Windrush Road. 'No junk mail' and 'No door-to-door salesmen' stickers are common – never before have I seen the one saying 'Loan sharks not welcome here'.

Emerging from Harlesden station are a slightly worthy-looking white couple with their two children, obviously tourists. As we wait at the lights together, curiosity gets the better of me. 'What have you come to see round here?'

'Excuse me?' The woman's accent is German.

'I wondered why you'd come to Harlesden. Not many tourists do.'

She points north, towards Neasden. 'We are going to see the temple.'

Of course. The Shri Swaminarayan Mandir, the biggest Hindu temple outside India. I, on the other hand, am bound for Willesden Junction station, which when I get there brings back memories of the Seven Sisters Road on my Victoria Line walk, in that several of the cafés and shops round it are Brazilian. Several properties are for sale with an estate agency called Margo's, while round the corner on the High Street I pass 'Hair by Pauline – Le Coiffeur'. Leaving aside the fact that this should surely be 'La Coiffeuse', these names remind me of my all-time favourite business name in London: Patisserie Sharon.[6]

The Church of God of Prophecy, run by Open Door Ministries, inhabits a traditional redbrick church built in 1901. This much is clear from the not one but four foundation stones bearing that date, each inscribed with a different name. I always look at the representatives of the great and good who've got themselves carved into history this way, and wonder how sharp their elbows were. No need for such jockeying between men of the cloth – the Reverends Mann, Fyffe and Ellis and Charles Storey Esq. shared the honours between them.

---

6. It's on Store Street in Bloomsbury. Very good reviews, apparently.

I stop at a newsagent's for a drink, and am amazed to find that the can of fizzy orange has the old-fashioned if-you're-not-careful-you'll-slice-your-finger-open type of ring pull; surely these became illegal years ago? The good thing about being this far from Central London is that there are still bins in which to dispose of the can. At the top of Scrubs Lane is a sign saying 'Welcome to Hammersmith and Fulham'; never knew their patch came this far north. Not that I'm taking that turning – it's eastwards along the Harrow Road for me. Eight and a half miles into the walk and I'm at Kensal Green Cemetery.

London's living may have colonised Metroland in the twentieth century, but its dead were a century ahead of them. The city's churches had pretty well filled their graveyards by the 1830s, which was a problem not only for grieving relatives with loved ones to bury, but also for everyone else whose water supplies were becoming contaminated. So Parliament decided that the time had come for London to export its burials. Land was set aside for what became known as the 'Magnificent Seven', privately run cemeteries on what were then the capital's fringes. The locations included Highgate, West Norwood and Mile End, but the first, in 1832, was the one that decades later would inspire G. K. Chesterton's lines: 'For there is good news yet to hear and fine things to be seen,/ Before we go to Paradise by way of Kensal Green.'

It's now home to, among a quarter of a million others, Anthony Trollope, Harold Pinter and Terence Rattigan, but there are two other inmates who stand out for me today. One because he inspires a look forward along the Bakerloo Line

– Isambard Kingdom Brunel, architect of Paddington station – the other because he inspires a look back. On 13 July 1985 Wembley Stadium belonged, by common consent, to Queen; having rehearsed their Live Aid set for three days they were easily the best band there, causing Elton John to tell Freddie Mercury, 'You bastard, you've stolen it.' Yet only six years later, Mercury was here at Kensal Green to be cremated.[7] It's strange: this cemetery, supposedly a place of death and grief, actually feels alive, sparking as it does memories of world-famous people and inspirational achievements. Whereas the rest of the walk has been the other way round: supposedly the realm of the fit and well, it's had a miserably lifeless feel to it.

Back out on the Harrow Road I pass my first gastropub of the day, offering tickets to its forthcoming Notting Hill Carnival Garden Party (£12) and a menu whose starters include Serrano ham with cantaloupe melon (£5.50). Just before the next station (Kensal Green), and yet another turn into a residential road, the tops of the BT Tower and Canary Wharf appear over a roof in the distance. Halfway down the road is a church whose foundation stone was laid by HRH Princess Henry [sic] of Battenberg in 1899. Several years later the royal family would be translating that surname to Mountbatten, to reassure the plebs that they were on the right side in the First World War.

It's the Citroën DS that does it. The gastropub was a clue, but the car is confirmation: I'm finally in London.

---

7. As with John Lennon, there's never been official confirmation of what happened to his ashes.

Specifically, I'm in one of those areas of London where people with money aspire not to a new car but to an old one. (Let the estate agents argue about whether it's Kensal Green or Queen's Park.) The Citroën, like the one de Gaulle uses in *The Day of the Jackal* (except spotlessly white rather than spotlessly black), was made in 1972, a couple of years after the guy who owns it now. He reads the *Guardian*, freelances in multi-media, and wears faux-nerd black-framed glasses. Actually the only facts I'm sure of there are the ones about the car, but I'd put money on the rest. If the car isn't owned by someone like that, how come there's a shop on the next corner selling retro furniture (and possibly repro-retro furniture, it's hard to tell)? And then Queen's Park itself, owned by the City of London,[8] where Boden-clad children gad about with their Gap-clad parents? It's just as well that for most of their history Queens Park Rangers have concentrated on the last word of their name rather than the first two:[9] most of the cheering round here must be for Chelsea and Man United.

It's an attitude, London. The streets round here don't look any different from lots of those I walked through in Harrow and Kenton and Harlesden. This isn't about geography or architecture: it's about aspiration. The shoppers at T. K. Maxx in Wembley aren't bothered about whether they live in

---

8. The park accounts for 30 of the Corporation's 10,000+ acres of green space in and around the capital, provided as breathing spaces from development. The others include Hampstead Heath, Epping Forest and smaller parks as far out as Surrey and Buckinghamshire.

9. They'd settled at Loftus Road in Shepherd's Bush by 1917.

London or not. But Mr Citroën DS and his friends are; it's just that property prices in Maida Vale are beyond them. So they settle in (and settle for) Queen's Park, distress a few sofas and gentrify the recreation areas, and . . . hey presto! The capital has expanded by a mile or two. Judging by that gastropub back in Kensal Green the next exodus has begun, which ought to please Mr Citroën DS – not because he'll have somewhere else to enjoy saffron and mozzarella rissoles, but because it makes his house that fraction nearer to Central London.

Just the other side of the Tube line are First Avenue, Second Avenue and so on up to Sixth. This area was developed in the 1870s by the Artisans, Labourers and General Development Company, who wanted New York-style street names, numbers for those running north–south, letters for the east–westers. They got the numerals through, but the prospect of living on 'A Street' proved too much for the locals, or the ones who were going to become the locals. The developers had the last word, though, or rather words, all of them in alphabetical order: look at the map and you'll see parallel streets called Kilravock, Lothrop, Marne, Nutbourne and so on.

After Queen's Park station there are some of those modern apartments with triangular windows hanging off the front to create more space, followed by a building that was once the Brondesbury Arms but has now forsaken the sale of Reid's Stout and Watney's Ales (though not the tiles advertising them) to provide residential space for several flats. The Kilburn Salvation Army Community Church displays a poster exhorting us to 'Stop the Traffik'. This turns out to be of the human variety; have campaigners changed the spelling to distinguish the practice from the traffic in drugs?

Finally, at 5.37 p.m., over four hours into the walk, I encounter something that's been horribly absent until now: an attractive Tube station. Kilburn Park is an example of that definitive design seen also at Covent Garden, Oxford Circus and several other places, clad in ox-blood terracotta blocks, the station name spelled out above wide arches, next to the 'UNDERGROUND' logo. The design's effect, despite its beauty, is solid and venerable, so it's a shock to learn that its architect, Leslie Green, died aged just 33, in 1908. The rush to get so many stations built – he was working for Charles Yerkes's rapidly expanding UERL company – is thought to have contributed to his ill health. His assistant Stanley Heaps (people had *real* names in those days) stepped in to continue the fine work. Kilburn Park was one of his.

The territory is proper posh now. The mansion flats on Randolph Avenue lead me to Maida Vale, the first Tube station to be manned without men: when it opened during the First World War the ticket collectors, porters and booking clerks were all female. I cross Elgin Avenue, where one of the flats is part of Stirling Moss's property empire. A girlfriend of mine used to live there, and testified to his qualities as a landlord; any problem with the kitchen sink and the ex-racing driver was there, spanner in hand. Further down Randolph Avenue a designer-clad blonde lifts her own hair to smell it. A man on an expensive mountain-bike calmly reasons with his screaming daughter. The door of a large detached house bears an engraved brass plaque reading 'NO JUNK MAIL – PROSZE O NIE WRZUCANIE ZBEDNE POCZTY'. Yes, the last six words really are Polish for the first three.

Past Warwick Avenue station, another surprisingly considerate series of pedestrian subways guides me under the Westway. A brushed-metal footbridge curves sinuously over Regent's Canal, on the other side of which new cafés and restaurants continue the process of turning Paddington into Paddington Basin. Then it's a temporary shortcut through the building works, and we're into Brunel territory – the station itself.

Somehow Paddington never feels quite as big or grown-up as London's other mainline stations. Perhaps it's because the layout hides some of the platforms, making the main space appear smaller. Perhaps it's because the commuters here are bound for the Cotswolds and the West Country, making it harder to take them seriously as downtrodden members of the rat race. Perhaps, tonight, it's because of the businessman cyclist on platform 8, whose one concession to bikewear has been to change his suit trousers for shorts, meaning his hairless legs extend down to black socks and black brogues.

But really we all know the reason Paddington must inhabit the Junior League of train stations. That reason comes from Lima, wears a duffel coat and likes marmalade sandwiches. A whole generation of us are unable to utter those three syllables without a faint echo coming back in Michael Hordern's voice. So I'm unable to pass the official Paddington stall without stopping to buy my one-year-old son a book.

'Do you ever get anyone from Peru here?' I ask the assistant as she counts my change.

She laughs. 'We've only ever had one. She was with her English boyfriend. She'd never heard of Paddington.'

Exiting the concourse on to the ramp that leads up to Praed Street means passing through a nicotine pea-souper. Smokers now have to stand outside, and there are dozens of them. One or two, having been banished from smoke-free pubs, drink from cans of lager. It suddenly strikes me as being slightly inhumane. Around the corner is St Mary's Hospital, which bears, like many buildings in London, a blue plaque. By and large I hold the opposite view on these from Lord Rosebery, who in 1903 asked 'anybody who is in the habit of taking long walks in London . . . whether it is not an immense relief to come on some tablet . . . which recalls to the mind the career of some distinguished person'.[10] Most of the ones you see now commemorate people you've never heard of, and the bar not only of achievement but also of longevity seems to get ever lower. A typical blue plaque now reads 'Charles Total-Nonentity, Secretary of Upper Norwood Bowls Club 1932–3, ate a sandwich here, 1925'. But standing on Praed Street – and it *is* standing, the plaque having literally stopped me in my tracks – I can't help but think that Lord R. had a point. Because this one says 'Sir Alexander

10. He also praised plaques for easing the 'intolerable pressure of the monotony of endless streets'. Given that Kenton and Wembley were still undeveloped in his day, and that his London walks can't have been much further afield than Westminster, Mayfair and the like, the man was clearly off his Prime Ministerial rocker.

Fleming, 1881–1955, discovered penicillin in the second storey room above this plaque'. The fact that you can look up to see the window itself, imagine the great man standing there as he realised the implications of his happy accident with some mould, makes this a wonderfully specific plaque.

A little over 12 miles brings me to Edgware Road station. Or rather one of the two Edgware Road stations. The use of the same name for two pretty distinct stations (Circle, District and Hammersmith and City Lines south of the Westway, Bakerloo to its north) provokes regular calls for one of them to be retitled. I can see both sides of the argument, but in the end think that 'endearing quirk' wins out over 'need for clarity'. Then it's Marylebone station, into whose mainline section the Beatles are chased by fans at the beginning of *A Hard Day's Night*.

Through Dorset Square, where Thomas Lord had his first ground before taking the Marylebone Cricket Club out of Marylebone to its current home in St John's Wood, then it's Baker Street station. Chiltern Court, the residential block on top of it, was home during the Second World War to the Special Operations Executive, Churchill's 'Ministry of Ungentlemanly Warfare', charged with encouraging espionage and sabotage in Nazi-occupied Europe. Past the institution started by a French woman who once made death masks from the heads of guillotine victims (Louis XVI, Marie Antoinette, Robespierre *et al.*), so that the revolutionaries could parade them through the streets in triumph. Marie Tussaud's later, more famous, works included the rest of her models' bodies too.

Regent's Park station is always annoying when you're heading south, because the private gardens immediately next to it block your way. You have to head either west or east, then round the gardens' curved edge. So tonight, after about 50 of my steps have been retraced, I find myself on Portland Place, heading past the latest extension to the BBC's Broadcasting House. Previous extensions were known (when I worked there over a decade ago) as BHX and BHXX; it'd be nice to think the new one will be BHXXX, as though Auntie was getting ever ruder.

A few yards later, opposite the Langham Hotel, I reach what feels like a momentous point: the first time I've crossed a previous route. This was where the Victoria Line walk took me north-east into Fitzrovia. As of now, today's south-easterly trek is drawing an X, one that marks not so much a spot as a process, that of joining up this city, linking it together. Each step further helps make my mark on the enormous ballot paper that is London. The election metaphor seems an appropriate one; taking part makes me feel included, tied in, bonded to the capital. It feels cocoon-like. It feels good.

My last sight of the Langham was at teatime. Now it's 7.30 p.m., dinnertime, which is pleasing as it was at a dinner here in 1889 that an American publisher not only commissioned Oscar Wilde to write *The Picture of Dorian Gray*, but also commissioned Arthur Conan Doyle to write *The Sign of Four*. Not bad for a single sitting. Map sensibilities are offended further down Regent Street, where one of the other-wise excellent information boards provided by the City of

Westminster and Transport for London turns the street plan upside down so that 'south' is ahead of you, as it is in real life, putting Oxford Street to the north of Regent's Park. Tourists may be tourists, but surely they still know how to read a simple map without being patronised?

Past Oxford Circus station, then Great Marlborough Street appears on the left. You wouldn't normally associate the mock-Tudor building that takes up much of its south side with anyone called Arthur, but that was indeed Mr Liberty's Christian name. This very English street, with its Palladium stage door and magistrates'-court-turned-luxury-hotel, was also the birthplace of so-called all-American hero Marlboro Man: the firm started by British tobacconist Philip Morris used to make its cigarettes in a factory here, hence the brand's name. Regent Street curves round into Piccadilly Circus, and then becomes Lower Regent Street. Or rather, I notice from the street signs, it doesn't. The 'Lower' was dropped well over a hundred years ago (a map of 1888 refers only to 'Regent Street', as does the modern *A to Z*) but no one seems to have noticed.

Thoughts of Wilde and Conan Doyle exchanging bon mots over the bouillabaisse have got me hungry, so of the many routes I could take to Charing Cross I choose the one that includes Panton Street. Quite why theatre-goers insist on paying through the nose for what goes into their mouth mystifies me when here, a few steps from Leicester Square, in its fifty-second year of trading, is the West End Kitchen. Avocado vinaigrette, aubergine parmigiana and a can of Coke (safe ring pull) set me back £8.95 plus tip. Thrown into the bargain are the three cabbies at the next table discussing their recent rounds of golf. During a rant about green fees I hear my first-ever irony-free use of the phrase 'diabolical liberty'.

In Whitcomb Street, on the way through to Trafalgar Square, is a flashing neon sign offering 'Massage'. Unusually for Central London this turns out to be an invitation to have a massage. A semi-reclined businesswoman gazes vacantly out of the window as the soles of her feet are rubbed. Then it's the square itself, where in the shadow of Nelson's Column, while waiting to cross the road, I find myself next to a woman in a wedding dress and her besuited husband. With them is a photographer.

'Congratulations,' I say.

'Thank you,' come the smiling replies.

'Where was your wedding?'

'Oh, we did not get married today,' says the bride. 'We got married two weeks ago, back in Poland. That's where we're both from. But we live here, and wanted photographs in places that were special to us.'

I round the hotel next to Charing Cross station, which was the venue in 2003 for the drink that cost Andrew Gilligan his job at the BBC and Dr David Kelly much more. Then it's down to, and through, Embankment station. To the right is Northumberland Avenue, off which runs Great Scotland Yard, not only the Met's original home but also starting point in 1865 of the earliest attempt at a Tube railway. A pneumatic system would have used air pressure to push trains under the Thames to Waterloo station. But money ran out, and the excavations now form the National Liberal Club's wine cellar.

Up on Hungerford footbridge, another Brunel element to the day (he built its predecessor, whose suspension chains were rescued for reuse in his bridge at Clifton), I notice that one of the London Eye's 32 capsules is missing.[11] They're being individually cleaned in the run-up to the Olympics – each one floated, like a lonely testicle, down the river to Tilbury, then driven by lorry to Worcester.

Outside the Festival Hall a couple stand between fountain jets that surge upwards in ever-changing configurations, the next alteration trapping them in a cell with walls of $H_2O$. Down the side of the National Film Theatre to Waterloo station, then it's back westwards along York Road to the roundabout at the back of County Hall. Famed for years as the ugliest traffic feature in Christendom, the monstrosity of a building that stood on it (actually a 1970s annexe to County Hall itself) has now made way for the state-of-the-art Park Plaza Hotel. Passing reception, which is on the outside of the island, I ask a staff member if there's a tunnel under the road to the rooms.

'No, sir.' His resigned smile indicates that this is not the first time the question has been posed.

'Really? Your guests have to pick their way through the traffic?'

'There's a crossing over there,' he says, pointing to the Westminster Bridge side of the roundabout. 'But I know what you mean. Even we were saying to management, "Are you really not going to build a tunnel or a bridge?"'

And so I gaze up at the world's most dangerous hotel. On

11. One for each London borough. Though they're numbered up to 33 – superstition did for 13.

the fourth floor a Japanese man stands immobile in trousers and a vest, fruitlessly trying to work his TV remote control. Directly underneath him an excited kid uses a bed as a trampoline. Feeling unnervingly like James Stewart in *Rear Window*, I decide to move on. The bend of the road suddenly takes you out of Central London, as though Big Ben and County Hall and the Eye were in a different time zone, not just round the corner. The area round Lambeth North station feels boring, plain, even a little dispiriting. Certainly a man who died here in 1772 (reports identify him only as 'John G. E.') had had a less than happy time of it. 'It was my misfortune,' his will read, 'to be made very uneasy by Elizabeth my wife, for many years from our marriage . . . she seemed only to be born to be a plague to me; the strength of Sampson, the knowledge of Homer, the prudence of Augustus, the cunning of Pyrrhus, the patience of Job, the subtlety of Hannibal, and the watchfulness of Hermogenes, could not have been sufficient to subdue her . . . therefore I give her one shilling only.'

The area's sombre history continues with the Imperial War Museum. It stands in Geraldine Mary Harmsworth Park, where in 2004 Kevin Spacey was robbed of his mobile phone; asked what he was doing in the park at 4 a.m. he said, 'My doggy had to go.' The museum itself used to be the notorious Bedlam, the Bethlem psychiatric hospital, whose patients doubled as a freak show for paying Londoners. It migrated here in 1815 from the site where Liverpool Street station now stands, and in 1930 travelled on once more to Beckenham, where it now (incredibly still called Bethlem) forms part of the South London and Maudsley NHS Foundation Trust.

Strangely the one thing that doesn't feel sombre round here is the War Museum itself. Without in any way painting war as a good thing, there's something about London's long experience of it, and of violence in general, that's at one with the city's dynamism. Any physicist will tell you that energy can take different forms, not all of them desirable. The same life force that builds palaces and makes fortunes can also turn bad, snuffing out life itself. Hellish as that is, the capital seems to accept it; as someone said during the Blitz: 'There's one good thing about all this bombing, it takes your mind off the war.' More than accept it, in fact: relish it. Sexual abandonment during the war affected even the historian A. L. Rowse, who had the only carnal experience of his life with a man he met during a blackout. And there's something sexual in the words of a woman whose house was bombed during the Second World War. 'I lay there feeling indescribably happy and triumphant,' she wrote. '"I've been bombed!" I kept on saying to myself . . . It seems a terrible thing to say, when many people were killed and injured last night; but never in my whole life have I ever experienced such pure and flawless happiness.'[12]

\* \* \*

12. I'd like to borrow her phrase 'it seems a terrible thing to say' as a prelude to noting that London's 7 July bombings somehow didn't feel as shocking as I thought they should. There was certainly no happiness, pure and flawless or otherwise, but neither was there outrage, or fear, or for that matter defiance. It just felt like a day in the history of a city that had seen lots of similar days. When I tentatively mentioned this to a friend, he replied that his sister, another Londoner, had said exactly the same thing.

Final few yards now. St George's Road, one of the several that congregate at the Elephant and Castle, is dark and uninspiring. Normally, and like most people, I'd have pretty much the same opinion of the Elephant and Castle itself, with the caveat that it's now half-past nine and so the lights on the traffic islands and their surrounding buildings shine brilliantly against the night sky. The Elephant's architecture is typified by Metro Central Heights, now an apartment block, designed as government office blocks in 1959 by the Hungarian modernist Ernö Goldfinger.[13] Can anything bode less well for a building than the phrase 'Hungarian modernist'? Not without due cause did Adrian Edmondson's character in the Comic Strip film *Mr Jolly Lives Next Door* illustrate Cockney rhyming slang to a Japanese businessman with 'Elephant and Castle – stick it up your arsehole'.

But tonight, somehow, the Elephant looks good. Maybe it's because I've got 17.1 miles' worth of endorphins surging round me, maybe it's because I've completed another line, maybe it's because the 133 bus I need for Liverpool Street appears right on cue, but instead of Metro Central Heights I notice the Metropolitan Tabernacle, the large 1860s pillared Baptist church. Rather than looking at the hideous shopping centre, I gaze up at the Strata skyscraper, recent poacher (from the Barbican towers) of the title 'tallest residential building in London', informally known as the Razor because of its similarity to an electric shaver. Quite

---

13. Yes, he is the man who gave his name to the Bond villain. Not that he was very happy about it. He threatened to sue, at which Ian Fleming proposed a change to 'Goldprick'.

Gothamish: you can imagine the Batman logo projecting out of the three enormous holes at the top that house the eco-friendly wind turbines. I feel happy, full of good cheer towards this unfairly denigrated corner of London. I savour the impish way its Tube station (like several others) teases reality by being simultaneously in both Zone 1 and Zone 2. Good old Elephant.

Then, on the bus, I pick up a copy of the *Standard* and read how residents in the Razor are complaining because their eco-flats don't have air-conditioning and are far too hot. Crappy old Elephant.

The next day, I'm sitting at home with three of my nine new maps stretched out on the sitting-room floor. I'm poised over them all, black magimarker in hand, contemplating the strokes that will make a record of my Victoria and Bakerloo Line walks. For a while contemplation is as far as it gets. Actually putting marker to map proves too much, an act of desecration, as though drawing these lines will permanently scar London itself. I even wonder for a few foolish seconds whether defacing a map isn't illegal, like defacing currency. But then I remember Piotr's words about mapmaking being an art. What Sting said about albums, Truman Capote said about novels: you never feel as though they're finished, people just take them away from you. There are always more changes you want to make. Why shouldn't it be the same with maps? The Geographer's A to Z Map Company Ltd have done their bit; now it's my turn.

Within the first inch or so nervousness gives way to

exhilaration. Not only does drawing the route feel like an artistic statement – I *know* that belongs in *Private Eye*'s Pseuds Corner, but honestly, that is how it feels – it also gives me a sense of reliving the walks, taking each step in my mind rather than with my feet.

Jo comes in and watches for a minute. Then she says: 'That's two down, then.'

'Mmm.' It's quite a muffled 'mmm', owing to the fact I'm concentrating so much. And have a magimarker top in my mouth.

'How many are there in total?'

'Ebeben.'

'How many miles?'

'Ibobal, or sobar?'

'In total.'

'Bour unbreb.' I waver my left hand to indicate that this is an estimate.

Jo nods. 'And how many so far?'

There's no way of saying 'thirty-seven point three' with a magimarker top in your mouth, so I remove it. And, having given the figure, add that those miles have been completed at an average speed of 2.256 miles per hour.[14]

'So you haven't even done a tenth of it yet?'

'No.'

Jo watches my magimarker travel up Seven Sisters Road.

---

14. All this talk of average walking speed being four miles an hour is nonsense; try it and you'll see how much effort that requires. A comfortable pace is down towards three; plus I've been stopping to make notes, read the map, eat and drink and so on.

As it nears Tottenham she says: 'No one would know if you didn't walk it all, would they?'

The magimarker stops. It's best that it does so, as I'm in danger of sending it careering horrifically off towards Dartford. '*What?*'

'You know, if you . . .'

'If I what? Pretended?'

'Yeah.'

I sigh, a very deep, ominous sigh. 'Jo. That's not true. One person would know. The most important person. Me.'

I'm expecting contrition, maybe even a little fawning, a hand clasped to Jo's forehead as she realises what a fool she's been, how could she not have seen that self-deception is the very worst deception of all?

Instead she just laughs, a laugh from the border of 'sympathetic' and 'patronising', the sort of laugh that says, 'OK, dear, whatever makes you happy.' Then she goes out.

When she gets back, Jo says, 'Close your eyes and hold your hands out.'

I do as I'm told. Jo places a present in my outstretched palm. Two presents, in fact. A can of anti-blister foot spray and some special padded plasters.

# 3
# Central Line

## Live in fragments no longer

It's at this stage that I recruit my research assistant.

Not that I was looking for one. But then that's part of Richard's charm: he makes things happen where you weren't expecting them. Captain of the local cricket team I sometimes play for, he has an insatiable, fact-based enthusiasm for all sorts of subjects. Football grounds, obscure bands, flags of the world . . . Richard doesn't always manage to successfully communicate the reasons for his enthusiasm. He once said to a group of us in the village pub – and, I promise you, he said it with a completely straight face – 'This is more interesting than I'm making it sound.' But nevertheless the fact that you know that *he* knows why something is interesting somehow makes it interesting. In his mid-thirties, Richard possesses the knowledge of someone twenty years older, though as that knowledge is held with the vigour of someone twenty years younger, he averages out at about the right figure.

One of his greatest loves, I remember as we have a drink in the village pub for the first time since my project started, is the London Underground. So when he asks what I'm working on at the moment, and I tell him, a look of respectful awe spreads across his face.

'What — *all* of it?'

'Yeah. All eleven lines.'

'How many have you done so far?'

'Two. I'm doing the Central next.' After the matching diagonals, a nice straight line across the middle feels appropriate.

'Longest line on the system. Forty-six miles.' You see. Richard *knows* this stuff.

'Yeah. I was worried about doing "the biggy" so early. But actually in my terms I don't think it *is* the biggy. What with walking between the ends of different branches, I think the District or Metropolitan will be the longest.'

Richard's eyes narrow as he consults an imaginary Tube map. 'Or the Piccadilly.'

'Maybe.'

'I could work it out for you, if you like?' No puppy has ever offered to fetch a stick with greater eagerness.

'Thanks, Richard. But actually I'm deliberately not working it out in advance. Want to keep a bit of mystery for out on the road.'

'Oh. OK.'

You can't leave a man crestfallen like that. You just can't. 'But if you wanted to help out with some more general research . . .'

'Really?'

'Of course.'

'Great! Thanks.'

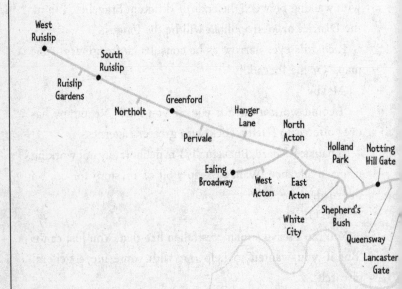

## CENTRAL LINE

Stations: 49

Line mileage: 46

Near-fatal incidents with
noise-free Toyota Priuses: 1

West
Ruislip

South
Ruislip

Ruislip
Gardens

Northolt

Greenford

Perivale

Hanger
Lane

North
Acton

Holland
Park

Notting
Hill Gate

Ealing
Broadway

West
Acton

East
Acton

Shepherd's
Bush

White
City

Queensway

Lancaster
Gate

N

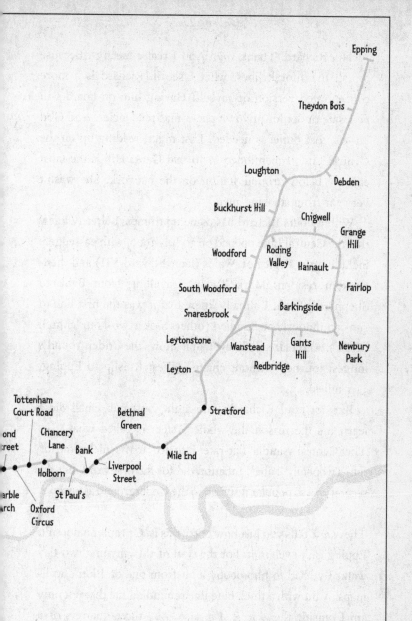

Epping

Theydon Bois

Loughton

Debden

Buckhurst Hill

Chigwell

Grange Hill

Woodford

Roding Valley

Hainault

South Woodford

Fairlop

Barkingside

Snaresbrook

Leytonstone

Wanstead

Gants Hill

Newbury Park

Leyton

Redbridge

Stratford

Tottenham Court Road

Bethnal Green

Chancery Lane

Bank

Mile End

ond reet

Holborn

Liverpool Street

arble arch

St Paul's

Oxford Circus

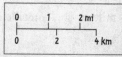

'No, Richard. Thank *you*.' And I really mean it. Because for all the anorak jibes, what I see in Richard is a more concentrated version of myself. Having him on board will be a safe outlet for my own pac-a-mac tendencies. And God knows, that outlet is needed. Last night, reading up on the Central Line, I mentioned to Jo that Gants Hill is the most easterly below-ground station on the network. She wasn't very far from stabbing me.

Within hours Richard has come up trumps. I already knew that the Central Line opened on 30 July 1900, with passengers including the Prince of Wales (later Edward VII) and then-London resident Mark Twain, travelling from Bank to Shepherd's Bush. I already knew that it was the first line to run continuously on Sundays (others took a two-hour 'church break'). And I already knew that it allows the Underground's longest journey without change (West Ruislip to Epping, 34.1 miles).

But not until Richard's late-night, post-pub email did I learn it's the reason the whole system is called what it is. The Central's initial flat-rate fare led to its nickname of the 'Twopenny Tube'. Inflation did for the first word, but the second was so popular it spread to the Underground as a whole.

The *A to Z* tells you just how crazy this is. Or rather it doesn't: Epping isn't even in it. For the start of this, my first two-day walk, I've had to photocopy a bit from one of Piotr's wall-maps. A bit with a thick blue line reminding me that not only am I outside the *A to Z*, I'm also – by three-quarters of a mile or so – outside the M25.

Not that the motorway's proximity feels real. Leaving Epping's respectable little nineteenth-century train station (this end of the Central Line has been only part of the so-called Underground system since just after the Second World War), you're quickly into countryside. Listen for the cars and you can just make out a faint rushing noise, but the route is so well-disguised that only once or twice can you glimpse the motorway through trees or over the brow of a hill. It's not yet nine o'clock, but three members of Epping Golf Club have already reached the tenth tee, and happily assure me that yes, that footpath across the fairway is indeed the one that goes under the M25. Increasing traffic noise gives extra confirmation, until someone else in a country lane tells me that what I'm actually heading towards is the M11. Hopefully the golfers have a better sense of direction when they're aiming for the pin.

The detour costs me half an hour, which, as tonight's intended resting point is Liverpool Street, feels like a lot. So it's full speed ahead through the pedestrian tunnel that takes me under all six lanes of the M25 (curiously, the tunnel is the one place from which you can't hear the motorway at all), then across a wide-open field. Two hundred yards to the right, on the other side of a hedge, runs the Central Line track. Trains pass in both directions, their blues and reds standing out against the greens and browns of rural Essex.

The residents of Theydon Bois[1] continue to vote against street lighting, for fear of ruining the village's 'village' atmos-

---

1. It's pronounced 'Boys', something I only learned from the recorded announcement on the Tube that brought me out here.

phere. The green is certainly pleasant, and there are even ducks on the pond, but it's just that bit too big to feel properly Miss Marple. The road along one side has a constant stream of traffic, and even on the quieter edge I pass a woman in expensive training gear working out with her personal trainer, a distinctly urban touch.

On the road to Debden is a property, invisible from the road, whose forbidding gates have an expensively carved stone sign reading 'NO TRESSPASSERS' – let's hope they weren't paying by the letter. Then there's an entrance to part of Epping Forest, the Corporation of London noticeboard reminding me of Queen's Park on the Bakerloo Line. It was in this forest that Henry VIII was hunting when he heard the gun from the Tower of London confirming Anne Boleyn's execution in 1536. Shortly afterwards I arrive in Debden itself, most of which is a post-war housing estate. As I overtake two old women, one of them is saying: 'I had to go 'cos if I hadn't I'd have wet meself.'

The station isn't far from the De La Rue printing works, whose contract to produce the country's banknotes explains why the nearby junction on the M11 only lets you join southbound, towards London; the police wouldn't want robbers heading north into open country. Loughton is more of the same (estates, both housing and industrial), then there's Buckhurst Hill, where Dick Turpin began his life of crime selling deer meat poached from Waltham Forest. Now they've got a Waitrose.

It's here that my project reaches its first complication, or as London Underground calls it, branch. Imagine a letter 'b'.

Epping was at its top. Buckhurst Hill was just before the start of the loop. Woodford is the next stop down on the vertical, but I've also got to do all the stations on the loop, from Roding Valley round to Wanstead. The map tells me it's quicker to do them first, before heading all the way back up to the start of loop then back down to Woodford.

So Roding Valley it is. Named after the river that passes nearby, it's a thoroughly average 1930s station. Nothing special about it. Except for just one thing: it is the least-used station anywhere on the London Underground network. In the league table of 269, this poor creature props up the other 268. Victoria has more passengers in a day than Roding Valley has in a year. Surveying it at midday on a Tuesday, the first day back after a bank holiday, I can't help but feel a pang of sympathy for it. To stop myself actually patting its brickwork and muttering 'there, there', and knowing Jo won't understand, I text Richard to tell him where I am. He, needless to say, is aware of the station's claim to infamy. He manned a trade stand there once, he replies, while working for the Essex Wildlife Trust. 'There were literally tumbleweeds.'

A footpath leads towards the M11, and this time that's actually the motorway I need. Just before the footbridge that carries me over it, unmarked on the map, is Tottenham Hotspur's training ground. A Sky Sports crew wait outside it, preparing for a link-up with the studio.

'What's going on?' I ask the reporter, a heavily-pancaked blonde.

'Transfer day. They might be signing someone.'

I nod.

'Are you a Spurs fan?' she asks pleasantly.

'No.' And then, because I've been doing this for nearly four hours today, and thinking about it every day for several weeks, it seems the most natural thing in the world to add, by way of explanation for why a non-Spurs fan *would* be here: 'I'm walking the Tube system.'

All of a sudden the reporter seems to have something of great urgency to check on her mobile phone.

Just the other side of the motorway is Chigwell. In his 1929 book *London's Countryside*, Edric Holmes wrote that 'how long the old village will retain its rural character is a matter for anxious conjecture'. Well, Edric,[2] 80 years on and your anxiety still isn't justified. Not totally, anyway. Yes, they've built some big houses on the High Road (they've even set a sitcom called *Birds of a Feather* in one of them), and in the 1950s they built a parade of shops near the station,[3] but essentially Chigwell is still rural. Within a couple of minutes I'm walking along the edge of a field that's being ploughed by a farmer (though he is using a tractor rather than horses), with nothing to see beyond it but more fields. Then through a wood. Then past a paddock containing half a dozen horses.

And then on to Manor Road, part of the Grange Hill estate.[4] This is not very rural at all. In fact, it's very

---

2. No, there isn't a 'C' missing. He really was called Edric.

3. One of which is a health food shop whose window contains a neon sign saying 'Belgian Chocolates'.

4. Not where the TV series was set – that was a fictional North London area called Northam.

Sprawlsville suburban. The sort of suburban where wooden fences at the end of cul-de-sacs block pedestrians from taking the cut-throughs they want to take. This pedestrian, though, has only done 12 miles by lunchtime on a day when he'll need to do about 30, so it's up and over the fence. (Soon I'll do something I wouldn't normally consider: use a shortcut over a section of chain-fencing that kids have torn down for precisely that purpose.)

This geo-inconsistency continues for the next few stops, as though the Central Line is a succession of wormholes transporting you from 'countryside where you can't imagine a house let alone see one' to 'housing estate where even the notion of a tree is pure fantasy', then back again. Hainault gives way to Fairlop's playing fields, the area taking its name from an oak cut down to make a local man's coffin in the eighteenth century; when the tree grew back, his friends said they must have made a 'fair lop'. Then modernity reappears just before Barkingside – a barber's shop with gold lettering on a black plastic sign is called Geezer's – while after the station a footpath cuts through a farm. To the west a line of trees blocks any view of buildings, while to the east you can only see fields.

Dickens said of London's ever-expanding nineteenth-century edge that it was 'neither of the town nor of the country'. This bit of the walk is like that, except that it's of the town *and* of the country, just never both at the same time. The dividing line zig-zags madly, blocks of countryside punching their way into the city and vice versa, leaving the border like one of those agreed after a war between two obscure African states. The limbo finally ends when I hit the A12 and turn right; it's going to be all city from now on. Were I to turn left, though, there would be several farms within a mile either side of me as I headed for Romford just down the road. You don't see them *from* the road, that's the thing. I've driven this way back to Suffolk many times and never suspected their existence.

On balance, though, it's London that wins out. There's something urban about Essex, and it's probably the accent. Henry Higgins could no doubt hear a difference, but to an untrained ear a conversation in London's eastern county sounds very much like a conversation in its old East End, for the simple reason that what we used to think of as Cockneys have all moved out here. And even before that, they used to come here for their country breaks. As James Thorne observed about nearby Wanstead (where I'm heading) in his 1876 *Handbook to the Environs of London*, 'East-end holiday makers . . . come here during the summer months in vans and other vehicles in prodigious numbers, and amuse themselves with swings, donkey and pony races.' There's a frankness, a lack of pretension, an in-your-faceness about Essex that ties it very much to London, in a way that is not true of other outlying areas.

Soon I'm at my next station, Newbury Park. As the crow flies this is nine miles from the Bow Bells on Cheapside, well outside the auditory range that marked true Cockneydom.[5] And yet it feels Cockneyish – Londonish – in a way that I

---

5.  Modern studies suggest six miles to the east, five to the north, three to the south and four to the west.

can't believe, say, Queen's Park (only five miles from Cheapside) ever has.

When we were house-hunting in Suffolk, that journey along the A12 used to drive my partner and me mad. But today it's beautiful. Yes, it's loud; yes, it's charmless; and yes, the only bit of colour is the yellow of the speed cameras. But I've been weaving and winding (and fence-hopping) for six hours now. A nice straight easy bit is just what's needed. Including Newbury Park, the next four stations are on this road.

From Gants Hill onwards, the stretch of Tube tunnel beneath me has a proud claim to having helped Britain win the Second World War. Completed just before the war as a connection between Liverpool Street and the old above-ground rail lines in Essex, the extension hadn't officially opened by the time hostilities started. So five miles of the tunnel were converted, Bond-villain-style, into an underground factory where Plessey could make aircraft components, free from the attentions of the Luftwaffe.

After Redbridge, having negotiated the subways under the North Circular, I pass some allotments. An old man, tall and white-haired, works away dressed only in tracksuit bottoms and shoes. Anyone younger wearing this outfit would look either ridiculous or slovenly, but he has an air of dignity. Then it's Wanstead, one-time haunt of the people Dick Van Dyke so feebly imitated, now home to one of the Belgique chain of cafés ('Patisserie, Bakery, Delicatessen, Coffeeshop, Chocolaterie . . .'). Because of my 'walk every bit of line' rule I have to continue to the Green Man roundabout, where the Central Line continues westwards to Leytonstone but where I head north for the long slog up the side of that 'b', back to Roding Valley.

Keeping a street or two away from the stations I'll do on the way back down (don't want to visit them out of order), it's impossible not to notice the number of cars with private registration plates. Vehicular veneration has been a theme of the walk all day long. There've been Porsche 911s with '911' on the plate, Jaguar XJRs with 'XJR' on the plate, and even a bog-standard motor home with 'BMW' on the plate (the make of his other car). Virtually every house you pass has a car parked outside, and most have two. Even the residents of modest semis have perfected their parking arrangements so as to get as many cars as possible on to the tiny areas in front of their dwellings. One woman back in Barkingside retracted both her wing mirrors before edging into a garage that allowed two (*possibly* three) inches either side. I can only presume the building opened out at the far end, otherwise she'll be in there even now. OK, all suburban areas depend on their cars. But not all of them worship their cars. This bit of London's Tube system definitely feels Londony, but it doesn't feel very Tubey.

The walk up to Roding Valley is tiring, mentally as well as physically – it's tough going back to somewhere you've already been. A woman wheeling her mother out of an old people's home says patiently, 'You should say thanks to them, you know.' Life goes full circle. Two men in their fifties stand studying some half-relaid paving slabs, one with left hand on hip, the other with his right, so that they look like mirrored teapots. A poster announces the disappearance of a cat with 'an extra digit on each paw'.

And then, at 4.22 p.m., I return to the least-used station on the network, boosting its visitor, if not passenger, numbers. Heading back down the 'b' feels easier, largely because this time I can tick the stations off. Woodford serves a peacefully well-off area (with grammatically inventive residents: 'Please don't put leaflets here nor under this door'), while the internet café next to South Woodford serves me a much-needed latte.[6] Much-needed because as of this point I've walked 26.2 miles – a marathon.

After Snaresbrook there's the Crown Court of the same name, whose main Victorian building is far more inspiring than the ugly modern extension they always show on the news. It used to be a children's home; sadly several former residents have returned to appear at the venue in its new guise. Then through the pedestrian subway formed by Leytonstone station, lined with tiled mosaics in honour of Alfred Hitchcock, once of this parish. The *Psycho* shower scene features in one, with a quote from Janet Leigh putting paid to the urban myth about how Hitchcock elicited realistic screams: 'at least he made sure the water was warm'.[7]

---

6. Richard has emailed to say he's bought an old Bakerloo Line map (the horizontal ones inside the carriages) off eBay. 'Happily having it framed to the obvious dismay of the wife.'

7. It is true, though, that Leigh was put off showers for the rest of her life. If she had to take one she left the door open, together with the door to the bathroom, having first locked all other doors and windows.

Halfway along the long street of terraced Victorian houses leading to Leyton, I get my first glimpse of the Gherkin, the Heron Tower and Tower 42. Wonderful the way they jump around depending on which part of London you view them from, like ornaments rearranged by a cleaner. The walk from Leyton to Stratford – partly down Angel Lane, where the Beatles filmed the promo for *Penny Lane* because they didn't want to travel back to Liverpool – is dominated more and more with every step by the burgeoning Olympic site. The main stadium looms good-naturedly over the smaller structures (including the new station itself), the evening sunlight bouncing off their metal surfaces in detergent-ad sparkles.

But soon dusk descends, both in reality and in my soul. Over 30 miles walked now, and while weary legs can feel good – a sense of having earned your dinner – I'm heading into exhaustion territory. My fingers have pork-sausaged (pointing down all day, they've had blood draining into them), and even though I know the depression stalking the edges of my consciousness is purely a result of tiredness, and therefore unreal, I don't feel that confident about repelling it. I think back to Stratford and can't stop myself visualising the Central Line's interchange there with the Jubilee, then across to Westminster, where you can change to the District, which takes you out to *Wimbledon*, for God's sake . . . The whole Tube map's unfolding before me and for the first time I find myself asking what the hell I've got myself into. Crossing a street as a van turns into it, I find that my legs won't hurry. Like a stubborn New Forest pony I maintain the same pace, knowing that the van will stop. Further along the Bow Road, dumped by a rubbish bin, is a car's front passenger seat. It looks very tempting.

But no – on to Mile End, a reference to the Roman road from London to Colchester (it was a mile from Aldgate), then it's Bethnal Green, reached by Roman Road, so-called because . . . well, you can guess.

This was the station that in 1943 saw the Second World War's largest loss of UK civilian life. With a horrible irony it wasn't due to bombing itself, but rather to someone falling in the scramble to get into the station after an air-raid siren. In the resulting crush, 173 people were killed. My route to Liverpool Street includes Brick Lane, so there's really only one option available for dinner. Halfway through chicken hunza (made with oranges) and lemon rice, I realise I've accidentally ordered an Indian version of one of the most famous nursery rhymes about London. Finally, at 10.08 p.m., over 13 hours since that first step in Epping, I reach Liverpool Street. A couple of minutes past the station (though tonight it's more like ten) is the hotel where I'm spending the night. Unsurprisingly, after walking 35 miles sleep doesn't take long to claim me, though in the few moments before it does I notice the dull rumble of a Tube train passing beneath the hotel. And my brain's last thought, before it finally logs off for the night, is just *how* parochial London can make you. 'That's not a Central Line Tube,' I'm thinking. 'It's got to be a Circle. Who cares about that?'

There have been easier times to admit this during the last few decades, but I love the City of London. Yes, its bankers have double-or-quitted the nation to disaster, and yes, they have passed the tab for that to the taxpayer with one hand, while using the other to help themselves to never-diminishing bonuses. But even so, there's something about the place – as opposed to its institutions – that gets me every time. It's not just the depth of the place, the knowledge that wherever you walk your feet are treading upon 2,000 years of history, walking on land that's been London ever since the Romans bridged the Thames in AD 43. It's also the energy, the crackle and hiss that radiates from every square inch of the Square Mile, the fizz that gets inside your head and makes you believe anything is possible.

From the 1980s onwards, the financial district's soaring ambition has taken a very physical form. Its first skyscraper, built by NatWest and now known as Tower 42, lies on my route this morning, between Liverpool Street and Bank. Every sighting of the tower on my previous walks – together with its smaller neighbour the Gherkin, and the ever-growing Heron – has brought to mind the very horizontal nature of my own project. And so, as the first of two appointments I've got before this second day's walking really gets under way, Tower 42's owners have kindly agreed to indulge me with a moment of verticality. They're going to let me survey the Central Line walk – the whole of London, indeed – from a height of 600 feet. They're going to let me stand on their roof.

As we take the lift to the top, the building's operations manager, Nathan O'Reilly, talks me through the figures. 'Obviously Vertigo [the champagne bar] is the forty-second floor; that's where the name comes from. Then there are five more beyond that, so the roof is forty-seven.'

'Glad the lift's working.'

He smiles. 'You know about Vertical Rush?'

I don't.

'Running up the stairs for charity. It's an annual thing.'

'All the way?'

He nods. 'Ground floor to the champagne bar.'

'How long does that take?'

'Depends on how fit you are, obviously, but the serious ones can do it in just over four minutes.'

'Sorry?'

Nathan laughs. 'I know. Four-twenty-two, I think the record is.' By now we're up at the top (though away from any windows, so the height isn't apparent), heading for the cubby-hole office of Alan and Bradley, the men in charge of the tower's plant and machinery. Alan responds to my amazement at the Vertical Rush record by mentioning Steve Galloway, a semi-professional footballer from the 1980s. 'His day job was in the City,' says Alan. 'Every morning, as part of his training regime, we let him run up the building.'

The roof is in three sections, because of the way the building was designed in the shape of NatWest's logo. The lowest section is accessed simply by stepping out of Alan's office. 'Be careful as you get near the edge,' he says, indicating my binoculars. 'Anything that drops from here doubles its weight every sixteen feet.' The view over the chest-high parapet produces that wonderful mix of elation and terror

– but it's not quite what I'm here for. To reach the very highest section of roof, Bradley and I have to return inside and ascend several more staircases of diminishing width. The last few are just iron ladders bolted to the walls of plant rooms, and at different parts of the floorplan, meaning we have to clamber over pipes and under bits of machinery, taking care not to hit our heads. A final few rungs deliver us up through a trapdoor and there we are, out in the fresh – the very fresh – air.

The roof isn't that big, about the size of two tennis courts, and has cumbersome bits of technical gubbins bolted all over the place. One section is given over to satellite and radio dishes – 'make sure you don't stand in front of those,' says Bradley, 'you'll interfere with their signals.' Railings keep you well back from the edge. It's a clear day, meaning we can see well into the distance. The big surprise is how much greenery is visible from above. Not just the famous pockets – Hyde Park and so on – there seem to be trees *everywhere*, lining every street, surrounding every tower block. Height and perspective play weird tricks, making the three huge reservoirs between Tottenham and Walthamstow look like buildings, their expanses of water appearing as white roofs. Closer to hand, the only structures anywhere near as tall as this one are the Gherkin and the Heron – somehow the fact you're in this exclusive club makes them seem even nearer than they are, literally as though you could reach out and touch them.

By lining up my *A to Z* with landmarks to the east – the reservoirs are a help – Bradley and I pin down a dark patch that has to be Epping Forest. Just beyond that was where my walk began yesterday morning. At the other end of the line Ruislip proves more elusive, there being no real landmarks to look for. Apart from knowing it's just to the right of the Wembley Arch, we're stumped. The only notable feature out there is Harrow-on-the-Hill. Through the binoculars we can just make out the church that stands near the famous school.

It's great to be up here, gazing out across the city that's inspired my project. But I can't help feeling, as Bradley and I negotiate the ladder assault course on the way back down, that it wasn't *quite* as great as it should have been, or at least as I was hoping it would be. It's as if there was something missing, a frustrating fault not in the view itself but in my experience of it.

As it turns out, there was. But I won't understand what until later on in the project.

The next station is Bank. It was here, in front of the Royal Exchange, that Britain's first municipal public lavatories opened in 1855. A poem commissioned for the occasion included the line 'wherein a penny opens the gate to Heaven's mercy'. Yes, this was the coin-operated convenience that gave rise to the phrase 'spend a penny'.[8]

Between Bank and St Paul's, just north of Cheapside, is the Guildhall, the City's town hall. The fifteenth-century part is still used for official functions, such as the state banquet where President Sarkozy found himself sitting opposite the

---

8. Its modern successor is in the subway leading from the Exchange down into Bank station.

statue of Wellington.[9] The modern extension is where I have my second appointment of the morning, this time with a man rather than a building, albeit a man in charge of buildings – every one constructed in the City for the past 25 years, in fact. As Planning Officer for the City of London, it's Peter Rees who decides whether or not the Gherkins and Herons and Cheesegraters go up in the first place.

There's something of the skyscraper about 61-year-old Rees himself. The way he carries his 6'3" frame seems to add another inch or two, though the reason for that is less Manhattan swagger than Celtic pride. The lilt of his Swansea valley childhood is still there in Peter's precise diction, every sentence delivered crisply but with a passion and conviction you just don't associate with the phrase 'urban planner'. Nor do you expect sharply tailored grey trousers, a fashionable white shirt and a vibrantly coloured tie. But then that, after all, is why I'm here. Having read some of Peter's comments in the press, I know that he and the views he brings to his job are as animated as the City itself.

After we've seated ourselves in his office, I ask him why he thinks the Square Mile has such a magic about it.

'It's the combination of not just its energy,' he replies, 'but also its secrecy. That's what gives it the mystique.' It was a lesson Peter learned early. 'My first contact with the City was when I was thirteen, on a family holiday to London. We were on the top deck of a number fifteen bus, and as we went past

---

9. At another Nelson Mandela was fascinated by the official measurements of an inch, a foot and a yard, made of metal, counterparts to the ones on the north side of Trafalgar Square.

the site of Temple Bar, my father said, "We're going into the City now, it's a different sort of place – even the policemen are taller."[10]

Peter used to come to the capital for holidays, staying with an aunt in Blackheath. 'She worked in Holborn, and I'd travel with her on the Sardine Line into Blackfriars. Arriving in the City in the rush hour, seeing people rushing off down tiny alleyways and secret rabbit burrows, really caught my imagination. It was the back-doubles that got my interest. It's the same wherever I go. In Paris I hate the Haussmann bit; I love the parts they never got to, the quirky bits. It's the same here – the City's full of quirky bits.'

Paris's love of a plan is only to be expected in a country that as recently as 1993 forbade parents from giving their baby a name that wasn't on an official list. It's also been pointed out that Paris's uniformity was guaranteed by France's readiness with a pen whenever a surrender document appears. London's appetite for destruction, on the other hand, be it by war, riots or terrorism, has ensured a constant rebuilding process that results in the architectural pic 'n' mix we see today.

'We're lucky,' says Peter. 'London's unplannable. I say that as a planner, and I'm thrilled by it. Grand plans and London have got nothing to do with each other. Every now and then a monarch-in-waiting crashed his way through en

10. This is actually true: in those days City policemen had to be six feet tall, whereas everywhere else in the country five-ten would do. Equalities legislation has done for that, but to this day the City police call the Met 'the Bantams'.

route from his palace to Regent's Park, or something of that ilk. But it usually leads to problems; think how Regent Street damages travel in London. The historic routes go east–west. But most of the buses that come along Oxford Street have to turn right at Oxford Circus and insist on pushing their way through to the Strand, only to have to turn north again when they hit the City. Madness.'

After school Peter decided that he wanted to study architecture. 'Not surprisingly the only place I wanted to go was London. By then I knew the Tube map by heart, and on those trips to my aunt I'd always go to get the latest copy.' He arrived at UCL in 1968. 'The very first project we were given was being divided into groups and going to different parts of London to see how well they worked. I was sent to Paternoster Square.[11] Little did I know it would take decades of my real career sorting it out.' Ending up in his current job sits well with Peter. 'I'm the second Celtic City Planning Officer, the first being Boudicca. I see this as reclaiming territory lost by her. She didn't have a great deal of success at controlling the Italians and their grand planning ideas.'[12]

Peter's outsider status reminds me of Disraeli's comment that London is 'a roost for every bird'. It's my experience too; after a childhood spent in the Midlands and university

---

11. The area just north of St Paul's was then at the nadir of its popularity, due to a post-Blitz reconstruction that would have done Stalin proud.

12. Her final battle with the Romans wasn't far from the start of my Central Line walk, in Epping Forest. It's thought that, seeing defeat was inevitable, she and her daughters committed suicide by eating poisonous berries.

in Manchester, London was the only place I wanted to live. Almost every Londonophile I've ever known has been the same. The comedian Chris Addison once observed that, after 12 years in London, 'I don't know any Southerners. I only know people who've come to London.'

Peter agrees. 'There'll always be someone else in London who has your peculiarities, or your interests, or something you can share. The other day I was emailed by a Beijing newspaper, wanting to know why London was a world city, and how Beijing could become one. If I knew the answers I wouldn't be telling them anyway, but I emailed back and said the secret to London's success was that it's the best party on the planet. It has the best free sex in the world – it's full of young people looking for other young people to go to bed with. If they really wanted to know why London was a success and Beijing had yet to achieve this, they should ask the hundreds of Chinese in the gay bars of London. They'd be able to tell them why they weren't in Beijing.' He raises an eyebrow. 'They didn't print it, strangely.'

It becomes apparent from this and other references in Peter's conversation that he himself is gay. Although we don't address the question directly, it isn't hard to imagine that someone growing up with that identity in a 1950s Welsh valley might feel more comfortable in London than back home. Speaking more generally, he talks of the capital being 'full of misfits from all over the world who find London more conducive, because they can be themselves'. Not that it's just a question of human interaction. 'Sometimes what I want is to connect with a place, more than with people. There are times that I fancy a beer but I don't want to chat, I just want to sit in a corner and listen and observe and eavesdrop. That's a great pleasure to me; it's part of enjoying a place. You don't actually have to connect with a person. That is something very interesting about London – people say "it's so unfriendly". It isn't, but you have to make sure first that the person wants to connect. If you can't catch their eye, or if when you do you smile and they don't smile back, then don't go any further.'

Our conversation turns to the importance of pubs in City life. 'Going out to the pub at lunchtime has always been a valuable thing to do in the Square Mile,[13] and not simply as a way of getting inebriated. Not only are you likely to bump into someone you can exchange gossip with as you wander down the alleyways to get to the pub, you'll be able to eavesdrop when you get there. The English pub, although it's a dying breed, differs from a French café by people standing up to drink. This means you can be closer to people you don't know than if you're sitting at a table. The gossip you get in a French café is the gossip of your group. The gossip you get in a London pub is the gossip of other people's groups. If you're careful and clever. Now that's very valuable, because you can take that back to the office and put two and two together and make some money.'

Gossip, in Peter's eyes, is – as it always has been – the fuel on which the City's engine runs. The layout of the area's

---

13. The City of London really was once exactly one square mile. Then in the 1990s the pesky Boundary Commission made minor changes – including adding the Golden Lane estate just north of the Barbican – to produce an annoyingly inexact 1.16 square miles.

streets and lanes and alleys – many of them centuries old – is what gives the City its primacy in world finance. 'It's like a collection of beehives on a compost heap. The bees are going out of their banks and cross-pollinating, and coming back with the nectar to make honey. You don't get that at Canary Wharf, or La Défense in Paris, or in Beijing. You get it to some extent, or you used to, in Wall Street – but not in most American cities. They're too organised. People are compart-mentalised into their own buildings.'[14]

Peter returns to the racial mix. 'It's very important for business. If you're trying to find a solution to a problem, the last place you'll get it is from your own family, or close friends. They probably think in a very similar way to you. What you want is someone with a very different perspective on things, ideally from a different culture.' Proof of this, he says, can be seen in the car industry. 'Ford have their world design headquarters in the middle of Soho, in a building that isn't labelled. It's very anonymous.[15] Why? Because London

---

14. All this talk of beehives reminds me of one of my favourite places in the Square Mile: the Little Gatsby, a sandwich bar hidden away in a warren of alleyways just north of the Bank of England. One of the alleys leading to it – the one off Tokenhouse Yard, which in turn leads off Lothbury, the street running round the back of the Bank – is only wide enough for one person at a time. It's not so much the bacon sandwiches that have got me addicted to the place, but the chatter among the ad-hoc pinstripe conventions. And I don't even *understand* most of it. Imagine what it's worth to someone who does.

15. The modern building – designed by Richard Rogers – on the corner of Berwick Street and Broadwick Street.

is the most creative city in the world. You don't get that in Detroit, or in Tokyo. They're mono-cultural.'

As his next appointment is the other side of St Paul's – my next station – Peter joins me on the walk there. He tells me that, when the City was deregulated in the 1980s, US banks wanted to build new skyscrapers while South American ones preferred old historic buildings ('possibly to show dependability because their currencies were unstable'), and muses on Norman Foster's displeasure at his Swiss Re building acquiring the nickname 'the Erotic Gherkin' ('he had just remarried – some influence on the design, perhaps?').

Through on Cheapside, taking up the entire south side of the street from St Mary-le-Bow (home of the bells) to St Paul's, is the huge retail and office development nicknamed 'the Stealth Bomber', due to the futuristic angularity of its tinted-glass frontage. Workers scurry about making the final tweaks to electrics and plumbing and air-con that will bring the giant to life, and as always at such sights I'm reminded of the London Walks guide who said, as we passed a building project, 'London – it'll be a great place when it's finished.' Retail is the one thing the City has lacked until now; workers have had to hop on the Central Line to Oxford Circus for a nifty lunch-hour dash round John Lewis. But wouldn't it be a shame if the Square Mile provided *too* much retail, becoming a West End clone and losing its uniqueness?

'Absolutely,' says Peter. 'We don't want this to be a shopping mall – I deliberately use the American pronunciation, because that's how you feel when you come out of one: mauled – we want somewhere where you'll find something you weren't expecting to find, not more of what you know you're going to find. We can have retail with flavour that's an adjunct to the business district.' At weekends, he hopes, people from newly gentrified areas like Clerkenwell and Bermondsey will do their shopping here, instead of travelling across town to the King's Road. 'For retailers to come here they need seven-day-a-week trade. Twenty-five years ago the City was dead at weekends, the image of it was those bowler-hatted people trudging to work across London Bridge.[16] Now it's just as much tourists coming over the Millennium Bridge from Tate Modern to see Wren churches and wonderful modern architecture.'

And beyond any financial considerations, Peter sees the project as 'resurrecting the City's high street – that's what Cheapside always was. "Chepe" *means* market. The streets around here took their names from what was sold on them: Bread Street, Milk Street, Honey Lane . . . [17] I actually now buy my bread in Bread Street, albeit Belgian bread from Le Pain Quotidien.' Goldsmiths were ordered to locate their shops in Cheapside by Charles I, to impress foreigners as they passed through to St Paul's. Showing off in the City is nothing new.

We gaze up at the building's enormous façade, the dark

---

16. When the late Tory politician Peter Walker got his first City job in the 1950s his letter of appointment included the line: 'You will wear a bowler hat to and from the office.'

17. As well as Poultry and Friday Street, where good Catholics bought their weekly fish. 'Chepe' is also how market towns like Norton and Campden got their 'Chipping'.

glass designed to give off vague hints of red depending on where you stand. Above it peeps St Paul's, the top of the dome directly over the spot where Nelson is buried in the cathedral's crypt. The new and the old together: one of London's recurring themes. 'I'm glad we're doing buildings like this now,' says Peter. 'Twenty years ago there wasn't this level of imagination. When we talked to the designers of Minster Court [mock-Gothic building near Fenchurch Street station] I said, "Come on, there's so much you can *do* with an office building; you don't just have to turn the handle on the machine and produce a copy of the last one you did. Look at the Prudential building in Holborn, for example – that was in the 1870s, what a magnificent job they did there." So they went away and designed a copy of that instead. No passion in it. No individuality.'

Certain views of St Paul's are protected by law: this is why the Cheesegrater will be the Cheesegrater (its upper floors having to slope away to avoid getting into shot from the west), and why a particular holly bush in Richmond Park has a parting that's kept constantly trimmed.[18] Fair enough. Some people do go on about architecture, though (no names, but he's first in line to the throne). How does Peter respond to traditionalists?

'There have always been complaints: UNESCO started campaigning to stop us putting up tall buildings in the City because of the impact on the Tower of London, which is a World Heritage Site.' A phrase to chill the blood. 'I say

18. There's a telescope behind the bush for checking that St Paul's is indeed still visible.

to them, you have to understand that this is the Tower *of* London, not London of the Tower. The thing was only built in the first place because the Normans wanted to protect the City of London, knowing it was a good earner – not for any other reason.' He indicates the bustle all around us. 'And as you can see, the City has continued to thrive. It's important that from the Tower you should be able to see the City that it's there to protect.' He sighs. 'The maddest thing was when they wanted to reflood the moat. I opposed that. They said, "We want to turn the clock back." I said, "No, you don't. It was a muddy ditch, full of shit and dead dogs. It wasn't clean water." All they wanted was a theme park.'

One of Peter's final comments is that London's skyscrapers are 'a mountain range'. This stays with me after we part. The capital's cityscape has always struck me as natural, in the sense that it's a part of nature, made by nature. Quite literally *rus in urbe*. The view from Waterloo Bridge, often (and understandably) cited by many as their favourite – Big Ben to one side, the City to the other – feels like it's been there forever, as permanent and could-be-no-other-way as the Pyrenees or Niagara Falls or an African savannah. Inspired by the view from Westminster Bridge, Wordsworth wrote that earth had not 'anything to show more fair': 'Never did sun more beautifully steep,/ In his first splendour, valley, rock or hill'. London's buildings are, to me, as old as any valley, rock or hill. No matter that some of them are 500 years old and others five – each new addition wipes the memory, reprogrammes the sense of what is elemental. The new and old together, yes – but the new looking as though it's been there just as long as the old.[19]

Before restarting the walk, I take one last look at the Stealth Bomber, and a placard reminds me of its proper name, taken from its address on the street running south off Cheapside: One New Change. What's more, the architect who designed it is called Jean Nouvel.

Just past St Paul's is the Old Bailey, which until 1902 was the site of London's most infamous prison, Newgate.[20] The jail took its name from the gate in the Roman city wall here. It's almost as hard to believe that this is where London once ended as it is to believe that all the matter in the universe was ever contained in a single tiny dot.

Then it's Chancery Lane station, possessor of London Underground's shortest escalator. Fifty steps, linking the east- and westbound platforms; they had to be on top of each other because this first section of the line was built to follow the road, and there wasn't room for side-by-side tunnels.[21] The dragons just before the station mark the end of the City, but like a lot of London 'traditions' they haven't been

---

19. All this is the opposite of the viewpoint expressed in a letter written by an evacuated child during the Second World War: 'They call this spring, Mum, and they have one down here every year.'

20. The victim of the first murderer convicted in the current building was William Whiteley, founder of the department store on Queensway.

21. Tube lines did this back then because tunnelling under buildings would involve potentially large payments to owners. The government, by contrast, granted free 'wayleave' under streets.

around for as long as you'd think: since 1963, to be precise. Past Holborn and Tottenham Court Road stations (between which lies a wine merchant called Planet of the Grapes) and then we're on to Oxford Street.

Rathbone Place is off to the north – and off that is the passageway that housed the bent lamppost Terry and Arthur tried to straighten every week in the *Minder* credits, something Westminster City Council has sadly since achieved – but my motto for the next few hours is simple: go west. It's all Roman again, of course: this is the A40, the road linking the Bank of England with Fishguard Harbour in Wales.[22] Oxford Circus station becomes the project's first triple tie-up, and then it's into John Lewis for a comfort break. The packed lift contains three old women chatting busily away, one of them the other two's mother, a fact that only emerges when one daughter, unable to conceal her pride any longer, announces, 'She's a hundred and two today.'

Bond Street, then Marble Arch. A plaque at the bottom of the Edgware Road marks the site of the Tyburn Tree gallows, whose Catholic victims are prayed for by the nuns of the Tyburn Convent, a few hundred yards away along the Bayswater Road. Barely distinguishable from the buildings around it, this brick structure, once you're inside it, provides an incredible sense of peace, and my aching legs need little excuse to find their way to one of the benches facing the shrine. Three other

22. Or not quite. Annoyingly the technical starting point is now, for some reason, St Martin's Le Grand church, just west of St Paul's station. A change instigated by the sort of bureaucrat who makes the Square Mile 1.16 square miles.

people, all women, have done likewise, and one of the nuns sits silently praying before the shrine itself. A cleaner polishes the benches, spraying her Pledge directly into the duster to avoid breaking the silence. Then a Tube rumbles underneath us, and unlike last night at the hotel it's a Central Line train, giving me a gentle reminder that I need to get shifting.

Lancaster Gate station sits almost unnoticed under the hulk of the Royal Lancaster Hotel (where in *The Italian Job* Michael Caine, faced with seven women dressed only in bikinis and asked what he wants, replies 'everything'), then it's Queensway. Both places are named after Queen Victoria, the second for obvious reasons, the first because (like all reigning monarchs) she was the Duke of Lancaster. A dog walker heading for Hyde Park successfully corrals two labradors, three King Charles spaniels and a red setter, but when the St Bernard decides it wants a pee everyone has to stop. By now it's gone midday, and the legs are talking again, saying, 'Yes, Mark, you *do* deserve an early lunch.' I would ignore them, but for the fact that Café Diana appears on the right.

Its walls lined with framed pictures of the woman who lived over the road in Kensington Palace, this place has always fascinated me, in the same way that Channel 5 documentaries about Elvis impersonators fascinate me. Never been in, though. I stare at the pictures as I wait for my egg mayonnaise sandwich, and suddenly Diana begins to seem very unreal, like when you look at the word 'the' for too long and start to doubt it. The owner, a softly-spoken Arabic man in his forties, brings my order, and I mention that today is the anniversary of Diana's death. 'Yes,' he replies. But instead of an unhinged monologue on how she captured our hearts and how she made you feel like you were the only person in the world (one of the pictures is of the owner proudly standing next to the woman herself), all that follows is a respectful nod. Years of snobbish disdain drop away; what's wrong with putting up pictures of someone you liked? After all, it can't be bad for business.

Just past Notting Hill station is the Oxfam whose typical item is a pair of Jimmy Choo sandals for £149. All change from 1902 when the poverty here was 'as deep and dark a type as anywhere in London', and the 1840s when the nearby area known as 'the Piggeries' hosted 3,000 pigs per acre. Then it's Holland Park, named after the aristocratic family who were great friends with Napoleon, sending him jars of plum jam when he was exiled on Elba, as well as a refrigerator to keep them in.

Shepherd's Bush marks a change of tone, even though it's climbed a few notches since Steptoe and Son lived here. Central to the regeneration is the Westfield Shopping Centre, just north of the green and stretching its whole length. Part of the site used to be the White City exhibition ground, where in 1908 the attractions at the Franco-British Exhibition included a 'Senegal Village', inhabited by 150 Africans specially shipped in. And that was just *part* of the site: Westfield is staggeringly, unnaturally vast, the sort of shopping 'maul' to which specially chartered coach trips of middle-aged women pay pilgrimage. It's certainly imposing, and that's a pity as it should be welcoming. I walk round rather than through it. It takes 20 minutes.

I pass White City station and then the BBC complex, built on the site of the 1908 Olympic Stadium. A plaque just underneath *The One Show*'s window commemorates the medal winners, including the City of London Police team who took gold in the tug-of-war. (Hardly likely to be the Bantams, was it?) As the event was then dropped from the Olympics, they're still the reigning champions. Over the Westway and past Wormwood Scrubs, which was built by its inmates: the first nine inhabitants constructed enough cells for 50 more, who took the capacity up to 100, and so on. Then East Acton station, huddling in a secluded network of streets whose dainty terraced houses make you feel that nothing has changed since the Edwardian era. The knowledge that during the Great Fire of London charred leaves of burning books were blown as far as here ties the area even more firmly to the past.

But as quickly as that feeling registers it disappears, the route to North Acton being a tortuous twist under dripping railway bridges and over tracks carrying rusting brown freight trains. Then *that* backdrop gives way, just as speedily, to respectable suburbia, the streets between West Acton and Ealing Broadway lined not just with half-timbered houses but half-timbered garages.[23] It all brings back Peter's comment about this city being unplannable, as well as the words of Geoffrey Fletcher in his 1962 book *The London Nobody Knows*: 'a characteristic London feature [is] the quick transition from a well-off to a seedy area at the drop of a hat. A single street becomes a sort of Mason-Dixon Line of demarcation.' It's worse than that, Geoffrey – very often London fails to make sense even within

---

23. Only to be expected: in the nineteenth century Ealing called itself 'the Queen of the Suburbs'.

a street. That sense was there on the Victoria Line walk (Mrs Mamas and Papas passing the afternoon drinker), and it's grown with every step since. Both architecturally and in terms of its people, this place is a mess.

Part of you rebels against that, wants to tidy the city as though it was a child's nursery, putting all the toys into boxes, all the boxes into neat stacks ordered by size and colour and style. But then you remember Christopher Wren. Dab hand with a church he might have been, but his ambitions extended dangerously far. Thank God Charles II rejected his plan for the reconstruction of London after the Great Fire. The drawing looks beautiful, but only as an exercise in geometry: roads diverge and meet to form neat triangles, the whole block south from Newgate and the Guildhall to the river is a New York-style grid, and every so often piazzas gather streets together in precise radials. *Piazzas?* In London? The city where Marylebone Lane takes its shape from a winding river?

Sometimes mess is good.

Ealing Broadway marks the end of this branch, and at a café overlooking the green I give the caffeine tank a boost, throwing in a couple of Paracetamols for good measure. The 'every bit of line' rule means I now have to return eastwards to North Acton[24] before walking the Ruislip branch, even though the first

---

24. Or, if you want to be an absolute stickler for detail – Richard, this footnote is for you – to a point on Western Avenue just before North Acton. I'd reached this point on the North Acton–Ealing Broadway walk. The first bit of the North Acton–Hanger Lane walk would be the same, and has therefore been walked already.

station, Hanger Lane, is due north of here. It's going to add about half an hour to the journey. And the state I'm in, that's a very unwelcome half an hour. When I cough it hurts my lower back. The feet aren't too much of a problem – the anti-blister spray is doing its job – but the legs are getting seriously mutinous, especially when there's a climb involved. And by climb I include pavements, which today feel like the Eiger. Plus the road-crossing problem from last night has returned, made even worse in Holland Park by the sudden appearance of a noise-free Toyota Prius; when are they going to add an artificial engine noise? (And please can it be the noise from a clown car?) What's more, the sun has now overtaken me – it's three o'clock – so for the rest of the walk I'll be heading into its glare.

But overall the pain's worth it. A walk on this scale, I'm coming to realise, doesn't just bring a heightened awareness of your surroundings, it also brings a heightened awareness of yourself. Only when it starts to malfunction do you really appreciate what an incredible piece of engineering the human body is. You become attuned to every little change. My finger-nails, for example, are noticeably longer than they were this morning. William Blake wrote that the road of excess leads to the palace of wisdom. Nothing to say the road has to be a metaphorical one.

To avoid trudging the same streets on the way back I go via Ealing Studios. As so often, a place with a famous name is disappointingly normal, though the cartoon logo of a St Trinian's schoolgirl on the whitewashed wall is nicely done. Ealing as a whole feels prosperous, respectable, defiantly suburban, as though it's trying to get away from London, deny that it's part of the city at all. The complete opposite of yesterday in Essex, which pushed inwards, equally insistent in its clamour to be *in*cluded.

After such tranquillity, the multi-lane Western Avenue mugs your senses. I never thought that 'so loud you can't hear yourself think' could actually be true, but it is here. It's only looking back that I register astonishment at there being houses lining the road. All have net curtains or blinds in the window, but can even modern double-glazing be that sound-proof? One front door has a poster taped to the inside of its glass picturing a bulldog above the words 'Piss Off'. A huge billboard pictures a blonde model above the word 'Beauty', but that's only for the benefit of perfume-buying motorists; not much beauty for anyone who lives here.

Hanger Lane adds to the air of intimidation. In traffic reports it's always followed by the word 'gyratory', which sounds like an enchanting child's toy but just turns out to mean 'roundabout'. This intersection of Western Avenue, the A40 and Hanger Lane itself was once voted Britain's scariest junction. Although the subway that takes you under it also lets me tick off another Tube station, I can see why. This is one of those stops you only get off at to take a bus. Waiting further along Western Avenue is the Hoover factory. Derided by the architectural critic Nikolaus Pevsner in 1951 as 'the most offensive of modern atrocities', it has now (nearly 80 years after its construction) secured a place in the capital's heart, so I'm looking forward to it brightening up my day. But, you realise as you approach on foot, your memories of it are as seen from a car.

From a distance its art-deco frontage acts as a familiar marker: 'nearly in London now'. Up close, however, the concrete looks tired, the style dated, and it reminds you depressingly of that other icon, the old Wembley Stadium. Like Wembley it works better as an idea than a reality. Hoover have left the building; it's now a Tesco. As if to rub it in, they sell Dysons.

The rest of the walk passes uneventfully. Perivale leads to a welcome bit of greenery, and ten peaceful minutes along the Grand Union Canal. In a park a young girl on a pink bike asks her mother something in Polish, then switches instantly to English as she tells her friend, 'We can go to the bottom and back.' After Greenford (the only station on the network where you take an escalator up to the trains) is an industrial estate on which a row of lorries wait for tomorrow's workload. Each cab displays a road atlas and, as far as I can see, no sat-nav: a pleasing sight for a map-purist. The Hovis factory pumps out a delicious smell of warm bread, then at Northolt a friendly West Indian woman in the ticket office advises me on the quickest route to South Ruislip (she's walked it herself). The housing estate to the right was built on an old pony-racing track, hence Ascot Close, Wincanton Crescent, Goodwood Drive . . . Predictable but competent, unlike the estate in Birmingham that was themed around the Second World War and included a Bader Walk.[25]

It's closer to 'dark' than 'dusk' now, and it's definitely not

25. Actually, just who the hell does decide street names? There was one on the Bakerloo Line walk called Derek Avenue. Sorry, I don't care who Derek was — Nimmo, Randall, even Bo — there are some monikers that just don't work.

London any more. Hasn't been since East Acton, to be honest. Ruislip is the archetypal suburb: homely, dutiful, mundane. From the tiered seating around a swimming pool parents patiently watch their offspring. In many houses the curtains have yet to be drawn or the lights switched on, so I see families bathed in the ghostly flickering of a TV screen, shadows moving as Heston cooks or Kirsty haggles. The set of one middle-aged couple is tuned to Gok Wan; she's rapt, he's nodded off.

Ruislip Gardens at 8.36 p.m., West Ruislip at 9.03 p.m., and finally my journey is complete. 27.2 miles today, making a total for the whole line of 62.7. Every yard of that is making itself felt as, for once, I go through a ticket barrier and collapse on to a train. But it's the very best sort of 'dead on your feet'. The sort that allows you to say 'I did it'. And when you're as impractical as I am, that counts for a lot. DIY, car mechanics and sport are out of the equation – the only sense of achievement I'm going to get comes from putting one foot in front of the other more times than feels comfortable. A quick bit of measurement at home revealed that my average stride length is 28 inches. In the last two days I've walked three million, nine hundred and seventy-two thousand, six hundred and seventy-two inches. That means I've put one foot in front of the other one hundred and forty-one thousand, eight hundred and eighty-one times. Please forgive the words rather than figures. Sense of achievement depends on that sort of thing.

Despite the internal hum of self-congratulation, though, there's something bothering me on the Tube ride back to Liverpool Street. It comes to mind as I eavesdrop on a conversation. A Sloaney girl (yes, I know the term 'Sloaney' is out of date, but so is she) gets on at Holland Park, then recognises a man who joins the train at Bond Street. 'Kisses,' she says, before kissing him (both cheeks). They talk, swapping news; it's evidently several months since they last met. He leaves at Holborn. 'More kisses,' she says before kissing him again (both cheeks again). And my absorption in their exchange (does she like him? On balance I'd say not) brings back something Peter said this morning: 'Sometimes what I want is to connect with a place, more than with people.' More and more this is how I've used London. Peter called it the best party on the planet, and it is, but it's also the best human zoo.

'Only connect,' E. M. Forster told us. 'Live in fragments no longer.' But some of my happiest times in London – both when I lived here and now that I don't, and certainly more and more as I came to accept that this was my nature – have been spent as a fragment, watching all the other fragments. Friedrich Engels was evidently not in my camp, warning in 1845 that 'the disintegration of society into individuals . . . has been pushed to its furthest limit in London. Here indeed human society has been split into its component atoms.' A century earlier the historian Edward Gibbon criticised London for being 'crowds without company'. He meant it in a bad sense. It's one of the reasons I love the place so much.

Or, at least, that's what I've thought until tonight. Now there's a horrible nugget of doubt.

# 4

# Hammersmith and City Line

## The beauty of the North Circular

Richard's very excited about this. Which, as we know, doesn't always mean that anything exciting is actually happening. But this time even I can sense the importance of what's imminent: the route of my next walk will include the route of the first-ever London Underground line.

I've chosen the Hammersmith and City because I need another single-dayer. My right foot is taking ages to forgive me for the Central Line, and to pacify it I occasionally have to resort to a mild limp. But, as the Polish poet Stanislaw J. Lec said, 'He who limps is still walking.' Specifically, I'm walking to the pub with Richard. Need the odd pint to put some weight back on; despite the Central Line walk including a curry and plenty of energy-giving chocolate, it still lost me three pounds in two days. It's over this pint that Richard imparts the caveat about the Metropolitan Railway being a sub-surface rather than properly deep-level Tube line. Which, of course, I know from my Victoria Line walk, but I don't tell him that because I don't want to hurt his feelings.

The rest of what Richard has to tell me is new. The Hammersmith and City was opened in 1864, only a year after the Metropolitan. For a long time it was actually a branch of the Metropolitan, heading west from Baker Street to Hammersmith and east from Liverpool Street to Barking. It wasn't until 1988 that it got its own name. The hallowed Metropolitan stretch – from near Paddington through King's Cross down to Farringdon Street – opened on 10 January 1863. Hallowed, but not altogether pleasant. The Metropolitan Railway invested in gas lighting in the carriages, 'to dispel any unpleasant feelings which passengers, especially ladies, might entertain against riding for so long a distance through a tunnel', but that didn't change the fact that the trains were steam-powered. The company might have claimed that this 'invigorating' atmosphere provided 'a sort of health resort' for people who suffered from asthma, but they also quietly allowed their drivers to grow beards in a (doomed) attempt to filter out the smoke. One passenger who had spent time in the Sudan said the smell was like that of a crocodile's breath. Incredibly the last steam-powered trains weren't retired until 1961.[1]

The new mode of transport revolutionised life for poorer workers. Those whose jobs were in the City could now live outside it and not have to walk six miles in each direction.[2]

---

1. One person who refused to attend the 1863 opening was the Prime Minister, Lord Palmerston. Citing his old age, he said he wanted to spend as much time as possible above ground.
2. Six miles? Lightweights.

Needless to say, and as we've already seen out in Metroland, the sense of escaping London didn't last very long. London simply chased the Tube. In 1864 Hammersmith was still a village 'best known for spinach and strawberries'. By 1901 it had a population of 112,239.

Today, though, Hammersmith feels like one of those corners of London that's trying to drag you out of the capital completely. The presence of the flyover, even when you can't see it – and, facing the Hammersmith and City station,[3] I can't – pervades the whole area, never letting you entirely forget that the M4 is just a few minutes from here. So strong is the sense of westward pull that you're afraid to stand still for too long lest you be swept away, like Dorothy in *The Wizard of Oz*. You could be in Bristol before you know it.

In the early afternoon of this autumnal Thursday, therefore, I head resolutely north. Hammersmith Grove is tree-lined and affluent, quiet enough to stage a local primary school's cycling proficiency class. Then two teenagers wobble dangerously by on the same bike, one perched uncomfortably on the handlebars, showing the children exactly how not to do it. At the top of the street is the Goldhawk Road, whose eponymous station contains Ruby's Café. Always exciting when there's a café inside a Tube station.[4] Or a shop, or a flower stall. Puts you in mind of those science-fiction books where the network becomes a refuge for post-apocalypse survivors, people living their whole lives down there. There's definitely something womb-like about the Tube system.

---

3. The District and Piccadilly incarnation is over the road.
4. The one inside Temple is particularly good.

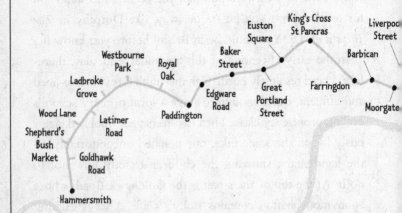

## HAMMERSMITH & CITY LINE

Stations: 29

Line mileage: 16

Different names for opposite
sides of the same street
near Paddington station: 2

King's Cross
St Pancras

Euston
Square

Liverpool
Street

Baker
Street

Barbican

Westbourne
Park

Royal
Oak

Ladbroke
Grove

Edgware
Road

Great
Portland
Street

Farringdon

Wood Lane

Paddington

Moorgate

Latimer
Road

Shepherd's
Bush
Market

Goldhawk
Road

Hammersmith

N

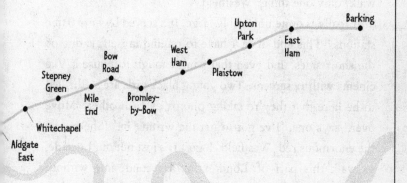

Barking

Upton
Park

East
Ham

West
Ham

Plaistow

Bow
Road

Stepney
Green

Mile
End

Bromley-
by-Bow

Whitechapel

Aldgate
East

| 0 | 0.5 | 1 mi |
|---|-----|------|
| 0 | 1 | 2 km |

Shepherd's Bush Market, hugging the line that sends trains 20 feet or so over the shoppers' heads, sells exactly what you expect any bog-standard market to sell – cheap handbags, kitchenware, saris, a mobile-phone unlocking service – then surprises you with a carpet stall offering fake grass at £20 per square metre. Very popular with your lazy urban gardener, apparently. I pass the station that now takes the market's name – until 2008 it was just Shepherd's Bush, another of those Edgware Road-style duplications – then round on to Wood Lane. Which means, as I know from the Central Line walk, only one thing: Westfield.

It really is quite unfeasibly large. It's served by *three* Tube stations.[5] This end of it, I have to remind myself, is one of the short sides, and even that's big enough to house a Vue cinema with 14 screens. Two young black girls are so thrilled to be here that they're taking photos of each other. 'Move over,' says one, 'I've got to get the writing in.' (She means the enormous red 'Westfield' logo.) It's just not on, I decide, to walk this part of London for a second time without experiencing the building that has so radically changed it. After ticking off Wood Lane station, opened in 2008[6] to ferry Westfield supplicants to their shrine (very good job they did of it too – nice marriage between the new metal and the old brickwork of the arches), I double back and head for the nearest entrance. There's a momentary faltering at the sign announcing Jamie Oliver's new restaurant inside, but I gather my courage and plough on.

---

5. Shepherd's Bush, Shepherd's Bush Market and Wood Lane.
6. It's the newest station on any of my walks.

You're expecting me to say it's hideous, aren't you? You're expecting a tale of spiritless consumerism, empty grandiosity, retail without heart. Well, I hate to disappoint you, but you're absolutely right. If it's possible to organise an area of 30 football pitches into a more depressing shopping experience than this one, I'd like to see it (or rather I wouldn't). Over two levels – was it two? Might have been three, or 3,000 for that matter – people wander the fridge-white floors in that special slow-motion state of reverence reserved for Awesome Retail Experiences. That's what it is, after all: an experience. Shopping itself is secondary, and quite often non-existent. Just to be here is enough, in a place whose atmosphere is sealed with medical precision against the possibility that somewhere in this world there might, just might, be something so unspeakably foul as a speck of dust.

Actually it would be unfair to say there isn't a single good thing about Westfield. There is: the security guard who tells me how to take a shortcut out of it. Against the rules, and because using the proper exit would take me well off the route to Latimer Road station, he reveals which lift will take me to an exit in the car park that only taxis are supposed to use. On the way I notice a sign saying 'Limousine drop-off'.

Outside a footbridge leads over the big link road between the Westway and the Holland Park roundabout, delivering me into the quiet streets south of Latimer Road. Just before the station itself is a trendy junk shop called Last Place on Earth (several chairs re-upholstered in the Union Jack, which after a decade or two of St George's Cross prominence seems to be making a comeback), a sign that we're entering the land of Portobello/Notting Hill chic. I'm just trying to weigh up whether this is one of the poorer or richer pockets, when within a few hundred yards either side of the next station (Ladbroke Grove) I see a Virgin Active gym offering a 'dedication holistic studio' and 'organic juice bar', an elegant old woman in George Burns glasses and one of the actresses from *Cold Feet* collecting her child from school.[7] This would appear to settle the question, but as ever the answer is far from definitive. On the streets leading to Westbourne Park station there are multi-million-pound houses overlooking pavements scattered with abandoned TV sets. This sort of thing always reminds me of my brother, who still lives close to our childhood home in the Warwickshire countryside. When the news mentions that, say, David Cameron lives in Notting Hill, Steve will say, 'That must be a nice part of London', and I reply, 'Yes', before adding, 'But then again . . .'

After the station comes St Stephen's Church of England Primary School, still housed in its 1897 building, the front door topped by a stone plaque engraved so attractively with various quotes (e.g. Isaac Newton: 'True religion is an habitual recollection of God') that I stop to take a photo of it. The headmistress, supervising the collection by their parents of the last few children (it's now nearly four o'clock), closes the door. I curse myself for being thoughtless, but also can't help feeling miffed that it's something necessary of thought in the first place. On with the eastward trek, knowing

---

7. To avoid having to call her 'the sour-faced one' I've looked her up: Hermione Norris.

that just round the corner from here is Newton Road, erstwhile home of Cornelius Ignatius O'Leary, charged in 1940 with defacing council posters about air-raid precautions. His defence, according to *The Times*, was that 'there was a split infinitive on one of them'.

Past Royal Oak station the streets develop that 'suck you out of London' feeling again; the Westway is a matter of yards to the north. Indeed Gloucester Terrace is the final stretch of a one-way system that feeds motorists on to it. Or at least the northern side of the street is Gloucester Terrace; the southern side is called Porchester Square. I've heard of streets being split between councils, but never one that had full-blown schizophrenia. The terraced houses that line it are seriously big, but not in an elegant, Holland Park way. Rather they're tall, as though too many cardboard boxes had been piled on top of each other, daring gravity to do its worst.[8] The street as a whole looks like two sheer white cliffs facing each other. Every property has been subdivided into flats, the porches containing entryphone grilles that in *Money* Martin Amis likened to the 'dashboards of ancient spaceships'.

Round the corner, parked just off Bishop's Bridge Road, is a Range Rover, its front seats occupied by two men in business suits having a discussion; the driver still wears his seat belt, as though he doesn't quite trust his passenger. Then it's into the side entrance of Paddington station, the bit where taxis drop off and pick up passengers in a chaos that never

---

8. This happens a lot in these parts: here, Gloucester Road, Earl's Court . . .

quite loses its choreography. The Bakerloo Line walk took me down the station's far side, so I failed to notice the statue of Brunel that sits cross-legged just off platform 1. Not bad from a distance, but look closely and you see he has no eyes, as though birds have pecked them out. Doesn't really do the man justice. Better to adopt the St Paul's/Wren approach, and seek his monument by looking around you.

As I walk the whole length of the station twice (this is a Hammersmith and City Line walk, so pedantry dictates a trip to the correct Tube entrance[9]) I think about the really great London statues, from the modern – Lord Woolf in the Royal Courts of Justice, made entirely from wire coat hangers set at different depths to construct his profile – to the traditional, such as Churchill in Parliament Square. So realistic is the lapel of his coat that I sometimes think I can see it flap in the wind. In 2000 it was defaced by a protester, though why he needed to simulate blood coming out of the mouth with red paint was a mystery. His other amendment – a Mr T haircut achieved with a strip of turf – was undistilled genius. You like to think the great man himself would have had a chuckle at that.

On the way out I pass a man getting on to the Heathrow Express carrying nothing but a single long-stemmed rose. Past Edgware Road station (the one just south of the main Marylebone Road, not the one from the Bakerloo Line walk), then it's on to said main road, the one they dug up in the

---

9. The authorities have laid two thin stripes along the whole length of platform 8, one pink and the other yellow. If only all London signage was as witty as this.

1860s to lay the first underground line. The 'underground' didn't become 'Underground' for another 40 years, however, when the different line operators – such as Charles Yerkes's UERL – agreed to a common name and system map in a move to encourage business.

It isn't just the Tube that has its roots here, though. Just to the south, off York Street, is Shillibeer Place, named after George Shillibeer, who on 4 July 1829 launched London's first omnibus service. Starting from a Paddington pub called the Yorkshire Stingo, it followed pretty much the same route as the Metropolitan Line would a few decades later.[10] Shillibeer's coaches were drawn by three horses abreast of each other, and carried 22 passengers, all inside. Newspapers were provided free of charge – in the days before *Metro* this was a big deal – and soon Shillibeer's sixpenny fares were bringing in £100 a day. Rival operators liked the sound of that, and soon competition was not just fierce but fatal: in 1842 a man was knocked down and killed by an omnibus doing 12 miles an hour along the City Road.

Just past Baker Street the pavement is halved in width by an ugly green Portakabin, on top of which are various ungainly pieces of equipment, not unlike Jonathan Pryce's plumbing system in *Brazil*. It transpires that this eyesore is an emission-monitoring station. To protect the environment the authorities have ruined the environment. A little further on a couple are embracing. Only when the hug shows no sign of ending do I notice that the woman's

10. Except that at King's Cross it carried on up the Pentonville Road, then down the City Road and Moorgate to Bank.

shoulders are shaking. The street they've emerged from is Harley Street.

Great Portland Street, then Euston Square, outside which is an old woman, five feet tall if that, her clothes ragged, her hair dirty and her gait unsteady, but whose cigarette is being smoked through a tortoiseshell holder. I take a *Standard* from the pile outside Euston station and see that Andrew Flintoff's knee injury has caused him to retire. Not the sort of example I need now that my foot's playing up again. (Has been since Royal Oak, actually, but I didn't want to go on about it.) Soon I'm outside the station that my mother calls St Pancreas. This place is a huge great refutation of the theory – you can see why it's popular, though only if you don't think about it for very long – that London has nothing to do with the rest of Britain, that it stands arrogantly apart from its fellow cities, and all the towns and villages too. Indeed that it is, in Disraeli's words, 'a nation, not a city'. Fine, grumble if you like at the fact that Britain's government, media and cultural life is run predominantly from London. But remember that many, if not most, of the people doing that running aren't *from* London. They're from all over the country, and as that country is so small they usually spend a lot of time back where they came from. In fact, the most successful ones – the ones you'd think would be most out of touch – often invest the financial fruits of that success in a weekend pad, living Monday to Thursday in London and Friday to Sunday in Not London.

St Pancras is the architectural embodiment of that human traffic. Not just in the sense that its trains do lots of the ferrying – the building itself is a massive slab of the Midlands in the heart of London. Its famous red bricks are that colour because they're made from the red clay of Nottinghamshire. Its golden limestone came from Lincolnshire, the slates on its roof from Leicestershire. All of this happened because the station was built by the Midland Railway; why look elsewhere for materials when your trains are doing the journey anyway? The hotel part of the station was designed by George Gilbert Scott,[11] the train shed by William Barlow – and even here the Midlands set its stamp on things. Barlow's solution to the problem of getting over Regent's Canal just north of the station was to build the platforms above ground level. The iron columns that supported them – hardened by being soaked in horse urine – were positioned three Bass beer barrel-widths apart, so that the Burton-on-Trent brewery could use the sub-platform space to store the ale they sent every day to London.

These days St Pancras is connected not just to the rest of the country but also to the rest of the continent, after its 2007 inheriting of London's Eurostar duties.[12] As I walk away from the station I reflect on those who accuse the capital of isolationism, of carrying on as though it's the only place on earth, of not caring about anywhere else. Typically the charge is made by someone who brags about how they hate

---

11. What was it about his family and red? His grandson Giles designed London's famous phone boxes.
12. It's annoying that the French no longer have to arrive at Waterloo, but on the other hand, as you sit in the departure lounge, you do get to see those precisely positioned columns.

going to 'that there London', about how their little place does them just fine, how it's got everything they need, thank you very much. Someone, in other words, who doesn't care about anywhere else.

Time for a break in the Starbucks opposite the station, to meet up with a cabbie. Or at least someone who's about to become a cabbie. The exhaustive element of my project – the need to do every station, to hit 100 per cent, in the hope that this will enable me to 'own' London – has been preying on my mind. In particular whenever a clipboard-enhanced scooter has passed slowly by, its driver scanning the streetscape to implant it in their memory, I've been reminded of the Knowledge, the even more exhaustive project that would-be cabbies have to undertake. As I said at the start, walking every street in London failed to appeal; it would have no structure, no rhyme, no narrative. That and the fact that it would take years.[13] Nonetheless, those scooters, and especially the maps on those clipboards, have got me thinking about the similarities between the Knowledge and what I'm doing. However different in scale, there's something we share in principle: a need to relate how London looks on a map to how it looks in reality, and thereby to say we've conquered it. It's a theme I want to explore.

---

13. Whisper it quietly, but any serious London-lover and/or walker will tell you that, however beautiful the *A to Z* is, both as a concept and a tool, they simply don't believe the claim that its inventor Phyllis Pearsall walked every one of the city's 23,000 streets in a year in order to compile it.

The Knowledge student who's going to help me do that is in some ways very typical of the Identikit London cabbie – white, middle-aged, chatty, down to earth, born and bred in the city (New Cross) – but in other ways completely atypical. For a start, she's a woman (over 98 per cent of cabbies are male), and furthermore she's one who, I discover during our conversation, is 'not going to tolerate racism in the back of my cab'. Rachel Martin-Pe'er owes the first half of her surname to a family who've been 'Deptford for generations', the second to her husband Meni, a Georgian-born Israeli she met while travelling in India. Fortunately her family had a more enlightened attitude to foreigners than many white working-class Londoners of their vintage. Both Rachel's parents were community workers, her mother being an innovator in anti-racist campaigning.

No problem recognising Rachel: she's the one carrying a crash helmet. She doesn't have a scooter, though. She has a *bike*. 'A CBF250,' she says with the nonchalance of a true biker. Not being a true biker, I have to look this up later; it's made by Honda. 'For a lot of people who do the Knowledge, the hurdle is getting on a motorbike. But that didn't bother me: I've been riding them for thirty years. That was a pleasure for me. My hurdle was the map. I did *not* understand maps.'

As we get our coffees and find a table I ask Rachel whether she does now.

'I've had to. I never had a *bad* sense of direction, but I'd never had to deal with maps like this. That's what the Knowledge is all about: driving across that map in your head. You're aiming to have a complete picture of it in your mind.'

How does she visualise things when she's reciting a route street-by-street ('calling' it, as it's known)? Does she see the map or the streets themselves?

'If you ask me the general direction we're going to need to take, I see the map. But as soon as I start to call it I see the picture of how it'll look when I'm driving. That's how you have to do it. There's one examiner, he can tell you, as you say a street, every shop down that street. He's amazing. I'm in *awe* of that man.'

I've heard that it's impossible to do the Knowledge just from a map – there's no substitute for getting out there and driving the streets. Is this Rachel's experience?

'Oh, absolutely. I have heard people say they know people who've done it from a map, but I'd challenge that. Same as I'd challenge someone who says they've done it from a sat-nav. I just don't think it's possible. Visualisation is a tried and tested way of the human brain learning things. That's why it works so well for people who aren't academics.' I tell her a story I once heard about a Knowledge boy[14] who cockily turned up for an 'appearance', one of the regular tests that punctuate the training period, and called a route that took him right from Holborn Viaduct on to Farringdon Street. 'You do realise,' said the examiner, 'that you've just driven off a forty-foot bridge?'

Appearances are designed as a test not just of knowledge but also of character. An ex-prisoner, for instance, might be asked to call the route from Wormwood Scrubs to Pentonville,

---

14. As students are called – Rachel assumes she must be a Knowledge girl, though there are so few that she's never heard the term used.

just to see how he reacts. 'I've had all that,' says Rachel. 'I had one examiner, he wasn't one of the chatty ones, he was just saying "take me from here to here", and I was doing the routes. Then he starts with, "I see from your file you're from South London." I say yes. He says, "You obviously won't have been going out [driving the streets for practice] then." And I *know* what's happening, I know what he's doing. I mean, he can see I have been going out. He says, "What are you going to do when you leave here?" I say, "I'm going to go out on my bike, sir." That was my test, to see if I'm going to turn round and go, "Oh yeah? What you saying?" You don't want people like that driving taxis. It's a constant battle out there against road rage. You do need those kinds of tests.'

Politeness to the customer now increasingly extends to assuaging their 'why don't you use sat-nav?' complaints. 'You can't put the sat-nav up against the human brain,' says Rachel. 'Sat-navs can't think on their feet. Most of the people you see trying to turn right into a no-entry are using sat-navs. You should go and see Derek at Knowledge Point [one of the Knowledge 'schools' that coach you through the process]. He told me about one of the cabbies being put against a load of the latest sat-navs, and he won.' The problem is worse now that so many phones have sat-nav functions. 'A woman got into my husband's cab the other night [Meni himself is a cabbie, inspiring Rachel to follow in his tyre-marks]. She had an app on her iPhone, and punched in the route, said, "I want to go this way." Meni tells her it'll be quicker his way, but she's not having it, so he does as she asks. Fifteen quid extra, her route. Forty-five quid. He knew his would have been about thirty.'

It took Meni four and a half years to complete the Knowledge. By the time Rachel's completed her 'suburbs' – as well as knowing every one of the 25,000 streets within six miles of Charing Cross, applicants have to show a more basic knowledge of the area out to the M25 – she will have done it in three years and ten months. Her final appearance is due in a few weeks, and anyone who reaches this stage is pretty sure to pass. 'I've beaten him,' she says with a smile. 'But no, it's not his city, not his country . . . And besides, without him, I'd never have done it. I was so proud of him, seeing how he turned our family's life around [the couple have two teenage sons] – he was on minimum wage, had come from a country where he was told he wasn't going to achieve anything, but now . . . Well, you're not going to be a millionaire as a cabbie, but if you're a hard worker you can do all right.'

The Knowledge is comprised of 320 'runs', each of which is simply a starting and finishing point; for instance the first run (as mentioned on the Victoria Line walk) is Manor House Tube to Gibson Square in Islington. Not only do you have to decide and memorise the quickest route between the two (as well as the return route, which because of one-way streets is almost certain to be different), but you're also expected to know the major points of interest within a quarter-mile radius of the run's starting point, and ditto at the end.[15] Points of

---

15. Memorising the two circles joined by a straightish line is known as a 'dumbbell' of knowledge.

interest include parks, government offices, hospitals, places of worship, football grounds, hotels, police stations, schools, art galleries, societies and associations, courts, theatres . . . in other words, just about anything anyone could want to find in an area stretching from Willesden to Blackheath, Wood Green to Tooting, Acton to Stratford. It must do your head in, I say to Rachel.

'Oh, I had to have therapy,' she says. It's a second before I realise she isn't joking. 'I had NLP [neurolinguistic programming], hypnotherapy . . . I'd have worn a dead goat's head round my neck if I thought it was going to help. There've been lots of times I was close to giving up, times I've been in tears, thinking "I can't take it any more." It's such hard work, seven days a week, up at six, all the time till you go to bed. I've never had moments of sadness like I've had doing the Knowledge.'

It really got that bad?

'Yeah, but too far in to stop. I'd told everyone I was going to do it, so I couldn't lose face.' She thinks for a minute, looking out at the traffic on the Euston Road. 'Twenty-eights, probably. That's when it was that bad. When I was on twenty-eights.'

She means when her appearances were at 28-day intervals. They get more frequent as time passes: every 56 days, then 28, finally 21. You don't even get on to 56 until you've learned the Knowledge as best you can, then taken a written test. In this you're given a blank map of an area of London with just one road name filled in, and have to identify certain other roads. This fascinates me, another example of maps being something you can play with, be creative with. It must seem as though you develop a relationship with the map?'

'Absolutely,' says Rachel. 'That's what it's all about. I draw on maps, colour them in. I'll write my route out in bright colours to try and bring it out in my memory. Anything to get that map into your head.' The thought occurs to me later that it's almost like pursuing a lover with notes and letters. 'I draw pictures, too. Say, if I'm trying to remember the layout of St James's Square I'll draw it, put the London Library at the top left-hand corner and so on . . . Or if I'm trying to remember the streets off Wardour Street, I'll imagine myself sitting on the bike at the top of it, then draw it as I drive it in my head, all the streets off the left and right.'

As well as that there's a lot of Never-Eat-Shredded-Wheatery. 'Like the wet T-shirts in Covent Garden: the roads that get you through from the Aldwych to Charing Cross Road. It starts Catherine Street left Exeter Street, then to remember the next few I do "right *W*ellington Street, left *T*avistock Street, right *S*outhampton Street, left *H*enrietta Place . . ." Then there's Geales fish restaurant in Notting Hill: it's a mad point to get into and leave. An older driver told me, "Have you just had fish?" *H*illgate Street, left *U*xbridge Street, right *J*ameson Street, right *H*illgate Place, right *F*armer Street, set down on right. Creating the image makes the whole thing flow. The fact that I remember making the connection almost matters more than the rhyme itself.' Rachel calls the routes so fast they become musical, like a Deep South auctioneer. The language of the Knowledge is beautiful in itself. *Comply Silvertown Roundabout, leave by*

*Capston Street South, forward North Woolwich Road, comply North Woolwich Roundabout . . .* It's poetry.

Every time Rachel rehearses a route she relives a trip she's done for real, takes the journey again in her mind.[16] Reminiscent of me marking up my maps at the end of a walk, I say.

'That's what we call being "on the cotton",' she replies. 'You decide on a route, then draw it on the map and get a piece of string to see how straight your line was. If it's as straight as it could have been, you were on the cotton.'

Rachel says that doing the Knowledge has revealed her home city to her. 'It's really opened London. New Cross has always been my home, so I've always been travelling from there to somewhere, then from somewhere back to New Cross. Now, though, I've had to go from one place to another. I'll say, "I never knew that was next to that – I thought it was miles away." You go round a corner and suddenly you're in Camden.'

Were there any bits that were completely new to her?

'Oh yeah. There were parts of London I never even knew existed. Like Southfields – since when was *that* London? I'd never heard of it.'

What else has she noticed about the capital?

She thinks for a moment. 'I tell you something about South London – you don't get so many pockets of people from one nation staying together. There's a lot more mixing, I've definitely noticed that. You go to Stoke Newington and it's

---

16. And has she done some trips – 19,000 miles in all, four-fifths of the way round the world.

very Turkish, and so on, but South London's a lot more diverse.' Rachel has also registered the 'poor and rich together' thing. 'That's true just about everywhere I've been. Whenever you see a high street that looks really hardcore, and you're thinking "no way would I want to live here", you go a few streets back and it'll get really affluent. And if there's a hill, then you *know* it's going to be affluent.'

Really? Why?

'I don't know – maybe because people want views? Whatever it is, anywhere there's a hill it starts to become very middle-class.'

Whenever we mention a specific area Rachel's got a memory of it, something unexpected she encountered while out on her bike. This is one of the things we've both enjoyed: wondering what a place will actually look like in comparison to the map, on which a road is just two parallel lines, a park just a green shape, even a church just a small black cross. Rachel remembers the Gothic village on Swains Lane in Highgate. 'It was early in the morning, everywhere was covered in mist and dew, and all of a sudden I found this little village; they looked like miniature gingerbread houses. They were built by Byzantine monks, apparently, but you could just imagine fairies and pixies building them. Incredible. I had to turn the engine off, just sit there for a minute. It's things like that that have kept me going.'

This reminds me of my own 'stumble across it' moment on Swains Lane. More specifically in its most famous landmark, Highgate Cemetery. I'd gone there to see Karl Marx, simply because his grave had cropped up in so many pub-quiz questions that I felt it'd be rude not to. As usual in such cases the reality couldn't help but be a disappointment, so I wandered round a bit, and was delighted to encounter Ralph Richardson's grave. He'd always seemed a beguiling chap – stark raving mad, and aware (unlike Olivier) that in the end acting was just a bit of a lark. I said hello, then went happily on my way.

The conversation with Rachel comes round to the question of whether Londoners – meaning those born in the city – take it for granted.

'I know what you mean,' she says. 'I never really took it for granted as such, I was always out and about getting my education, going to museums and stuff, because my mum educated me at home. But, yeah, I think until I started travelling the world, I took it for granted just how great London is. I really do think it's the best city in the world.' Rachel doesn't mean this in an American-tourist, look-at-the-Beefeaters-aren't-they-wonderful way. She means how London *works* as a city, how its people behave. 'The tolerance – we're way, way in front of anywhere else. Miles in front.'

She agrees that a lot of Londoners fail to make proper use of the city. 'Especially working-class Londoners, they don't come into the centre of town because there's an assumption it's going to cost you a lot of money. People don't realise how much is out there for free. Especially on the South Bank. And eating – we've been going to the *bhel puri* houses [Indian street-food restaurants] on Drummond Street since the kids were babies.' She pauses, gives a laugh. 'Not how it used to be. I remember my nan saying her mate had never been across the water. We said, "What, she's never been to France?" She said, "No, she's never been across the Thames."'

At this point Rachel's mobile goes (theme from *The Godfather* – if you're going to have a musical ringtone, have a good one), and she scrambles to answer it: she's expecting a call giving the date of her final appearance. But it's someone else, and as she deals with the call I look at my *A to Z*, noticing some of the side streets near here: Doric Way, Brill Place, Polygon Road . . . Now *they're* street names. None of this Derek Avenue nonsense. With 25,000 streets to learn, it's no wonder studies have shown that the hippocampus in a London cabbie's brain gets larger as they do the Knowledge.

Rachel finishes her conversation, and we fall to talking about maps again. 'I got myself two copies of the *A to Z*,' she says, 'took all the pages out and stuck them together, so I've got a map of London that's huge – the size of that wall.' She obviously needed two to have both sides of the same page. Rachel's also a Stanfords fan, and particularly loves their floors, which are enormous maps: the London *A to Z* in the basement, the National Geographic map of the world on the ground floor, with the same company's map of the Himalayas on the first floor, centred on Everest. 'Forty grand that cost them. I went and asked.'

Rachel thinks about her own huge map of London. 'It's given me the city as a gift. I suppose I did use to be quite parochial about New Cross, but that's changed now, after doing the Knowledge. London's *all* mine. It all belongs to me.'

Opposite King's Cross station, in the middle of a row of convenience stores and cheap Indian and Italian restaurants, is a hardware shop. A proper, old-fashioned hardware shop, with those yellow boards on its walls pitted with tiny holes to hang display hooks from, and men behind the counter who know exactly which box on which shelf to go to, pausing only to throw the question 'crossflam or gribbet?' over their shoulders. Actually I don't know for sure about the men behind the counter, because I didn't go in. I never do go into these places, finding it hard as I do to distinguish a screwdriver from a spanner. It's just nice to know that they're still here, that there's a shop in this part of Central London that sells *proper* things, rather than *Time Out* and heated pasties.

Just off the Farringdon Road is one of those 'look at me, I'm saving the planet' cyclists, signalling with his left hand but steering with neither. (Shortly, going through the Beech Street tunnel just after Barbican station, I'll see another one air-drumming to his iPod.) After Farringdon station is Cowcross Street, so named because it was where cattle crossed the River Fleet on their way to Smithfield Market. There's been a meat market here for over 800 years, from the days when it was a 'smooth field' beside the water. But the Smithfield-inspired place names don't stop there. The Holloway Road was hollowed out by cattle coming from the north, while the Kent delegation came up the Thames to 'the place where cattle are shipped', or 'Rotherhithe'. (They journeyed from there to the market by hoof.) Another location that owes its title to Smithfield was walked earlier today: the shepherds really did rest by the bushes in W12. Geography keeps these points separate, but history, and the growing awareness of it that this project is giving me, ties them together. The process is marshalling the city's disparate corners into a cohesive whole. Everything feels like it's coming together.

Passing through the market, its ornate Victorian shell resting quietly before the lorries and porters descend for another night of activity, I bump into a friend who works in the City.

'Off home?' I ask. Martin lives in St Albans.

'Yeah. I get the Thameslink from Farringdon.'

I adopt a suitably sympathetic expression. 'The commuter's daily grind, eh?'

'Oh, it's no hassle at all. Twenty minutes.'

'To St Albans?'

'Yeah.'

Good God. Another London wormhole. Martin and I chat for a bit, then he heads off to the station. It's surprising how often in this city of several million people you chance upon someone you know. There's even one of those dubious statistics that says if you wait all day at Piccadilly Circus it's more likely to happen than not – *wherever you're from in the world*. Whether that's true or not, the general tendency towards 'surprise' encounters is easily explained. It almost always happens in the centre, and how many people do I know who live and/or work there? Dozens. The real surprise would be if I *never* bumped into any of them. It stands to reason, also, that from time to time I must *nearly* bump into someone I know. Maybe we pass unseen either side of a double-decker bus stuck in traffic, or one of us leaves a pub by one door just as the other enters it by another. The sort of moments you see in films and think 'that would never happen'.

Like the thing that happened to me a few months ago. What's more it happened right here, at Smithfield, though in the days before the internet I would never have known it had happened. Jo and I had met my parents for lunch at Carluccio's, a few yards south of the market. A week or so later, several links in a chain of thought took me to a guy I'd met nearly twenty years earlier, when we both worked on a project that lasted only a few days. Never encountered him again, but his unusual surname had stuck in my memory, and we'd had a few laughs together. Just for something to do I googled him. Turned out he'd died, suddenly, in his late forties, in his office a few yards north of Smithfield Market – at the exact time I was enjoying that lively family lunch.

On Long Lane, which forms the south side of the market, a gaggle of motorcycle couriers eat bacon sandwiches from one of the caffs opposite; I guess they know the bacon here's going to be good. Less satisfactory was the transaction that took place in 1729. 'Last Wednesday,' reported the *Country Journal*, 'one Everet . . . sold his wife to one Griffin of Long Lane for a 3/- bowl of punch; who, we hear, hath since complained of having a bad bargain.'

After the next station, Barbican, comes Moorgate. Heading towards it are a couple of office workers, a man and a woman, discussing a colleague. 'He makes the same bloody joke every time,' complains the man. '"No, I haven't got one leg shorter than the other; I've got one leg longer than the other."' 'I know,' says the woman. 'Gets on your nerves, doesn't it?' They walk a few paces in silence. 'Mind you,' she adds, in a conciliatory tone, 'I suppose "one leg longer than the other" does sound a bit more glamorous.' Then it's Liverpool Street station, by which time I have walked exactly 9.99 miles. Opposite the main entrance are two police horses, as white as their famous forebear Billy, who controlled the crowd that spilled on to the pitch at the 1923 FA Cup final, but thankfully without the same workload.[17] Commuters, including some seemingly hard-faced businessmen, break into smiles at the sight. One of the horses whinnies and tosses its head and is generally a bit of a tart, but the other remains statue-still. Only after a minute or so do I detect movement, a faint Mr Ed-style judder of the lips, as if to say, 'I could have made it to Aintree, you know.'

Cutting through the City back streets towards Aldgate East I pass the beginning of Leadenhall Street, home to St Katharine Cree, one of the few churches (indeed the few buildings) to escape the Great Fire. In 1769 the man employed to dig a grave here for a Mrs Osborne 'laid a wager that he would dig it ten feet deep'. He did, too, but before he could climb out and collect his winnings, the earth

---

17. In Billy's honour the footbridge outside the new Wembley Stadium has been named the White Horse bridge.

'fell in and caught him up to the middle, from which several people endeavoured to extricate him, but in vain . . . the earth gave way a second time, and the poor man was smothered.'

Within the space of a few Whitechapel yards I pass three things for which the area is famous. First, a Jack the Ripper walk. Always easy to tell the Brits on these: they're the ones looking miserable. Despite the fact they've chosen to come on the walk – *paid* to come on it, indeed – they stare back at the guide with an ennui bordering on malevolence, as though they were schoolkids being marched forcibly round a museum. The Americans and Japanese smile, respond to the guide's jokes, generally do their best to make him feel like something other than an enemy. Then, at number 34 Whitechapel Road, is the foundry responsible for Big Ben and the Liberty Bell, still casting bells today. Finally, the East London Mosque, its entrances thronged with those attending Maghrib, the fourth of the five daily prayers, delivered just before sunset. I say 'entrances' because men and women have to use separate ones. This reminds me of St Stephen's, the primary school I photographed back in Westbourne Park this afternoon. Its two doorways were marked 'Boys' and 'Girls', and I remember thinking, 'Imagine if they tried doing that today . . .'

The next thing I notice is very un-Whitechapel and all the more surprising for creeping up on me so insidiously. More and more of the people passing by are young men in suits, looking not unlike young men in suits in London at any point over the last century or so, except for one thing:

the vertical line of the tie is absent, replaced by the diagonal line of a bag's shoulder strap. Then it dawns on me that many of these young men are accompanied by young women, also in twenty-first-century office-casual. The couples carry shopping bags full of Sainsbury's ready meals and mid-range Merlots. Just back there, I remember, was a new Starbucks . . . Yes, Whitechapel is being yuppified. Not in the eighties sense of the word (braces, floppy hair, enormous mobiles), but in the strict, acronymistic sense: Young Urban Professionals. Twenty-five years ago it was Fulham. Now the tribe's more restrained members are colonising the east.

I should have seen it coming, after what happened to Jo and me five years ago. It was our last summer in London, and after leaving our respective flats we needed a base from which to go househunting. As the hunting ground was Suffolk, the east side of London made sense. But, we told estate agents, that was the east side of *Central London*: we didn't want anything beyond Aldgate. In the end we plumped for Clerkenwell, though not before a representative from one firm – subsequent conversations have revealed that almost no one has a good word to say about them – loaded us into his branded Mini Cooper with an assurance that he had a 'stunning property, absolutely stunning' that was 'a little way' along the Whitechapel Road. 'We did say nothing east of Aldgate,' was our reply. 'I know, I know,' he said, 'but honestly, this place is *stunning*.' 'And it's just up the road?' we asked. 'Absolutely,' came the assurance. 'Couple of minutes tops.'

In the Millennium Falcon, possibly. His Mini was still going a quarter of an hour later, by which time I was asking if he was sure he had enough petrol for the return journey. To this day whenever Jo and I hear that firm's name we slaughter a chicken and circle the body three times – but now, as I head towards Stepney Green station, I see that the trail taken by that Mini was ripe for blazing. Whitechapel Road still *looks* as grotty as it used to, but mixed in there are those signs of incipient middle-classness. The Urban Bar, with its tiger-stripe frontage, offers 'events', including DJs and weekly poker nights. Next to the 'Halal Bite' café is a billboard ad for M&S lingerie, displaying far more flesh than lingerie, and the slogan 'Ooh la la!', while outside the Red Dragon with its 'halal Chinese buffet' (nothing like covering all the bases) a twenty-something couple do their warm-down after jogging. This still isn't Chelsea – one pub's happy hour includes 'Carlesburg' (probably the worst spelling in the world) – but neither is it the cool-free zone of a few years back.

Time for a short rest at Mile End, up on the 'Green Bridge', a wide lawn-covered walkway that carries Mile End Park over the main road. One of those initiatives that smacks of Worthy Councillor but in practice is just a bloody good idea. Sitting down, I remember how I walked here from Essex on my Central Line trip. So did 60,000 people in 1381, though they weren't following the Tube line, they were revolting peasants. Stepney Green Park, just to the south-west of here, is the last remaining part of the greenery in which they camped. The 14-year-old Richard II came out to meet them and negotiations went well. Only when the king headed back to Smithfield to meet rebel leader Wat Tyler and his men did the atmosphere sour, particularly for Tyler, who ended up with the Lord Mayor of London's sword through his neck. I'm beginning to wonder if there isn't a link between Smithfield and every single part of London.

Back on my feet, 50 per cent of which are working admirably, I head for Bow Road station. The area owes its name to Matilda, wife of Henry I, who in 1110 was walking this way to Barking Abbey (as indeed am I – the Abbey's ruins are near my final station). Crossing the ford of the River Lea, she went dress-train over tiara, and reacted by ordering a bridge to be built, the finished design of which was an unusual bow shape. Hence the title of the next station, which requires a cut down from the main drag and past some railway arches, all of them used as garages. One or two mechanics are working even at this hour (7.56). A carwash sign offers 'the best hand job in London'.

A short row of Georgian houses have different arrangements of shutters in place. Under the top half of one set I see a couple's four hands eating chops and peas; over the bottom half of another I see a woman peeling potatoes watched by her Siamese cat, which sits on the work surface. Those urban professionals block the way with a huge half-constructed apartment development, sending me further south than I'd like, but eventually Bromley-by-Bow station appears. East of this is an industrial estate, presided over by several hulking great gas-holders, whose silhouettes against the night sky would look intimidating but for the powerful beam of green light being projected upwards from the O2. Although it goes nowhere near the gas-holders, somehow this evidence of millennial technology feels as though it's protecting you from these disgruntled industrial dinosaurs.

West Ham, which I reach next, tries to mediate between the two worlds. Its bus garage is a huge old building powered by a twenty-first-century wind turbine whooshing doggedly away. The Tube station just up the road feels similar – the Jubilee Line extension shot through here in the late 1990s, and it's also getting ready to accept the DLR, creating a multi-level miracle of interchange, whose well-lit platforms shine down on the street below. A crumpled piece of paper flaps half-heartedly across the pavement in front of me. I can never resist these. This one turns out to be a CV for a television director. Its presence here would indicate that he didn't get the job. In sympathy I read of his exec experience on a 12x60 series for BBC1, his 1x90 for More4. The most affecting document I ever picked up was a lunchtime sandwich list, one of whose entries was 'ham salad, white – no mayo'. You could have given me that person's bank account details and all their internet passwords – it wouldn't have felt anywhere near as intrusive as knowing that they didn't have mayo on their ham salad sandwich.

After West Ham the darkness returns, and it soon becomes clear that the border of Urban Professionalville has been crossed. Come back in ten years and further encroachments will no doubt have been made, but for now this – being Plaistow, and everywhere from here to Barking – remains unglamorous, unkempt, unloved, even by those who live here. Nor do they hate it, either, you sense. They just accept that this is life, and they must lead it. They have signs in their windows saying 'Sod the dog, beware of the kids'. They add shallow plastic conservatories to the front of their small Victorian terraces – shallow not in any judgemental sense but simply the physical one: these structures add at most a couple of dozen square feet to the living space, which is used to store shopping trolleys, pushchairs, shoe racks. We all yearn for that little bit more territory, our own personal *Anschluss*.

The Tube line and the streets that follow it run east–west, the main roads that house the stations – Plaistow, Upton Park, East Ham – run north–south, rising up to get over the line so that each station is on a bridge. It is on these roads, teeming with people queuing for buses, eating at cafés and shopping at multi-marts, that the racial mix reveals itself: mostly Asian and Eastern European, the odd indigenous white, no one with very much money. Newsagent ads (often in Hindi or Polish) offer rooms in flatshares: 'TV, internate' . . . 'includes dinner, morning breakfast' . . . 'the first see it you will take'. At a Chinese restaurant near Upton Park station – well, one of those Chinese takeaways that has two plastic tables in the space between the door and the counter – I have some satisfyingly glutinous lemon chicken with egg-fried rice, and remember the caff down the road from here where I once had a fry-up on the way to a football match at West Ham's ground. A piece of purple day-glo card on the wall advised: 'Remember – bubble takes a little longer'.

Leaving the takeaway I say '*sheh sheh*', the only bit of

Chinese I know apart from '*nee-how*' ('hello'). The owner's surprise at being thanked in her own language turns to a smile, making me glad I had the courage to do it. Actually, why was that? I always want to say it but never do, the complexities of Mandarin pronunciation meaning you can easily call someone's mother something unspeakable. Only halfway down the next dark, uneventful east–west street does the answer strike me: it's because I'm walking. Walking this distance, I mean (up to the 18-mile mark now). The endorphins are giving me confidence, keeping my mood high.[18] They did this at the Elephant and Castle, but tonight they're almost cocaine-like.[19] Between East Ham and Barking, on a footbridge over the North Circular, I pause, leaning against the rail, looking down on the three lanes of white lights on one side, the three lanes of red on the other. The cool night air wafts around me. It's beautiful. The A406 in East London at 10.30 on a Thursday night is beautiful. It looks like a helicopter shot of Los Angeles in a Michael Mann film. *That's* how strong endorphins are.

Except – crap. By which I don't mean that the North Circular doesn't look beautiful, I mean I shouldn't have to apologise for calling it beautiful. What's so real about the non-endorphin-fuelled conclusion that it's ugly? As I finally reach Barking just before 11 p.m. (standard town-centre kit: Boots, Carphone Warehouse, station with lots of bus stops outside), I remember

---

18. As Henry Thoreau said, 'Me thinks that the moment my legs begin to move, my thoughts begin to flow.'

19. Actually, why is it called Bolivian marching powder? Marching seems to be marching powder.

a school I saw back on Plashet Grove, near East Ham. Its noticeboard advertised walktoschool.org.uk – 'We're walking to work once a week'. Good on them. But why not do it every day? Send them the long way round – it's better than drugs.

True, after a while, on the train back to Suffolk, and certainly the next morning, when the chemical effects of eight hours' pedestrianism have died away, the thought that London E6 could be described as picturesque is patent rubbish. But nonetheless a background certainty remains, a lesson that this project is gradually massaging into my consciousness: a place is never just a place. It's a place plus how you got there.

Rachel's sent me an email, following up on something we talked about. Advising on the Jubilee Line walk, which entails more than one crossing of the Thames around Docklands, she'd said that although you can't walk through the Blackwall Tunnel, you can through the Rotherhithe ('but I'd wear a mask if I were you'). She now realises she forgot to tell me why the Rotherhithe Tunnel has such sharp bends in it: built in the days when horse-drawn traffic was commonplace, the bends were designed to stop the animals bolting for the exit as soon as they saw daylight.

In the email exchange that follows Rachel says she'll let me know when she passes the Knowledge. And who her first fare is – by tradition cabbies do that one for free. I'm tempted to ask if it can be me, getting from one end of the Blackwall Tunnel to the other. But that really wouldn't be in the spirit of things.

# 5

# District Line

## The trackless path of a
## bird in the air

There's a bit in *The Day of the Jackal* where Edward Fox dismantles his custom-built sniper's rifle into its component sections, gathers them together in a bundle, then wraps them tightly in clear plastic sheeting. Prior to sliding this package into the short section of metal tubing that will later be disguised as part of one of his crutches (he gets through the security barrier in Paris by pretending to be a one-legged war veteran), he pulls the far end of the plastic sheeting tightly round the end of the rifle parts, so that they will fit neatly. It's all carried out with his trademark precision and care.

You'll have gathered from this second reference in the book to *The Day of the Jackal* that it's one of my favourite films. This is why I'm particularly chuffed that the walk for every line gives me not just one but two chances to re-enact that scene. Before handing me my maps in Stanfords, Piotr rolled them up, wrapped them in clear plastic, then put them in a sturdy cardboard tube. This is where they reside when not being consulted (pre-walk) or magimarkered (post-walk). Each operation offers a few seconds' opportunity to be a faux-Fox. Not, you understand, that I'm pretending the maps are rifle parts. Maps are way too exciting in their own right to need that sort of image boost. No, it's just the planning element that gets me. The idea of meticulous preparation, leaving nothing to chance, a series of calmly methodical steps undertaken in advance of a secretive urban operation. Get into the city, do the job, get out. In the Jackal's case that city is Paris, in mine it's London. In his case it's trying to evade thousands of police officers in order to kill the President, in mine it's just walking around a lot, which explains why he fails on the 'get out of the city' part and I don't, but no matter.

The very best cities do this – bring out the kid in you. The kid that wants to be someone else. By definition this is childish, but in case you think that means adults shouldn't be doing it, may I call in aid Michael Palin? His diary entry for 4 March 1988 (he was forty-four at the time, and, like the Jackal, though for different reasons, in Paris) reads: 'I walk, for an hour and a half, around the Left Bank, stopping at a couple of bars, enjoying what only certain great cities can provide – a marvellous set against which to invent and play your part. Like Venice, Paris dramatises everything.'[1] It's understandable that when a city has formed the set for as many iconic films as London has, you think of it as having

---

1. Just to mess things up I beg to differ on Venice: it's a tourist destination, not a working city. If Disney did a Venice it would be Venice.

a certain 'filmic' quality. But that quality was there before the films, indeed before there was film, as a couple of centuries' worth of novels show. The licence to be a character – to be two or more different characters, often in the same day – is what London offers you every time you visit it.

This stays true despite the fact that most of the things that happen to you in London are perfectly routine. It's the sense of *possibility* that keeps you coming – has always kept people coming – even when that possibility displays a stubborn refusal to hatch. At school in the Lake District, William Wordsworth knew a boy who had been to London. Wordsworth pumped him for information, and was disappointed when the boy couldn't remember anything. As Hunter Davies puts it in his biography of the poet, 'he didn't even look different'. Yet down to the capital Wordsworth came, to see for himself. As transport improved in the nineteenth century it became ever easier for others to do likewise. In 1888 the anonymous author of *Tempted London* noted that 'there is no parish, however remote or obscure, from the Hebrides to Cornwall, from which young men do not find their way to London. There is, perhaps, none who has not a relative or friend who has made his journey to the great city and fought his battle there.'

The battle might start as a rebellion against your home parish, fuelled by feelings of not belonging there, but as often as not it ends up as a battle against yourself, against the realisation that London can't – ultimately – give you what you dreamed of. It can't, as Wordsworth's classmate showed, make you look different. The thing is, though, you never

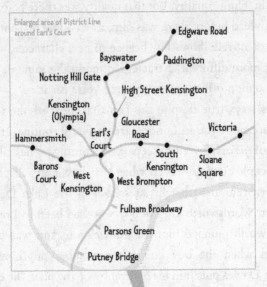

Enlarged area of District Line around Earl's Court

- Edgware Road
- Bayswater
- Paddington
- Notting Hill Gate
- High Street Kensington
- Kensington (Olympia)
- Gloucester Road
- Victoria
- Hammersmith
- Earl's Court
- South Kensington
- Sloane Square
- Barons Court
- West Kensington
- West Brompton
- Fulham Broadway
- Parsons Green
- Putney Bridge

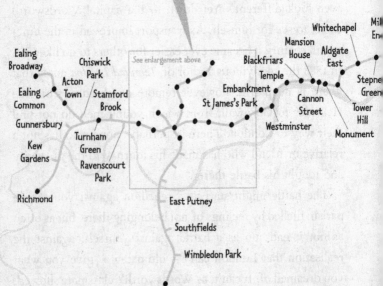

- Ealing Broadway
- Chiswick Park
- Acton Town
- Ealing Common
- Stamford Brook
- See enlargement above
- Blackfriars
- Whitechapel
- Mill End
- Mansion House
- Aldgate East
- Temple
- Embankment
- St James's Park
- Cannon Street
- Stepney Green
- Gunnersbury
- Turnham Green
- Westminster
- Tower Hill
- Kew Gardens
- Ravenscourt Park
- Monument
- Richmond
- East Putney
- Southfields
- Wimbledon Park
- Wimbledon

N

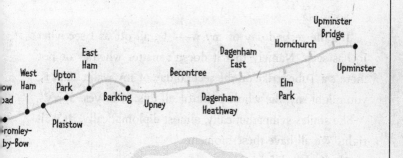

**DISTRICT LINE**

Stations: 60 (the most of any line)

Line mileage: 40

Words spoken by Russian woman in
Notting Hill pub to her own husband: 0

Upminster
Bridge

Hornchurch

Dagenham
East

Upminster

East
Ham

Becontree

West    Upton
Ham    Park

Elm
Park

ow                     Barking    Upney        Dagenham
ad                                              Heathway

Plaistow

romley-
by-Bow

0   0.5   1 mi

0    1    2 km

*quite* stop believing that one day it might. America, said F. Scott Fitzgerald, is a willingness of the heart. I think London is a willingness of the imagination.

'Damn!'

'What is it?' Jo is alarmed not just by my outburst but by the clatter of my knife and fork being put down at the same time. We're eating dinner, our conversation accompanied by the background burbling of a Radio 4 news bulletin.

'She just said about the Tube strike. Next Monday. I'd forgotten about that.'

'So?'

'It's the second day of my w—' I trail off as I see what Jo has seen. Namely that it doesn't matter whether or not there's a Tube strike on the second day of my walk. That is, you might say, the whole point of all this. 'Oh, yes. Sorry.'

She smiles sympathetically, almost diplomatically. 'It's all right. We all have these moments.'

The Jackal didn't.

Actually my alarm was *nearly* justified. A Tube strike on the second day doesn't matter, because all I'm doing then is walking from Earl's Court to the easternmost end of the District Line at Upminster. (There I'll catch a quick bus up to Romford, from where I can get a mainline train back home to Suffolk.) But on the first day of my walk, the Sunday, I do need the services of London Underground to get me out to Wimbledon. After much crouching over the maps with a pair of compasses to estimate distances, it seems clear that the quickest way to do the western end of the line, which resembles five octopus tentacles branching out from Earl's Court, is to start in SW19. From there the plan is as follows:

- into Earl's Court;
- out to Richmond. Here the walk requires something none of its predecessors has: an offline walk. It's pointless retracing my steps. Quicker to walk due north to the end of the Ealing Broadway branch (namely, er, Ealing Broadway), and then back to Earl's Court again;
- up to Edgware Road, followed by another offline walk down to Olympia;
- in from Olympia to Earl's Court, where the first day ends.

The reason for choosing Sunday as the first day is that none of the walks so far have been at a weekend. Now that autumn's well and truly here (this is the first week of October), bringing showers and darker evenings and pavements slick with leaves, it's struck me how fortunate London is in its latitude. Far enough away from the North Pole to be habitable, but not so near the equator that every day of the year is the same. Seasonal weather gives you four cities in one. And if the walks are varying in that respect – the aim is to finish just before Christmas – why not vary them over days of the week too? Sunday London is different from weekday London. The District Line will give me a slice of each.

\* \* \*

On Saturday night I stay with a friend who lives opposite Bromley-by-Bow station.[2] This is to avoid having to travel all the way in from Suffolk on Sunday morning, so wasting valuable walking time. The District Line looks like it could be an even longer trek than the Central. And it's certainly got more stations. The most of any line on the network, in fact: 60 of the buggers.

The first Wimbledon train (6.39) is surprisingly busy, well over half full, mostly with Asian people who, at this ungodly hour, can only be on their way to low-paid jobs. Central London replaces these with a few up-all-nighters (exclusively white) on their way back to Fulham and Putney. By the time the train reaches Wimbledon (7.40), I'm the only passenger left. Around the station itself are some cabbies, street-sweepers and Sunday-paper-buyers, but that's it. The Centre Court shopping mall (ha ha) is all closed up, wary of the heavy rain that's forecast for later. At the moment the skies are clear, but there's certainly a freshness about.

Right and right again takes me quickly out of pedestrianised shopping land into respectably residential suburbia, houses that date from around the time that the Metropolitan District Railway ventured out here in 1889. The company had been inspired by the Metropolitan Railway itself, and decided to get in on the act, so becoming the second oldest of what are now the Tube lines. They were cut-and-cover

---

2. Rob informs me that the station is missing from the map displayed in the Tube station on the *EastEnders* set. Not that you'd see it even in HD, but Bromley-by-Bow is replaced with the fictional station's own name, Walford East.

merchants too, opening their first section on Christmas Eve 1868 between South Kensington and Westminster. To build the tunnels and embankments the company had used 140 million bricks produced in their own huge kilns at Earl's Court. At Sloane Square they'd had to channel the River Westbourne over the platforms and tracks in a large square metal pipe.[3] The other branches opened up soon afterwards. The company even got permission to build a line across Wimbledon Common, but ran out of money, much to the relief of some of London's most important residents, the creatures first discovered by Elisabeth Beresford when one of her children, on a Boxing Day walk there, accidentally referred to the place as 'Wombledon Common'.

It's very peaceful out here, the streets deserted, every household asleep, apart from one where a toddler stands in the front room with a look that says 'entertain me'. Whichever parent is on duty must have retreated to the kitchen: there's a delicious smell of bacon. By Wimbledon Park station is the Café du Parc, then the first joggers of the morning (a couple, though almost all the others I'll see will be women, either on their own or in pairs), then a catering firm's van with a discreet 'By appointment to HRH the Prince of Wales' crest on the side. The roads here are in a grid pattern, built on land that as late as 1912 boasted the closest haystacks to Central London, between the villages of Wimbledon and Putney. But soon Southfields, as the area came to be known,[4] developed

---

3. It's still there today.
4. Hope this helps with Rachel's 'since when was Southfields part of London?' question.

a suburban prissiness, banning pubs from 'the Grid'. Only in the last two decades have they been allowed.

Raucous drinking is one of those things – like swearing and snooker – that the middle classes traditionally opted out of, despite the fact that the upper and lower classes got up to them at every possible opportunity. Another is violence, evidenced by the goings-on just west of here on Putney Heath, a traditional duelling place. It was the venue for the famous 1809 duel between politicians Lord Castlereagh and George Canning, and eleven years earlier even hosted a shoot-off between the serving Prime Minister, William Pitt, and another MP. (No one got hurt.) Up in North London, meanwhile, a Lieutenant-Colonel Montgomery duelled with a Captain Macnamara at Chalk Farm in 1803 simply because the 'dog of one snarled at the dog of the other'. It's not recorded which was the offending canine, but Montgomery was killed and Macnamara severely injured.

Putney Heath was also one of the calling points, in 1813, for Richard Phillips, author of *A Morning's Walk from London to Kew*. I've been looking at this as part of my research for today, and while Phillips does suffer from the slight disadvantage of being a pompous old tit, it's nevertheless a worthwhile read. His route obviously predated the Tube, so only crosses mine at a couple of points (he went from St James's Park down through Chelsea, Battersea and Barnes), but several passages hit home. As ever when you read something from long ago it's the *même chose* that strikes you as much as the *plus* that has changed. Complaining about the 'inconceivable millions which have been spent about Malta', Phillips bemoans what could have been achieved had that money been invested in the then-embryonic railways: 'we might . . . have witnessed our mail coaches running at the rate of ten miles an hour . . . or impelled fifteen miles by Blenkinsop's steam engine!' He points out that the rural idyll isn't always idyllic: 'Wandsworth . . . is like all the villages round London. Gay and splendid as they appear to the summer visitor, nothing can be more dull and monotonous than the lives of their constant residents.'

But London itself, seen by Phillips from the top of the telegraph tower on Putney Heath,[5] doesn't get an easy ride either. The capital looks 'like an anthill . . . Such is the estimate of the eye, nor is it heightened by that of the ear; for I was assured that during tranquil nights, particularly by listening near the ground, the confused hum of the vast British metropolis could here be compared only to the buzz of a BEEHIVE . . . What a lesson do these considerations afford to the pride of man.'[6] I like this. Important to keep things – and places – in perspective. I love my village in Suffolk, but if I never came to London, life would indeed be dull and monotonous. Similarly the vast metropolis itself can't fulfil all your needs. Whenever you're in one place, you dream of the other. Hence the famous comparison of the respective merits of travelling and arriving. Perhaps that's why I'm enjoying all these walks so much.

Up on the Richmond Road, opposite East Putney station, Caffè Nero is refuelling the joggers, of whom there are now plenty (it's twenty to nine). Among the few males of the breed

---

5. One of a chain, averaging 8 miles apart, stretching from the Admiralty to the South Coast so that visual messages could be transmitted to ships at Portsmouth and Plymouth.
6. Phillips is the second person, after Peter Rees, to liken it to a beehive.

are two blond late-teen twins, maintaining a frightening pace; disturbingly Aryan. Several people are on their way to the gym instead. All this health seems appropriate for the District Line, which when it opened was an early member of the anti-smoking movement. Only in 1874 did it join the Metropolitan in allowing the evil weed on its trains, 'for the comfort of passengers'. Round on Putney High Street it's Frapovia again: another Nero, a Starbucks, a Costa, though this lot cater mainly for the more sedentary. The well-heeled of SW15 are waking to their broadsheets and their free wi-fi. There's genuine wealth around here; many of the detached houses I've passed have been *seriously* large, as deep as they are wide, verging on 'mansion'. True, there have been post-war council flats too, but not many. Apart from Mayfair, this corner of London feels like the most sustainedly poor-free zone of the project so far.

The road rises as it nears Putney Bridge, and soon I'm out over the water. To the right is one of only two points on the whole Tube system where trains cross the Thames by bridge rather than tunnel, the other being the Richmond branch at Kew. The sun's still bright enough to reflect off the river, but the trees that line the north bank into the distance are rustling ominously; that rain's on its way. Still, for now, the overall effect – the sumptuous black lampposts, the rowing eight passing underneath,[7] the single bell tolling at All Saints Fulham – is all so calming that you can't imagine why Mary Wollstonecraft jumped from this bridge in an attempt to

---

7. This is where the Boat Race starts, though until 1845 it was where it ended, the crews having started at Westminster.

drown herself.[8] But then that was an October night (in 1795) rather than an October morning, and she had just found out that her lover was being unfaithful. She was pulled from the water and revived.

North of the river we're into Parsons Green.[9] It's still all Le Pain Quotidien, design stores called OKA, beauty salons offering Purity Facial Rituals from the Thalgo range. Street after substantial Victorian terraced street covers the ground from the north of here up to Fulham. One of them is Gowan Avenue, where Jill Dando lived and died. I've never walked round here before, but seeing it this morning, prosperous and ordered and still, makes the murder seem even more surreal than it always has, like a weird joke still awaiting its punchline. Outside Fulham Broadway station[10] a deflated white balloon bearing the slogan 'Join the revolution – Metro Bank' hobbles slowly along.

Down the Fulham Road is Stamford Bridge, home not just to Chelsea FC but also to a large hotel development. Even at half-nine on a Sunday morning there are Japanese and Russian and American tourists, taking photos of a truly bland set of

---

8. Unless you've seen *The Omen*, in which case no amount of Sunday tranquillity can sever the connection between All Saints Fulham and the image of Patrick Troughton impaled by the church's lightning rod.

9. Whose Tube station is one of four on the network to bear a name containing the colour of the line it's on. Two of the others are on this line – Turnham Green and Stepney Green – while the other is on the Central Line: Redbridge.

10. Where Gwyneth Paltrow both did and didn't make it through those sliding doors.

buildings. No, 'bland' is too complimentary – these are ugly in their blandness. I don't care if the snappers are Chelsea fans, why don't they take their cameras next door, into Brompton Cemetery? It's another of the Magnificent Seven, like Kensal Green. Carved into the stone gatepost are the words 'The public are permitted to walk in the cemetery daily', and even if this wasn't the quickest route to West Brompton station it's an invitation I'd be happy to accept. The graves and memorials here are some of the best London has to offer. Above a horizontal stone reading 'Sir William Eliot Peyton, K.C.B., K.C.V.O., D.S.O., Colonel, The 15th/19th Hussars' is a huge boulder marked 'BILL'. Beatrix Potter was a fan of the cemetery; it was on her walks here that she collected the names for many of her characters: Mr Nutkins, Jeremiah Fisher, Tommy Brock, even Peter Rabbit (though the original was a Rabbett). Also buried here, though I don't have time today to search the 39 acres for him, is Bernard Levin. I used to live opposite him in Marylebone, whose High Street he said was one of only two proper high streets remaining in the capital, the other being Hampstead. At the time he was right – there was even a hardware store. I'm glad for his sake that he left Marylebone (and indeed this life) in 2004, so didn't have to witness the Howard de Walden Estate's 'makeover'. Egyptian-cotton bedlinen is all very well, but a high street ain't a high street unless it can sell you a rawlplug.

The cemetery marks the end of both peace and wealth; emerging from its north entrance you're into Earl's Court, which is fine in a buzzy, touristy, here-for-the-Masterchef-Live-show kind of way, but certainly isn't exclusive. Between West Brompton and Earl's Court stations I pass a Chinese family taking photos of themselves outside their B&B, which is a large white stucco building, but is still only a B&B. There's the usual 'do I walk into shot and ruin the picture, or be kind and wait?' quandary. Nowadays I usually opt for the latter. When I lived in London it was different. No time, man. A friend of mine who lives and works in Central London says whenever he's caught on film like this (even in the background) it reminds him of the Native American belief that a camera will steal your soul, and he imagines the hundreds of snaps there must be of him, scattered across the globe.

Earl's Court marks the end of the first branch of my walk. A shade under seven miles, two and a quarter hours. Time for a late breakfast (sandwich and a coffee) opposite the station, reflecting on good old Bumper Harris. He was not, as someone once suggested, Bomber Harris's less aggressive younger brother, but the one-legged man who rode the station's escalator – the Tube's first – in 1911, to demonstrate how safe it was even for someone with a wooden appendage.[11] Sadly it's untrue that he was employed to do it all day long; once was sufficient to get people flocking to use the new invention.[12] But then what has this city earned if not the right to another bit of mythology?

\* \* \*

---

11. Early Tube escalators ended at a diagonal barrier, so that the stairway finished sooner for your right foot than your left. Those who wanted to stand rather than walk were therefore asked to do so on the right – the root of the modern convention.

12. Similarly you sense that Harrods' 1898 stunt of having brandy on hand to revive nervous users of the first escalator in London as a whole was just that – a stunt.

First stop on the next branch (out to Richmond) is West Kensington. Among its earliest users must have been the young Mahatma Gandhi, who moved to a house nearby in 1888; in fact my walk goes right past his blue plaque on Barons Court Road. This was during his first spell in London, to train as a barrister.[13] The area was new then, being developed by Sir William Palliser, who had connections with the Baronscourt estate in Ireland. (It's yet another London fallacy that he chose the name to ape neighbouring Earl's Court.) Barons Court station itself didn't arrive until 1905, but by God I'm glad it did. As you round the corner on to Palliser Road, the north–souther that humps over the Tube lines (shades of Plaistow and Upton Park on the Hammersmith and City walk), the station's terracotta façade hits – no, sorry – caresses your senses. Harry Ford's design is slightly paler in shade than Leslie Green's ox-blood, the tiles covering a structure combining arched windows, Art Nouveau lettering and a balustraded roof. The left-hand half of the building is an upmarket café and deli, while the ticket hall is lined with rich green glazed tiles. This, I decide here and now, without even having to see the rest of the competition, is the most beautiful station not just on the London Underground network, not just in the world, but in any world you, I or anyone else could possibly imagine. If you ever find yourself with time to visit – or even if you don't – you should treat yourself.

The centre of Hammersmith, with its busy shopping centre

---

13. His second, more famous, visit was also on the District Line, in 1931 when he lived in Bromley-by-Bow. His room at Kingsley Hall there has been preserved.

and its flyover and the Ark building, acts as a punctuation point. After here it's quiet again, a return to the quiet affluence of this morning, the line following the main road (King Street, then its continuation Chiswick High Road), the stations lying just to the north on quiet side streets. Opposite Ravenscourt Park a young woman, still in her pyjamas with a coat over them (it's 11.15, but then it is Sunday) loads bags into her VW Golf. Will she get dressed for the drive? Near Stamford Brook[14] is a postbox installed after the Royal Mail started using vans – you can always tell because the slot faces the road rather than the pavement. The quickest way to the next station is along sleepy Flanders Road, an appropriate place to see a front room dominated by a huge poster of Audrey Hepburn.[15] Further along a tree's roots have pushed a green plastic water pipe up through the pavement.

The park opposite Turnham Green station is called, as you would expect, Chiswick Common. Turnham Green itself is halfway down the road towards the next stop, Gunnersbury, past the yummy mummies stocking up at Jo Jo Maman Bébé and contemplating Dove Spa's offer of a complimentary Paraffin Wax Hand Treatment. In the Civil War this was where Cromwell's Roundheads halted Charles I's progress towards London. Today the green hosts a funfair. Gunnersbury takes its name from Gunnhildr, a woman of Danish extraction whose manor this once was – a rare case of a woman other than

---

14. Richard is happy to report that this was the first Tube station with an automatic ticket barrier – 5 January 1964.

15. She was Belgian – handy to keep up your sleeve for the 'five famous ones' game.

Victoria getting a look-in when it comes to London place names. Dominating the area is the British Standards Institution's HQ. While none of us wants risky kettles or car windows that break too easily, it is nevertheless depressing that the nanny state requires 18 floors from which to watch over us.

Gunnersbury's station was destroyed in December 1954 by a tornado. Despite the fact that the roof was ripped off and a car in nearby Acton was lifted 15 feet into the air, only six people were injured. Hopefully things won't get quite so bad today, but the first drops of rain are starting to appear. On go the waterproofs, up goes the umbrella, followed by a bit of jiggly rearranging as I get out the clear plastic cover, attached to a string round my neck, that will keep my map and notes dry. Glad I invested in this. At first it feels a bit geography-teacher-on-a-field-trip, but it certainly works: as I cross Kew Bridge[16] the rain gets stronger, and if there are any suspicions that it just feels like that because I'm over the river they're dispelled on the south bank. It is indeed stair-rods.

It is also, apparently, the eighteenth century. Bordering the road on both sides is Kew Green, rich in trees, its grass growing ever more lush by the second, and pretty well all the buildings you can see beyond it are Georgian. In fact George III learned he'd become George III while riding across the bridge here in 1760. Kew became his principal country retreat. On the right is Kew Church, where in the eighteenth century the Duke of Cambridge so enjoyed the preacher's warning against the evils of swearing that he called it 'a damned good sermon

---

16. Just upstream of Oliver's Island, so mentioned because Cromwell
   supposedly took refuge there during his aforementioned exertions.

by Gad'. My reason for pausing at the church today is that it's where Thomas Gainsborough is buried. The painter was born in Sudbury, my local market town in Suffolk, so it seems only fitting I should say hello. Richard Phillips did likewise on his walk here from London. He asked the church cleaners where the grave was: 'as is usual in regard to this class of people, they could give me no information [I did warn you about him] . . . I was therefore obliged to wait while the sexton or clerk was fetched.' He eventually discovered the tomb on the south side of the graveyard, which saves me some time today. The worn lettering on the horizontal stone is hard to read because of the rain running into it, but it's definitely him. I stand for a moment, reflecting on the fact that my trip from home to here has marked the geographical boundaries of Gainsborough's life.

Kew Gardens station, and the approach to it, are exactly as you'd expect from the name. The feeling of being a quarter of a millennium in the past continues, both because of the architecture and the slightly regal air to everything; not snobbish or self-satisfied, just very, very well-off. Secluded, too – Station Parade is a hidden horseshoe of delis, gift shops and an independent bookstore. The route south to Richmond takes me past the long boundary wall of the institution that sets the tone for the whole area: the gardens themselves. Phillips did the same journey (though in the other direction, coming as he was from Barnes), and noted that 'a disabled sailor has drawn in chalk the effigies of the whole British navy, and over each representation appears the name of the vessel, and the number of her guns'. As there were about 800 ships, each five or six feet long, the whole display extended more than a mile and a half. 'I was told the decrepit draughtsman derives a competency from passing travellers.'

Richmond – the bit of it I see – is slightly grubbier than the rest of the walk, being a busy terminus where people catch buses, its station brutally rebuilt in the 1930s (many of the others I've seen today retain their original Victorian glory). So I content myself with a quick lunchtime sandwich, then retrace my steps past Kew Gardens. This is actually now the offline part of the walk, up to Ealing Broadway, but the quickest way over the river is back the way I came.

As I walk, I read Richard Phillips's conclusions, which are safe and dry in the plastic pouch. 'I could not avoid,' he writes, 'feeling the strong analogy which exists between such an excursion as that which I have here described and the life of man . . . On emerging in the morning, I foresaw as little as the child foresees his future life, what were to be the incidents of my journey . . . At the end of my short career, I conscientiously looked back on the incidents of my course with the complacency with which all may look back in old age on the incidents of well-spent lives.' He thinks of the graves he saw at Kew. 'Was not life the mere dream of their now senseless tenants – like the trackless path of a bird in the air . . . ? May not the events of a morning which slides away, and leaves no trace behind it, be correctly likened therefore to the entire course of human life?'

At the church I stop and look at those self-same graves. I wander over to Gainsborough, recalling my thoughts of a while ago, how my journey here, his final resting place, began in Suffolk, where he was born. I remember something Rachel said to me on my Hammersmith and City Line walk, looking back on the emotional 19,000 miles of her Knowledge training: 'Our whole lives are a journey, aren't they?' At the time it seemed nothing more than a throwaway comment, a bit of a cliché. But now it seems a fundamental truth, one that helps make sense of a feeling that has been growing stronger in me the further I progress through this project: I don't want it to end. After this walk I'll have done five of the ten major lines (the Waterloo and City being too short to really count). One more step after that I'll be nearer the finish than the start. It reminds me of how I felt turning 35, remembering what the Bible says about three score years and ten . . .

My love of walking the lines, I see now, isn't just a love of London, or of exercise, or of achieving a goal; it's a love of life. Every journey you take is a mini-life, every journey's end an intimation of mortality, a (to borrow the French phrase about orgasms) 'little death'. However unpleasant Phillips was to church cleaners, on this I think he's absolutely right. Looking forward to a journey, planning it – especially a journey marked off, as mine are (at least on the Tube map) by regular little dashes on a lovely straight line – is a sub-conscious substitute for the thing we can't do, namely control our lives. Perhaps this is why airports and train stations are such magical places: they set you off on yet another mini-life, another leap into the unknown. And relishing a journey in the memory is the equivalent of immortality, or at least re-incarnation. I suppose that's why I've loved tracing each walk in magimarker. I remember feeling a pang of jealousy when

Rachel talked about qualifying, getting her green badge. Now I see why: that moment won't mark the end of her journeying, in the way that my last walk will. She'll carry on driving passengers around London, along a virtually infinite number of routes, theoretically for the rest of her life.

As the rain patters away on my umbrella, I think of the 'senseless tenants' in the graves before me, how each of their lives was 'the trackless path of a bird'. And I remember another conversation, this time with my editor, who once said he thought I wrote books for the same reason he published them: to leave something behind. A shelf full of objects that say 'I was here once'. I didn't agree then – immortality has never been my bag and I honestly couldn't care what, or whether, people will think of me when I'm gone. But now (and maybe it's relevant that since that conversation I've become a father) I wonder whether Nigel wasn't right after all. Is this project – this book – something to be remembered by? If you're trying to stop the path of your life ending up trackless, what better tool than over 200 miles of track?

North of the river, the southern outskirts of Ealing seem dated, but not in a charming sense like Kew, just very mid-twentieth-century, very suburban, not very London. Strangely Kew, although just as far west of Central London, and even further south, felt more tied to London than this area does, a tie that probably stems from the fact that the royals once commuted between the two places.

Near Ealing Broadway station a middle-aged couple argue in Hindi. She's broken down in her new little Mercedes, he's come to pick her up with his old big Mercedes, and there appears to be disunity over how best to fix the bright yellow tow rope. The next hour, as I head back into town, is pretty depressing, especially as the rain is losing its majestic fierceness and becoming a boring drizzle. Between Ealing Common and Acton Town is a branch of a well-known carpet firm. Just as Stella Artois markets itself as 'reassuringly expensive', so this store has a feel of 'reassuringly cheap'. Its red and turquoise sign also screams '1980s', which at least is a decade further on from Ealing's brown street signage. On a fashion advert in a bus stop between Acton Town and Chiswick Park, someone has written, across the forehead of an attractive blonde girl, 'Fuck off'. A row of abandoned factories, their windows covered in wire mesh, are filled to waist level with bags of rubbish and wrecked machinery. In one a life-sized plastic model of a generic cartoon character lies on its back in a skip, staring at the non-existent ceiling. I stop and look at it for slightly too long, until I'm convinced the thing might come to life any second. I hurry on. On the wall of a railway bridge is written 'Blonde busty man called Darren want's bumfun any time on—'. As this is the first thing that's made me laugh in quite a while, I stop to note it down. Too late I notice the woman walking past. She pretends not to see, which is good of her.

The next stop is Turnham Green, meaning this is where the Ealing and Richmond branches meet up, meaning in turn that I've already done all the stops back to Earl's Court. So now I can head due east along the A4 to my hotel, where I'm going to treat myself to a quick break before tidying up Edgware Road and Olympia. Along the way I pass the enormous 1880s building, now used for office space, whose intricate brickwork spells 'William Whiteley's Depositories – Removals to and from all parts of the world'. No point selling yourself short. That Whiteley could have built something as beautiful as this makes his eventual murder almost as shocking as Jill Dando's.

At 5.32 p.m., having walked 25.7 miles, I arrive at the Earl's Court Premier Inn, whose manager, having heard of the nature of my stay, has very kindly asked if I'd like one of their rooms overlooking the District Line tracks. There can't be many occasions when this side of the hotel is the preferred one, but his thoughtfulness is appreciated, and soon I'm looking down from the fifth floor on to the trains as they rattle into and out of the station a couple of hundred yards away. Not that there'll be so many of them in the morning – BBC News reminds me that tomorrow's Tube strike is still going ahead, and only limited services will operate. I won't be the only one walking the lines.

It's getting dark when I leave the hotel for the last section of today's walk. In one of the streets that feed the huge freeway-like road system round here a driver has indicated right, so blocking the left-only lane. A woman three cars back sounds her horn. 'Why are you *doing* that, you idiot?' she shouts through a lowered window. A pedestrian, an old man with a grizzled white beard, shouts back at her: 'Why don't you SHUT UP?' All very New York.

It's more peaceful after High Street Kensington. The only sound in the very expensive side streets leading up to Notting

Hill is birdsong. Shields over the streetlights protect first-floor rooms from anything so vulgar as the direct glare of a bulb. In the floor-to-ceiling window of Kensington Place restaurant a man and woman listen so attentively to their waiter that you know (a) it's a first date and (b) they're both bricking it. A sign outside Notting Hill station advertises its participation in a 'multi-billion-pound upgrade of the Underground' including 'improvements to all aspects of station ambience'. For that sort of money decent ambience would be the least you'd expect.

A couple of doors down from Café Diana in Bayswater, which provided my lunch on the Central Line walk, is a pub called the Champion, which now provides my dinner on the District Line walk. On the bar are pint glasses marked 'To Insure Perfect Service', showing that the staff believe the old story (attached to, among other London premises, the Jamaica Wine House off Cornhill) about this being the origin of the word 'tips'. As I nurse a pint of Timothy Taylor and wait for my lamb burger, I watch an elderly tourist couple (they look Russian) exchanging very few words indeed. She wears a look that says 'not easily will it be forgotten that this crap holiday was your idea'. At one point he risks a comment. She gives a palms-upward shrug of disdain, followed by a pushing-away gesture of disgust. He retreats to the Gents.

Now that the rain has cleared away once and for all, Bayswater is as busy with tourists as Earl's Court was this morning. I head along terrace after B&B-lined terrace, then up Praed Street to a Paddington crawling with wheelie suitcases. A tiny Japanese woman struggles gamely to hang on to one as it rolls away from her. As it's slightly bigger than she is it nearly ends up under a taxi, but with a final effort she just averts disaster. The same walk as on the Hammersmith and City Line trip takes me to Edgware Road, where this branch ends.

Offline again now. I could retrace my steps back to Notting Hill (from where it'll be west along Holland Park Avenue, then south to Olympia), but realise that an ever-so-slightly longer route will enable me to complete a London 'full set'. The Victoria Line walk took me past John Major's flat overlooking Vauxhall Bridge, while tomorrow morning's itinerary will include the Belgravia home of Lady Thatcher, and Westminster, where Gordon Brown has a flat near the Abbey. So it's only Tony Blair that stands between me and a clean sweep of every surviving ex-PM. And he now lives just off the Edgware Road, ten minutes' walk from here. Ten minutes' walk along a road whose pavements are lined with Arabic cafés, restaurants and supermarkets, all of which are doing a roaring trade this Sunday night. Given the event for which Blair's premiership is most remembered, his choice of London pad seems a little strange.

Connaught Square itself is very quiet and very shaded. In fact there are only two people visible, and as they're in police uniform, standing stoically outside one of the square's very pricey townhouses, and one of them is holding a sub-machine gun, they make my job very easy. I wander down to the house in question, gazing up at the third floor where two windows are lit.

'Can I help you, sir?' asks Sub-Machine Gun as he sees my pace slow.

'Just mooching,' I reply.

'Mooch away,' he says obligingly, seemingly glad of a break in what must be the brain-freezing monotony of his job. We have a short chat about Blair's property portfolio, how even though its details are regularly updated in the *Evening Standard* people still approach and say 'Is this where he lives?', as though to utter the name will bring instant arrest.[17]

Round the corner on Hyde Park Gardens a van bears the logo 'Stephen Fry Plumbing and Heating Limited'. The centre of Notting Hill is still busy, especially the store selling nothing but organic frozen yoghurt (if ever a store defined an area . . .). But west of that Holland Park Avenue carries me into darkness, the darkness of a Sunday evening in London. Today is the first full Sunday I've spent in the capital for quite a while, and it's been noticeable how much more alive it is than, say, five years ago. Even the charity shops are open, which they never used to be. But still, in a residential area like this, as evening becomes night (gone nine now), the cold chill of a London Sunday will always descend on your heart. Thomas de Quincey wrote in *Confessions of an English Opium Eater* that 'a duller spectacle this earth of ours has not to show than a rainy Sunday in London', while in the 1860s the French writer Hippolyte Taine said that on that day of the week the capital was 'appalling . . . After an hour's walk in the Strand especially, and in the rest of the City, one has the spleen: one meditates suicide.'

---

17. Tomorrow morning, passing a couple of minutes with the equally bored officer outside Thatcher's house – yes, she only merits one, and he's only got a handgun rather than a machine gun – I'll ask why there were no police outside Major's block of flats. 'I don't think he upset too many people,' is the reply.

I don't want to over-dramatise this, but I think Taine was nearer the mark with 'suicide' than de Quincey was with 'dull'. It's not just that Big City loneliness is a heightened form of the condition, though that memory certainly comes back as I pass a family house with its curtains still open. Son practises 'Piano Time Jazz' with Mother, while in the next room two siblings play an energetic game of Wii tennis. The atomistic nature of London life that Engels and Gibbon noted, and which I raved about, has got another edge to it, one that cuts pretty deep on a Sunday evening when you're between girlfriends. Because Sunday evening is when pretences are dropped, when the relationship-enabled friends you spend the rest of the week with scurry back to their partners. It's a time to keep you honest with yourself.

Honest not only about whether you're happy being single, but whether you're happy in London. Just about everyone who comes here is looking for something, a process that in the end means you are (and however much this phrase might have been soiled by hippies backpacking round Thailand, it's still true) looking for yourself. Yes, London is a great anvil on which to hammer out the truth, but eventually you realise it's the truth about what you're not rather than what you are. London, you see on a Sunday evening, isn't going to add a magical ingredient to your personality. As Jonathan Raban put it in his 1974 book *Soft City*: 'The city [he meant any great metropolis] has always been an embodiment of hope and a source of festering guilt: a dream pursued, and found vain, wanting and destructive.' As I traipse yet more deserted streets to Olympia station, where an empty train pulls in to collect passengers who aren't there, and then back through a quietening Earl's Court to my hotel, all those 'face the truth' London Sundays fill my memory.

God, I hate this place sometimes.

It would seem that a twenty-first-century Tube strike takes you back 200 years. On this gloomy and overcast Monday morning, London's pavements have become rivers of humanity. There are occasional islands formed by a bus queue or a taxi rank, but mostly the tide presses on, a tide of unsmiling but uncomplaining pedestrians. It seems offensive to employ the phrase 'Blitz spirit' about Londoners' reaction to a strike that hasn't even wiped out the service completely; most Tube stations are open, though quieter than usual, as people shun a long wait in favour of exercise. But it does take a lot to seriously upset this capital. The percentages this morning, therefore, probably aren't too different from those estimated by Richard Phillips as he started his 1813 walk to Kew from St James's Park. Of the 16,000 who came into London from neighbouring villages to work each day (seems very low, but then perhaps his maths was on a par with his manners[18]), '8,000 walk, 2,000 arrive in public conveyances, and 6,000 ride on horseback, or in open or close carriages'. The staggered timings seem similar too. Today's rush hour continues well into mid-morning, while Phillips observed 'clerks . . . before nine o'clock . . . from nine to eleven, you see shop-keepers, stock-brokers, lawyers, and

---

18. And indeed his vocabulary – his 'morning's walk' takes until six in the evening, which he eventually admits makes it a 'lengthened morning'.

principals in various establishments . . . At twelve, saunters forth the man of wealth . . . yet demonstrating the folly of wealth by his gouty legs.'

After Gloucester Road and South Kensington stations it's the King's Road, so-called because it was Charles II's private route to Kew. In 1711, when they grew hay in Chelsea, Jonathan Swift complained that 'the hay-making nymphs are perfect drabs . . . There is a mighty increase of dirty wenches in straw hats since I first knew London,' proving that nostalgia has always been a popular drug. After Sloane Square come the quiet streets of Belgravia, which since its construction began in the 1820s (overseen by Thomas Cubitt, who also built Pimlico) has always been the very poshest part of town, that tiny notch above even Mayfair. So nobby was it that the Duke of Bedford chose 6 Belgrave Square as his townhouse, rather than anywhere on his own estate of Bloomsbury.

Skirting the taxi queues at Victoria I head past the Catholic Westminster Cathedral, which almost no one seems to know will allow you up their tower for a fantastic view of London. The cathedral as a whole contains 12 million bricks – 2 million more than there are in the Empire State Building. The next station is St James's Park. The park itself was where James I kept leopards, crocodiles and elephants,[19] though by Richard Phillips's time they'd made way for beggars. 'One, a fellow, who had a withered leg, approached his post with a cheerful air; but he had no sooner seated himself, and stripped it bare, than he began such hideous moans as in a few minutes attracted

19. The latter allowed a gallon of wine a day each to get through the English winter.

several donations.' Deceitful pan-handlers, still debated today, have been part of London for centuries. In 1380 two men were convicted of pretending to be mutes by carrying 'a piece of leather, in shape like part of a tongue, edged with silver, and with writing round it, to this effect – THIS IS THE TONGUE OF JOHN WARDE'. They were sentenced to the pillory.

Crossing Parliament Square towards Westminster station I look down towards College Green, the patch of grass where the political media always hold their televised feeding frenzies, and remember their massed umbrellas during the 1995 Conservative leadership election (the one during which Michael Portillo made such inventive use of Brown's Hotel). I was there in a minor capacity for the BBC, and the reason I remember the umbrellas was that it was 13 minutes – I timed it – before anyone noticed it had stopped raining. This says a lot about the political media.[20]

Round on to the Embankment, and past the station of the same name. The tops of the City skyscrapers are lost in fog today, and the Thames looks choppy, though the river's appearance can change by the minute, which was why when Monet painted it he kept nearly 100 canvases on the go at one time. A Spanish-looking man consults his tourist map – at first it seems he's got something in his eye, but no, he's pulling down his lower eyelid simply to see the map more clearly. Passing the Embankment Gardens on my left, I imagine I hear the rumble of a Tube train. This project is clearly getting to me.

---

20. For the record, the first to notice was the ever-excellent Peter Allen of Radio Five Live.

Then I realise it's not my imagination — there's definitely a rumbling. I hurry into the gardens to investigate.

The sound seems to be coming from a brick structure behind a statue of the politician Henry Fawcett. The size of a decent garden shed, the structure is surrounded by railings that are clearly there to prevent further examination. But Mr Fawcett's plinth is at a convenient height, and with some slightly risky footwork I'm able to clamber up and see that the structure has no top, or at least only one made of wire mesh. Down there, perhaps 20 feet below ground level, are two sets of tracks. I wait a couple of minutes, and sure enough a District Line train passes beneath. It's thrilling to discover this Victorian ventilation shaft, doubly so when I text Richard and discover that even he wasn't aware of it. A real moment of bonding with the Underground, of realising how close it can be without us knowing.[21]

I pass the Savoy's river entrance, which until 1903 was the main one. When it was moved to the other side the hotel laid a rubber roadway from the Strand so that guests wouldn't be disturbed by horses' hooves. Then, after Temple station, it's the Embankment all the way to Blackfriars, and a cut up through the winding alleys just south of St Paul's. On Carter Lane is the poshest Youth Hostel in the world, an exquisitely detailed brick building, with Latin mottoes picked out in red, which used to be the school for choirboys from the cathedral. This morning, as ten o'clock ticks over, a City type wheels

---

21. Richard does tell me later that early District Line drivers were forbidden from sounding their steam whistles near Temple station for fear of disturbing the barristers.

his bicycle out through the front door – has he stayed the night to beat the strike? Just down the road a woman in red high heels is tottering uncomfortably; she hasn't got the hang of this walking-further-than-usual lark.

Then it's Mansion House, which isn't in fact the nearest station to the Mansion House (that's Bank), but is one of only two stations on the network – listen up, pub quizzers – whose name contains all five vowels.[22] On top of Cannon Street station a Meccano-style framework has been erected. Who knows what the building will be like that clings to it? All we do know is that it can't be any worse than its predecessor, a hulk of unloveliness that was designed by the 1960s architect John Poulson. He was later jailed for corruption. What he should actually have been done for was having a geometry set that contained nothing except a set square. Not a single curve or twist or undulation graced his office block. Whereas the just-completed Walbrook Building over the road has seductive black horizontals that curve in and out along the whole length of the structure, like the radiator grille of a massive car that's struck several closely grouped bollards.

As I've just passed the 40-mile mark, I treat myself to a tea-break at Leon, whose back-to-the-future hipness means a proper mug, and a proper milk bottle on the counter, rather than those stainless-steel flasks you get in Starbucks. It was probably this that attracted the old couple in sensible coats sitting in the corner. The woman, in her sixties if not older, taps her foot to 'Addicted to Love' by Robert Palmer. A group

---

22. The other is South Ealing.

of three businessmen huddle around a laptop as if for warmth.

Off again, past the Monument, which in November 1814 was climbed, as a publicity stunt, by a pony belonging to a local fishmonger (the Monument being on Fish Street Hill). The fishmonger's lad led it 'to the gallery . . . and several times round the same, and down again, without a slip or a stumble'. Unlike the seven people who either fell or jumped off the Monument before the top was enclosed, meaning that the structure killed more people than the Great Fire it commemorates.[23] The tourists at Tower Hill stand on the same ground where huge crowds used to gather for executions, including that in 1685 of the Duke of Monmouth, whose head was sewn back on so a portrait could be painted. Beyond the Tower itself is the bridge that took its name, scene in 1952 of some Hollywood-style heroics when the driver of a 78 bus thought he could see the road ahead sinking. Realising just in time that the bridge was being raised, he accelerated, jumping a three-foot gap to land on the northern half. He got £10 for his bravery.

Aldgate East turns out to be another station that's being built on, in part by a labourer who despite a pronounced Tennent's Tummy has chosen to tuck his T-shirt in. (*Why* do people do that?) Further down the Whitechapel Road is the London Hospital, which in 1842 failed to save John Glascott, who'd inadvertently proved the old saying about an elephant's memory. Said beast was part of a local circus, and according to a press report of the time Glascott 'took it

---

23. Figures vary, but the most commonly given is six.

into his head to amuse himself by teasing the animal . . . In the afternoon Glascott returned to the booth with his children and, whilst they were being entertained by the feats of the animal, it suddenly wound its trunk round the man's leg and did not uncoil it until the limb was fractured.' He died from complications caused by the injury.

The East End has traditionally had an 'essence of London' quality, as though you could dissolve a couple of drops of it in water and produce an instant copy of the capital. When Dick Van Dyke did a London accent it was a Cockney one (albeit an atrocious Cockney one), and even today when people from the rest of the country mimic Londoners it's in 'cor blimey, love a duck' tones. This may be because a Mayfair accent is neutral to the point of non-existence, and it may be several decades since Cockneys decamped from London to Essex, but somehow the image persists. To understand this area of the city, I've arranged to pause here, in a café on the Whitechapel Road, to meet a man who, because of his association with possibly the two most famous Cockneys ever, witnessed the end of the old East End and a fundamental shift in its relationship with the rest of London.

John Pearson was a successful journalist and author in his thirties, having worked on *The Sunday Times* and written a critically acclaimed biography of his friend and colleague Ian Fleming, when in 1967 he received an offer to pen the autobiography of Ronnie and Reggie Kray. Not the most straightforward of ghost-writing assignments, but then, as John puts it to me over our cup of tea (has to be a cup of tea, given the venue and subject matter), 'The East End back then was so unlike anywhere else in London. I found it fascinating.' John's diction is exquisitely precise, every syllable carefully demarcated from its neighbours. Funny how a posh English accent veers either to this extreme or the opposite one, where 'terribly' becomes 'te'bly'. Funny, too, while we're on extremes, how those so far apart on the social scale traditionally met up.[24] John's fascination with the Krays and their world, and the readiness with which they welcomed him in, were an example of how the upper and working classes felt comfortable in each other's presence, with only the staid, uptight middle classes left out, equally awkward whether faced with a duke or a dustman. John's an old-fashioned gent, his courteousness matched by 'a refusal to take myself seriously – perhaps I'd have achieved more if I had'. His eyes still have a mischievous shine, and he retains a natural curiosity that has produced books on topics as diverse as the Krays and the Sitwells, the Colosseum and Barbara Cartland.

'When I first met the Twins,' he says, 'going into the East End was like going into Eastern Europe. Like Vladivostock or somewhere, it really was. It was so scruffy. I had a flat in Richmond then, and I'd come over and stay for a few nights at a time. The Twins put me up in this terrible place they had, the Albert Family Dwellings, which had been built by Victorian philanthropists for the poor. By this time it had been condemned, but the Krays kept one of the ground-floor

---

24. Swearing, snooker, etc, as mentioned earlier.

flats as somewhere to keep people and torture them. It was terrible – but I loved the squalor. I remember hanging up a Warhol print of Mao Tse Tung. It was the sixties, after all.'

John got to know Reggie and Ronnie by spending nights with them in their favourite pubs, several of which they owned. 'They were like private clubs. The Duke of Devonshire had Pratt's,[25] the Twins had the Carpenters Arms. They would parade their associates, introduce me to them. They treated me as an oddity, because I'd been brought up in Carshalton, gone to school in Wimbledon, a South London bourgeois background – to them I was from Mars. In the Old Horns there was Teddy Berry, who owned the pub. He limped because Ron had shot him in the leg once during "a little misunderstanding" in a car park. Ron gave him the pub to say sorry. That was how you apologised if you were Ronnie Kray. There was Moysha Blueboy, who'd been on the racecourse gangs before the war, there was a lesbian called Linda who smoked cigars, a getaway driver called Collins who'd once escaped the police by driving a stolen Bentley the whole length of Bond Street in reverse . . . It was very much a pub culture, the Krays' world.[26] I think this came partly from their own oddity – not just that they were twins, but also that they were gay [although this is well-known about Ronnie – 'I'm not queer, I'm 'omosexual' – it's less well-known about his brother]. It was

---

25. The club where all the staff are called 'George' – or, in the case of a female steward who once worked there, 'Georgina' – so that members don't have to remember individual names.

26. Their tipple of choice was Newcastle Brown Ale, a curiously un-London drink.

a reassurance for them to have people around who respected and obeyed them. They were convivial gangsters.'

All of which – and John is well aware of this – can sound like so much 'they never hurt women or children' rubbish, as parodied by Monty Python's Piranha brothers Doug and Dinsdale.[27] 'Oh, sure,' he says, 'they were in the tradition of those old East End villains, which is to say they acted like animals at times. Uncaring thugs.' The reason John mentions the Krays' social standing – also the reason his writing about them fascinates me so much[28] – is that it highlights a characteristic of London that's striking me more and more with every walk: its parochialism. London isn't one place at all. 'The East End always stood apart,' says John, 'there was a sense that it was them against outsiders, even outsiders from other parts of London. That was why the Krays could be such heroes. The poverty there had been on a different scale: I remember Checker Berry, Teddy's brother, telling me their mother used to sew them into their underwear in the autumn; they wouldn't take it off until the spring. Life was poor there, and brutal too. A lot of the Krays' myth was that they were the one form of dissent, of rebellion against that, the one revolt of the no-hoper East Ender. It sounds like special pleading, and you can make too much of it – I

---

27. It's still being parodied by Mad Frankie Fraser, though I'm not sure he knows it; anyone who's seen his one-man show will confirm he can certainly murder an anecdote.

28. As well as *The Profession of Violence*, completed just after their imprisonment, he has published *The Cult of Violence* and *Notorious*, compelling analyses of their place in modern 'gangster-chic'.

think the Krays did make too much of it – but it's certainly true that they were local heroes. If it weren't for villainy, the only job they could have got would have been working at Smithfield Market as empties boys. They thought "fuck that".'

John contrasts this with the experience of Ian Fleming. 'His grandfather had been Scottish working-class, but made money. Essentially he invented the unit trust. And there his grandson was, going to Eton. One of those incredible jumps that Scottish families can make. The Macmillans were another. There was something more acceptable about a Scottish accent than a Cockney one. It was quaint.'

The capital's parochialism also shows through in the way the Twins ruled East London, while the Richardson gang stuck to South London. The 'manors' might as well have been in different cities, with entirely different cultures. 'The Richardsons weren't the same,' says John. 'It wasn't the same over the river, nothing like as tight or traditional as the East End. The East End went back to Bill Sykes, these terrible thugs who ruled the place. Like the Twins' great hero Dodger Mullins. His trick was to throw up a brick and smash it when it came down, just by punching it.' Yet another indication of how London was not one city but many is where the Twins went if they needed to lie low for a few days. 'There was a hotel in Finsbury Park they used to go and hide in. The notion that that's so very far from the East End seems incredible, but that's how it was. It was outside their manor, it was somewhere they could hide.'

Times, though, as John was to find during his months with 'the firm', were changing – largely due to the Krays themselves. 'They were the first ones to break down that wall between the East End and the West End. Iain Sinclair has compared it to the Berlin Wall coming down, and it really was like that. When the Twins got Esmeralda's Barn [their club in Knightsbridge] it was an extraordinary thing to do – no one had really done it before. And they'd go to the Astor Club in Berkeley Square – that was the great place for villains. East would come west after midnight. People like Mad Teddy, Freddie Foreman . . . I can remember it from way back before then, in the fifties. It used to be a respectable nightclub; I remember taking girls there occasionally.'

It was in the Astor that George Cornell issued his infamous verdict on Ronnie Kray ('fat poof'), which was to result in him receiving a bullet through the head in the Blind Beggar, a few yards from where John and I sit now. The relief with which John treated the news that we'd be meeting too early for the pub to be open tells you all you need to know about his opinion of today's East End boozers. Having visited the Blind Beggar myself, I can only agree. You get the feeling that if it hadn't been for the folklore concerning its most famous incident – how the jukebox was playing 'The Sun Ain't Gonna Shine Anymore', for instance, the gunshot supposedly causing the needle to stick on 'anymore' – the place would have closed years ago.

John remembers the atmosphere of those years in which London's great divide came to an end. 'Ronnie was taken by [Conservative politician] Lord Boothby to White's club in St James's. Boothby asked him what he wanted to drink. Ron said "I've always wanted to try one of those prawn cocktails."'

Like the Twins, Boothby was gay. 'Sex came into it a lot,' says John. 'There was this notion that East End gangsters had bigger balls. Poor old Francis Bacon was enthralled with the Krays, because he thought that was the supreme sexual switch-on, to be buggered by Ronnie. Who I think probably did bugger him. He certainly beat him up.' The traffic wasn't one-way. 'Narrow Street [in Limehouse] was very important – Bacon had a studio there, as did Tony Armstrong-Jones. The Grapes[29] at the end of the road became a very popular pub for people to venture into from the west. Then when Reg opened the Double R club, and the Kentucky, these were the East End welcoming the West End. A night out in the East End became something new. Until then the only people who'd ventured out there were homosexual adventurers, going for the male brothels.'

We talk some more, John recounting Kray tales that prove whoever said tragedy and comedy were the same thing knew what he was on about. Ron at his brother's wedding, for example. Irritated by the congregation's feeble rendering of the hymns, he marched up and down the aisle shouting, 'Sing, fuck ya, *sing*!' When it's time for us to go, John announces that he's taking the District Line back in the direction I've come from. 'Off to see my bookseller [John Sandoe, near Sloane Square]. Very old-fashioned, I know, like going to one's bootmaker . . .' Talk of whether he could live in London any more – John's home is now Sussex, but he and his wife still come up to town once a week – turns, via the Dr Johnson

---

29. In which Dickens supposedly used to dance on the tables for pennies when he went to collect his father.

Quote That Must Not Be Quoted, to John's memories of Samuel's old house, in Gough Court. 'When I was an undergraduate at Cambridge, very broke, the room at the top of the house, the room where he wrote the dictionary, was very useful.'

Useful?

'If ever I wanted to meet a girl, we'd have lunch in Fleet Street, then go round the corner to Johnson's house. That room at the top had an enormous sofa in it, and no one ever went up there. You had the place to yourself.'

As we step out into the Whitechapel Road, John and I muse on the draw of London, how we both feel the need to visit it regularly. 'Every time I come up here,' he says, 'I always think something wonderful is going to happen. And it never does.'

What stays in my mind about this is not that nothing wonderful ever happens, but that John always thinks it will. What was that about a willingness of the imagination?

The route between here and Barking has already been covered on the Hammersmith and City walk, though today's daylight reveals sights that the evening stroll kept hidden: the sign announcing that part of the River Lea after Bromley-by-Bow station is called 'Bow Locks' (clearly the person who came up with that name never said it out loud); the West Ham café where I stop for a cup of tea, wondering how its very camp Thai owner – earrings, touch of make-up – is viewed by the locals. Only as I'm leaving does one of those locals, a forty-something with a shaved head, respond to Mr Thai's 'it's as beautiful as me' (about a flower on the counter) with a 'yes, that wilts too', and I realise Mr Thai is in excellent company. The traffic cones outside the East London Cemetery are black and bear crosses and the word 'funeral'; hopefully this stops them being ignored or stolen.[30] In a small park near East Ham two men stand talking. 'I hate the fuckin' country,' says one, 'they're all going round shootin' animals and that.' Neither of them notices that ten yards away stands a fox.

After Barking the ethnic mix returns to monochrome. This is the land that twentieth-century municipal socialism built. On the huge Becontree Estate[31] (Bevan Avenue, Keir Hardie Way), which follows Upney station, the inter-war council houses now bear Cyfrowy Polsat satellite dishes, but there are almost no black or Asian faces to be seen. It feels very Essex, very working-class, very 1960s. There's obviously not much money about, but neither is there much graffiti or rubbish. Florists offer wreaths saying 'Mum', 'Dad', 'Nan'. Even though we're barely out of September one house has its (very extravagant) Christmas lights up. A garden gnome wears a West Ham kit. You half expect a front door to open and a young lad to run out shouting that the Russian linesman has allowed England's third goal.

After Dagenham (Heathway and East) there's a brief rural

---

30. The British sociologist Michael Young once visited a Cockney graveyard on Christmas Day to observe the East End tradition of sharing festivities with the departed. One family poured tea on the ground because their late grandfather had always liked a cup.

31. It's said that the old local name 'Beacontree' was one letter too long for bus destination boards.

interlude of playing fields and a nature reserve. In the dying light – it's nearly 6 p.m. now – this feels strange and unnerving, especially when I round some bushes to find half a dozen horses, one of which fixes me with a not very friendly stare, like that George Clooney scene in *Michael Clayton*. After Elm Park is the estate of that name, another constructed to hug the Tube line like pipe-cladding, though it contains larger houses than its more westerly cousins. This is where that young lad who was celebrating the World Cup win lives now he's grown up and done well for himself. Then it's Hornchurch, named after the stone bull's head on St Andrew's, surely the only church in the world with a stained-glass window depicting a red Ford Fiesta. Finally, having passed Upminster Bridge, I arrive at Upminster at a touch after half-seven. Those octopus tentacles at the other end of the line have made it a lengthy walk, to be sure, but not quite lengthy enough to grab the record. At 60.21 miles, the District has been a couple of miles shorter than the Central. The running total for the project is 171.4 miles, still not quite halfway towards my estimate. Stations-wise, though, I've broken the project's back: 154 down, 115 to go.

At home that night Jo tells me about our son Barney practising his walking skills on the playing field. Random directions, apparently, until he reached the football pitch, at which point he started following the lines.

That's my boy.

# 6

# Northern Line

## Nobody sees you,
## nobody hears you

That thought from the end of the Central Line has been nagging away at me for the past few weeks: how much should life in London revolve around being on your own? It really hit home on the Sunday night of the District Line walk, when I was thinking about my own lonely times in the capital. Does London drive you *towards* loneliness, make you more solitary than you might otherwise be? OK, it's menus for venues; there's no way you can – or should – translate patterns of behaviour and modes of thought from a Suffolk village to a vast metropolis. I'd no more want people blanking me in a country lane than every passer-by on Piccadilly saying a cheery hello. But have I become too averse to human contact while in London? I see friends there, and have met new people while walking the lines. The walks themselves, though, have been unaccompanied. Isn't it time for that to change?

What finally decides the issue is my latest research chat with Richard. He asks which line I'm tackling next.

'Not sure yet,' I say. 'Might do the Northern.' No particular reason, just pops into my head.

'Ah,' says Richard, his expression growing a little misty, 'the good old Northern. That's a *really* interesting line.'

This is the sort of thing that has Jo (and, for that matter, Richard's wife Ali) rolling her eyes in despair. I, on the other hand, eagerly don my mental anorak, and head off with Richard for a hearty yomp through Tubeland. 'Longest tunnel, of course,' I say, referring to that between Morden and East Finchley via the City branch: 17.3 miles. Used to be the longest in the world, never mind the longest on the Tube.

'And the deepest station,' responds Richard, in a tone that says, 'Another equally obvious fact, so obvious that neither of us need specify it's Hampstead, at 192 feet underground'. But then he adds: 'Did you know it's also got the *highest* point on the network? Highest that the line runs above ground, I mean?'

I did not.

'Dollis Brook Viaduct,' says Richard. 'Up near Mill Hill East. The trains run fifty-nine feet above the road.'

We swap more facts. The Northern Line has both the longest escalators on the system (Angel, 318 steps) and the shallowest lift (Chalk Farm, 30 feet). It serves the most southerly Tube station (Morden), and indeed 16 of the 29 stations that lie south of the river. Its 'Misery Line' reputation for unreliability received an unusual boost in 1946, when trains were delayed by a dog trotting happily along the City branch tunnel between Angel and Clapham Common,

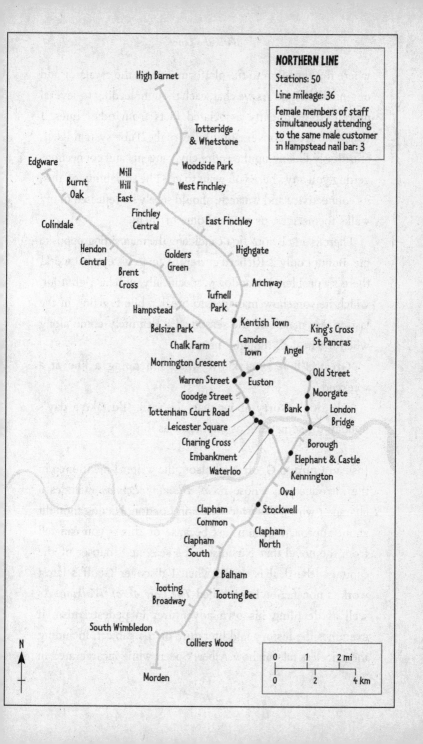

**NORTHERN LINE**

Stations: 50

Line mileage: 36

Female members of staff simultaneously attending to the same male customer in Hampstead nail bar: 3

High Barnet

Totteridge & Whetstone

Woodside Park

Edgware

Mill Hill East

Burnt Oak

West Finchley

Colindale

Finchley Central

East Finchley

Hendon Central

Golders Green

Highgate

Brent Cross

Archway

Tufnell Park

Hampstead

Kentish Town

Belsize Park

Camden Town

King's Cross St Pancras

Chalk Farm

Angel

Mornington Crescent

Warren Street

Euston

Old Street

Goodge Street

Moorgate

Tottenham Court Road

Bank

London Bridge

Leicester Square

Charing Cross

Borough

Embankment

Elephant & Castle

Waterloo

Kennington

Oval

Clapham Common

Stockwell

Clapham North

Clapham South

Balham

Tooting Broadway

Tooting Bec

South Wimbledon

Colliers Wood

Morden

N

0   1   2 mi

0   2   4 km

where it jumped on to the platform, ran up the escalator and out into the night. As we chat, each thought leading to several more, and frequently associated facts from other lines, I realise how the conversation mirrors the Tube system itself, effortlessly linking up the entire city, tangents and connections getting you anywhere you want to go. The sociability of this, its connectivity and warmth, should surely be reflected in my walks themselves, or at least some of them.

There is an obvious first candidate: the man sitting opposite me. But not only is Richard currently 'up to his eyes' at work, there's a problem lower down, specifically with his right foot, which he somehow managed to break while bowling in the last cricket match of the season. 'I'll definitely come along when it's healed, though,' he says.

'Great. I'll let you know when I'm doing a line at a weekend.'

'Oh, don't worry about that,' he says. 'I'd take a day's holiday for something as important as this.'

Instead I turn to Geoff Nicholson, the writer I mentioned in the introduction, whose novel *Bleeding London* includes a character who walks every street in London. Having thought about approaching him just because of this – you can tell from the novel that Nicholson is a seasoned traipser of the capital – the deal is sealed when I discover Geoff's latest work, a non-fiction book called *The Lost Art of Walking*. As well as detailing his own adventures in pedestrianism it examines the history and literature of the subject, including the priceless tale of how Albert Speer, while incarcerated in

Spandau prison, walked from Berlin to Heidelberg. He achieved this by completing 2,000-odd (very odd) laps of the prison garden. After this he sought a new destination. Fellow prisoner Rudolf Hess suggested Asia, but Speer rejected this as it would mean walking through several Communist countries. There's much about this story that echoes my own project: the fact that its pointlessness doesn't stop the proponent carrying it out; Speer's detailed records of how far he'd walked each day, including average and total distances; the fact that he needed a fresh challenge once it was over (really am starting to dread the end of the last line now . . .). Unnerving to find yourself mirroring Hitler's architect.

Geoff Nicholson lives in Los Angeles now, but still regularly visits his native England, and will gladly, he replies to my email, accompany me on a section of the Northern Line. A little diary-juggling results in an arrangement to walk from Camden Town to Highgate, which, as a co-operative providence would have it, is where he's staying while in London, and where my friend Matt lives, providing a convenient resting point at the end of my first day. The starting point is Morden.

I know what you're thinking: 'Why is he doing the Northern Line uphill?' Well, having spent several hours staring at the map, trying out various possibilities, I've decided my chosen route is, to quote Churchill on democracy, the worst option apart from all the others. The Northern Line is, in effect, a figure of eight with a straight line stuck on the bottom, the straight line being Morden to Kennington,

the lower loop of the eight formed by the Charing Cross and
City branches meeting at Camden, and the upper loop by the
Edgware and High Barnet branches, the top of it all being
the offline walk between the two. No matter which way you
do the loops, the best way to avoid doing chunks of them
twice is by starting at Morden.

Besides, the uphill element appeals to the Edmund Hillary
in me. Morden Tube station is 65 feet above sea level. High
Barnet Tube station is 345 feet above sea level. This means
a net climb of 280 feet. Mount Everest is 29,028 feet. I didn't
say there was *that* much of the Edmund Hillary in me.

In 1926, the year in which the Northern Line reached
Morden,[1] the then-village had a population of 1,000. Within
five years that figure had shot up to 12,600. The Tube, appropriately for its name, was doing its usual rolling-pin trick,
with London as the pastry. Though as I discover on a dank,
mizzly Tuesday morning in late October, the pastry wears
pretty thin around the edges. The buses outside the station
advertise destinations like West Croydon and Epsom. Neither
the shops nor the people using them are touched by glamour.
This is not, whatever else it may be, London.

On the road that leads to South Wimbledon station is a

---

1. The line being a marriage between the City and South London
   Railway – the one we encountered in the first chapter, the first
   deep-level Tube, running between Stockwell and the City – and
   the Charing Cross, Euston and Hampstead Railway, which started
   in the first decade of the twentieth century and whose route you
   can pretty well guess from its name.

health clinic whose waiting room is full, then a Chinese takeaway called Charisma (anyone got the number for Trading Standards?), which seems to be open for business even though it's not yet 11 o'clock. One senses that the area, even in its rural 1920s, was never the most sought-after – South Wimbledon's name was an exercise in social climbing, and even then the rail company couldn't quite bring itself to ignore the truth entirely, adding a guilty 'Merton' in brackets at the end.[2] The locale must have had at least something to recommend it in the early nineteenth century, as the land surrounding what is now South Wimbledon station is where Admiral Nelson had his country estate. The fact is commemorated in several street and business names, though Nelson Wines really haven't got the hang of things, specialising as they do in foreign beers. Equally inattentive to detail is the pub choosing to call itself the Nelson Arms. As if further to underline the error, the poster for their music night features a silhouette of Nelson with a guitar round his neck.

Further along in Colliers Wood naming rights pass to someone else: Robinson Road, Crusoe Road, Friday Road . . . Though strictly speaking Defoe Close shouldn't have its first two letters: dear old Daniel Foe added them to appear aristocratic, much as Mohamed Fayed is said to have added his 'Al'. The main London-bound road (at first Colliers Wood High Street, then Tooting High Street) is a grubby progression of plumbers' merchants, newsagents, launderettes, all topped by a floor or two of unappealing flats, the sort whose

---

2. At least one such roundel sign survives today – I saw it on the platform as my train passed through this morning.

numbers have wonky Bs and Cs next to them and whose communal hallways perpetually swim in pizza flyers. An estate agent called 'SW19' displays the tagline 'It's All in the Postcode'. Well, up to a point, Lord Copper. The early moments of my District Line walk were in SW19, and that was terrain of a very different kidney.

Tooting Broadway station can mean only one thing to a child of the 1970s: the *Citizen Smith* credits. No sign of Wolfie crying 'Power to the people' today, though. Even his revolutionary ardour would have been challenged by this weather. Already it's becoming clear that today the only thing of note will be that there is nothing of note. On Clapham Road I will see a girl dressed entirely in black except for pink tartan Ugg boots. In Kennington I'll pass a man who at first seems to be a meeja type in charcoal jacket and rimless spectacles, and only at the last minute will I see that he's drinking lager from a can held inside a plastic bag. But that will be about it. For whatever reason – the rain (which vacillates in strength between light and annoying), my own frame of mind (I'm feeling slow and weak after a stomach bug), pure and simple chance – London has nothing unusual or exciting to offer today. It is a day for putting in the work, getting through the miles, ticking off the stations. None of which are as depressing as they sound; the opposite, in fact. Like Stuart, the character in Geoff's novel, I find myself wanting 'the slog and the weariness of it'.

After Tooting Bec – the second word dates from the area's old owners, the Abbey of Hellouin Bec in Normandy – it's Balham. The author Arthur Ransome called this 'the ugliest and most abominable of London's unpleasing suburbs'. Its occasional wine bar and picture-framing store put it a notch above Morden, but I know what Ransome meant. Just as no one can now hear the word 'infamy' without thinking of Kenneth Williams in *Carry on Cleo*, it's impossible to hear the name Balham without mentally adding 'Gateway to the South'. Even locals accept that – there's a Gateway Hotel.

Clapham South, followed by the famous common, takes us up in the world. Apart from a spell in the twentieth century when its very ordinariness gave birth to the famous man on its omnibus,[3] Clapham has long had a history of housing the well-to-do. Benjamin Franklin was living here in 1783, and conducted one of his many scientific experiments on the common's Mount Pond, establishing that oil really did calm troubled waters (a teaspoonful spread out to cover half an acre). In the eighteenth and nineteenth centuries people grew asparagus and lavender round here, the latter explaining the name of the nearby hill.[4] Back in 1701 it was where Samuel Pepys came to live when he left London. Not that the country air of his 'Paradisian Clapham' (the words of his friend John Evelyn) did him much good – he died only two years later. Still, he was following in a noble tradition: lots of famous Londoners left the city at the end of their lives, so many in fact that it's hard to think of any who didn't. Johnson went

---

3. A more acceptable piece of slang than that of 200 years earlier, when 'to have been at Hadham and come home by Clapham' meant to have contracted gonorrhoea.
4. In the audiobook of his diaries, Alec Guinness curiously emphasises the final word when mentioning *The Lavender Hill Mob*.

to Islington, Dickens to Kent, Holmes to Sussex to keep his bees. H. V. Morton, whose pen portraits of 1920s London are required reading even today, left his beloved city for South Africa. Even the Krays, John Pearson told me, had a country home in Suffolk, though of course in the end the timing of their exit from London was out of their hands. In the shorter term, leaving London is something done every weekend by many of those who can afford two homes. If you love too intently it can turn to hate; some even say that the two exist simultaneously, opposite sides of the same emotional coin. Is that what happens to those who love London?

Clapham Common becomes Clapham High Street, where Belgo and the Rinky Dink bar and estate agents called Aspire are infiltrated by the red-and-yellow 1960s plastic sign above one office, announcing the HQ of the Socialist Party. Just to keep Sebastian and Jocasta from being *entirely* complacent. Then, after Clapham North, it's the main road up to Stockwell. As a reminder that walking really is the only way you can get to know a place, I notice something that never revealed itself to me all the times Jo drove us round here in her Brixton years: St Bede's Church for Deaf People. One of those things the need for which never strikes you until you see it, at which point it becomes the most obvious idea in the world. Stockwell station takes me back to the first morning of the whole project. There really is a sense of it all coming together now, connections on the Tube map translating into connections in my life.

Still it's the main road, up towards the Oval now. The

architecture lining it might be Victorian, but other touches are very twenty-first-century: the 'Cycle Superhighway' that explains why a chunk of the road is blue, and the mission statements outside Stockwell Park High School ('attitude determines altitude'). Opposite Oval station is St Mark's Church, outside which used to stand Kennington Common's gallows. When two men were hanged there for robbery in 1758, 'a child about nine months old was put into the hands of the executioner who nine times, with one of the hands of each of the dead bodies, stroked the child over the face'. A traditional cure for the wen, or cyst, from which the baby was suffering. To think that this sort of thing went on here makes 250 years seem a pretty short time. By the time 1896 came around the common had gained its current title of Kennington Park, and a seven-year-old Charlie Chaplin spent the day here, having been released with his siblings from the Lambeth Workhouse by a mother desperate to see them. Come the end of the day, however, the mentally-ill Hannah was forced to return to her asylum, her children to the workhouse.

Kennington station, just past the park, is where the line splits. It's 1.30 p.m. now, and I'm meeting Geoff in Camden at 4. I had planned to get there via the City branch, but post-bug torpor is still clinging to me, so I decide to take the shorter Charing Cross route instead. On one of the back streets up to Waterloo I experience a rare moment of practicality, fixing an unattended roadworks sign that's flapping dangerously in the wind, threatening to come away from its stand. Along the South Bank the high number of children being shepherded by grandparents is a reminder that this is half-term week. Over the river Villiers Street, the short climb up from Embankment station, is lined with depressingly touristy restaurants, though thank God Gordon's survives, the basement wine bar that claims to be London's oldest (1890), where candles light your way and they only serve wine.[5] At the top is Charing Cross. The fact that it used to be rhyming slang for 'horse' tells you how Cockneys pronounced it.

More equine thoughts as I pass the National Gallery: until 1829, when Trafalgar Square was laid out, the site housed the Royal mews. Round the back is a shop called Let's Fill This Town With Artists, a thought as absurd as a town filled with brain surgeons or plumbers. Just before Leicester Square station is St Martin's Court, the alleyway that leads to New Row, heading up into Covent Garden. In 1827, precisely because of the narrowness of New Street (as it was then called), two gentlemen chose it as the venue for a bet that proves London pedestrians have always been inconsiderate. 'Of the first 30 men who should pass,' ran the bet, '20 would have at least one hand in the breeches or coat pocket [so making it hard for others to pass], and 15 would have both hands so placed.' The actual figures were 23 and 18, 'the proposer of the wager thus winning it hollow'.

Opposite Tottenham Court Road station is Centrepoint, the first tall building in London not to need scaffolding during

---

5. It's a sign of how far the pre-Embankment Thames reached that the neighbouring garden contains a water gate. Were it not for engineer Joseph Bazalgette, Gordon's would be a riverside bar.

its construction (the H-sections were lifted into place by crane), and home of late to a private members' club on the top floor. Meeting a friend there I saw, for the first time (because I'd never been up a building of this height in the West End, there being so few of them), the familiar Square Mile scraperscape in a very unfamiliar order. Seeing the certainties of the City shaken up like that was invigorating. In one of the many electronics stores a Muslim assistant prays at his counter, alternately intoning the words then kneeling. The mobile phone he's in the middle of fixing lies in parts on the glass.

The Tottenham Court Road itself used to lead through fields to Toten Hall (roughly where Warren Street Tube now stands), a courthouse and then a tea garden offering games such as skittles. Local entertainment is now provided instead by Spearmint Rhino, which advertises in a phone box just down the road: 'call and order VIP collection from this point'. Since when have VIPs used phone boxes? A pickpocket on the Tottenham Court Road in 1946 chose the wrong target. 'Suddenly a yell was heard,' reported *The Times*, '. . . he had picked from the pocket of a magician a small non-poisonous snake, which wriggled down a drain and disappeared.'

Past another performance of that modern London dance, the Pret Shuffle, in which every sandwich must be considered before a choice is made, then at Goodge Street station a woman of a certain age meets her friend, though because of the 'work' with which she's sought to deny said age, her face is incapable of expressing emotion, so a hug is all the friend gets. At Warren Street it's a sharp right to Euston, then left up the side of the station to the Hampstead Road, where three huge tower blocks are topped in bright blue, bright red and bright yellow, as though the architects were trying to infantilise the residents. Mornington Crescent station can now mean only one thing, which is why the pub opposite has recently renamed itself the Lyttelton Arms, and why people left flowers here when Humph died.

The re-routing at Kennington means an early arrival at Camden Town, so there's a chance to recharge the fuel cells in Starbucks before meeting Geoff. They've run out of mugs, so even customers 'drinking in' are being given paper cups. I can't help noticing how many people (myself included at first) keep the protective lids on, sipping their drinks through the tiny hole. Maybe it's not just the residents of Camden tower blocks who have been infantilised.

Some very bad things happen in *Bleeding London*. Stuart is one of its three main characters, the others being a woman who wants to have sex in as many London locations as possible, and a man who's going round the city beating up several men who raped his girlfriend. This is as unlike the Richard Curtis version of the capital as you could get, and while that's one of the many fine things about it, the novel's stylish prose and dark viewpoint do lead you to expect a certain sort of author. Finding him to be the fifty-seven-year-old man sheltering from the rain inside Camden Town station therefore comes as a slight surprise. Geoff exhibits, if not shyness, then an unwillingness to impose himself on a situation. His soft tones still carry the accent of his Sheffield boyhood, unlost over the decades spent living in Cambridge (at the university), London, New York and now Los Angeles. The occasional 'a' sound undergoes a slight West Coast elongation, but that's all.

We set off, starting our conversation, as any two Englishmen anywhere in the world are legally obliged to, with the weather, though only to establish that we both like walking in the rain. I mention that it's established my mood for the day up to now, though before meeting Geoff I have deliberately (and easily) flicked that mood's off-switch.

'Ah, the joys of melancholy,' says Geoff. 'You don't need to convert me to those.'

He can't get much rain in LA?

'True. Though when it rains, boy, does it rain. When the sun doesn't shine there – and there are days when it doesn't – LA is the dullest city in the world, because everything was built to be seen in the sunshine. It's even duller than somewhere like Doncaster, because at least when they built Doncaster they knew it was going to be dull most of the time.'

Los Angeles has a reputation, much bolstered (not least in the second paragraph of this book), for being unwalkable. How could a committed walker like Geoff end up living there? The short answer is because of his American wife, whose work in publishing took them there from New York. The longer answer focuses on Geoff's refusal to accept reputations at face value.

'The perversity in me said it would be great to walk in LA, where you famously don't walk, or shouldn't walk,' he says. (A whole chapter of *The Lost Art of Walking* is devoted to this topic.) 'There are so many legends that back that up. Like John Paul Jones from Led Zeppelin – he was *arrested* for daring to leave his hotel room and go for a walk. And P. G. Wodehouse, when he was writing for MGM out there. There's the story – whether I believe it or not, I'm not sure – about him walking the six miles from his home to the studio for meetings, and the executives being horrified. One of them said to him, "Even the hookers don't walk in LA."'

According to Geoff, it's a myth that *no one* walks there. 'Sure, it's the exception. The city's too spread out; you just couldn't do the majority of your travelling on foot. But one of my favourite sights in LA is of someone walking to work: Wonder Woman. Outside Grauman's Chinese Theater on Hollywood Boulevard there are lookalikes – a Marilyn, an Elvis, Charlie Chaplin, Spider-Man . . . Because there aren't any changing facilities, they get into costume at home, and Wonder Woman lives just a block away, on Selma Avenue, so she walks there. You should see her coming out of her apartment block, getting into character as she strides up to Grauman's.'

If there was going to be any part of London to show us someone dressed as a superhero it would be Camden. But today's mundanity is well set in, apparently, and nothing noteworthy presents itself. Neither Geoff nor I seem bothered by this, and the conversation flows as we walk. Nigella Lawson says that the kitchen is the room of the house in which people talk most freely, because with at least one of you cooking, eye contact is minimised. Does walking together operate on the same principle?

It's not as though we need real-time stimuli anyway. We have my research notes, which tell us that Camden was named after the bigwig on whose land it was built, the 1st Baron Camden,[6] and that Kentish Town, which we reach next, has nothing to do with Kent: 'ken-ditch' means the bed of a waterway. It's never been fashionable: Professor Higgins in *Pygmalion* says that 'men want to drop Kentish Town, but they give themselves away every time they open their mouths', while current resident and *Channel Four News* presenter Jon Snow calls Kentish Town Road 'one of the slummiest high streets in London'. (He should check out Tooting.) In 1798 it was home to a rich miser called John Little, who was told by his doctor to drink the odd glass of wine. Reluctantly unlocking his cellar (he wouldn't trust his housekeeper with the key), Little fetched a bottle. Having been 'removed from a warm bed into a dark humid vault, he was seized with a shivering fit which terminated in an apopleptic stroke and occasioned his death'.

Apart from my notes, we also have Stuart's sightings from *Bleeding London* to discuss. Most of his appearances are in diary form, listing what he's seen: 'In Phillimore Gardens, Kensington, I looked in through a basement window and watched a heavy woman dressed only in a corset as she kissed a man in a suit and tie . . . In Broad Lawn, New Eltham, I saw a workman sitting in a van eating his lunch. I was surprised to see he was gnawing a raw carrot, which didn't seem like standard workman's fare. But then I saw the sign on the side of the van that said he was a piano tuner and that

6. Unsurprisingly chosen over his birth name of Charles Pratt.

seemed perfectly in keeping . . . I saw a woman pissing in the street in Wandsworth . . .'

Were Stuart's incidents real?

'Most of them, yeah,' said Geoff. 'There were certain days when I used to go out and pretend to be him, or rather do what he was doing. I knew London well enough to know there were vast swathes of it I didn't know. So I deliberately went to some bit that was completely off my map, as it were. Wormwood Scrubs, the first day. Everyone knows where Wormwood Scrubs is, but I'd never been.' As it happens I hadn't either, before my Central Line walk. 'On the one hand you're willing interesting stuff to happen so you can put it in the book. At the same time you don't want to make up dramas just for the sake of it. There were actually some things that really did happen that were too dramatic. Like in Soho Square, that little alleyway that leads to Charing Cross Road [Sutton Row] – there was this guy running full pelt with two coppers coming after him. I could have had a good go at stopping him, given him a shoulder charge. But by the time I'd thought "Should I do it?" he'd been and gone. That didn't quite belong in the novel, it would have seemed gratuitous. But actually you need a certain amount of "gratuitous" stuff, because that's the experience of walking around any great metropolis.'

As it happens, in real life the corseted woman happened 'somewhere round here, near Kentish Town. I can picture it now – I looked down through this basement window. The guy in the suit had just come into the room.'

Did Geoff get any sense of the context? It sounds like a situation where money was changing hands.

'It does, doesn't it?' He shrugs. 'Who knows? That's the nature of seeing these things round London.' He can't remember whether he really saw a woman pissing in the street. Jo saw it once, in the middle of Brixton.

Stuart is also fascinated by the names of the streets down which he walks: Artichoke Hill, Quaggy Walk, Yuletide Close, Pansy Gardens, Evangelist Road. 'And did I put any sightings of famous people in?' asks Geoff.

'Not that I can remember.'

'I always find that amazing,' he says. 'That you can be walking down the street and there's . . . I don't know, Felicity Kendal.'

Did he ever spot any real big stars?

'No. Cliff Richard was about as big as it got. Somewhere round Marble Arch.'

The only real biggie I ever had — on the street, that is, rather than in any media situation — was Madonna. Hyde Park. With one of her children, and a *very* big minder. The strange thing was that it was only after the event, or possibly just as we passed, that I realised who she was. OK, she was wearing sunglasses, but she was so tiny and inconspicuous that I never actually experienced a moment of physical recognition. It was just that there was something Madonna-ish radiating from her. I stopped and turned, not to watch her walking away, but to watch the people walking towards me. None of them recognised her until late on either. Two girls stopped, one saying to the other, 'Er . . . hang on . . . was that *Madonna*?' Other than that it was the B-list or lower. Anyone who spends any amount of time in W1 will tell you the same. Earlier, for instance, outside Tottenham Court Road station, I saw the politician James Purnell, for the second time in a year. The first was not long after his resignation from the government. He was outside the National Portrait Gallery, surely the first ex-Cabinet minister ever to wear Crocs in Central London. Tonight, in an off-licence in Highgate, I'll see Peter Capaldi. Once, in Boots on Marylebone High Street, I saw Brian May. He was examining – and I promise you this is true – the haircare products.

'The best one I ever had was working in a bookshop off Regent Street,' says Geoff. 'Angela Carter came in. I was a fan of hers. I was pretty sure it was her. Then when she handed me her credit card and it said "A. Carter", I said, "You're Angela Carter." I thought she was pretty well known at that point. But she said, "All my life I've been waiting for this to happen."'

By now our steps – which are leading us steadily, but pleasantly, uphill (nice to have something to work against) – have brought us to Tufnell Park. Those of us who like to think that this was where Spinal Tap's guitarist got his surname will be disappointed to learn that Nigel is a Tufne*l*. More myth-busting at the top of the next climb, up Junction Road, where Archway is the local station for the Whittington Hospital, so named because Dick Whittington is said to have heard the Bow Bells from here, telling him not to give up on London. Only problem is that his family home was in Gloucestershire, and no one with that sense of direction could have become Lord Mayor once, let alone four times.

As we pass the bus stops outside the station, Geoff laughs. 'I've just remembered – this is where the "seven-year itch" thing happened.' An incident in the novel that was inspired by an actual encounter. Geoff was once stopped here by two women who asked him what he understood by that phrase, and then whether he thought a man who goes off because of the seven-year itch always comes back. Stuart replies, as Geoff did, that sometimes he does, sometimes he doesn't – to the visible disappointment of one of the women. 'I just stood there,' writes Stuart, 'thinking I'd definitely said the wrong thing and wanting to say something more cheerful and optimistic, but I didn't know how to phrase it. Eventually, noticing my lack of ease, the other woman said, "Thanks very much, sir." The use of "sir" crushed me.'

'I was on my way back from the dentist,' he says. 'Don't know why but somehow that etched it into my memory.'

The buses lead to a brief Routemaster conversation. My story about hearing one drive past our cottage in Suffolk one night, and looking out to see that it was a 159, the route I used to take to Jo's in Brixton, is matched – no, let's be honest, trumped – by Geoff seeing a number 6, his local bus when he lived in Maida Vale, at Huntington Beach in Los Angeles.

We're on the Archway Road now. I ask Geoff why he felt the need to live in London.

'I always wanted to,' he says. 'Right from when I was growing up in Sheffield. It just seemed to be the place you had to go, needed to go. There was something of the "New York New York" thing about it, you know, if I can make it there I can make it anywhere. To see if you can live and survive there – or in New York, for that matter. It's about testing yourself.'[7]

This was my experience too, and one that marked me out from the rest of my family. Geoff's relatives were the same. His father had a very particular reason for staying put. 'He'd been in the navy during the war. He was part of that generation – he might have wanted to see the world as a young man, but he got to see it as a sailor and wherever he went someone was trying to kill him. At the end of it he went back to Sheffield and would have been very happy never to leave it at all. The day trips and holidays were for "the boy", for me. He accepted it as part of family life.'

Geoff's mother, though, was 'rather more adventurous. When my dad died she'd come and see me in London. We'd walk. She liked the shops, all that stuff. The ones who amaze me are the ones who grow up in Sheffield, go away to university, then go back and never leave it. The three years in Newcastle Tech was their adventure all done.'

Geoff's time at Cambridge was a springboard to the capital. 'I always carried an *A to Z* with me when I came here. It seemed that was the way to really get to know a place. I was amazed that some people *didn't* have a love of maps. The first time I was really away from home,

---

7. Part of the test being that these are cities where so many famous names have proved themselves. And indeed walked. On the plane back to America Geoff will read Keith Richards's autobiography, including Keef's fond memories of walking with his grandfather around London – including the Archway Road.

when I was seventeen, was for a job I'd got in France, in a youth hostel in Nancy. The first day I went out and bought a map – which I've still got; I don't collect maps as such, but I've got a big trunk full of them – and the other people thought this was a madly eccentric thing to do, to actually get a map of the place you were staying in. But to me it seemed the obvious first step. Once you'd got the map you sort of knew the territory, or knew *about* it, in a very specific way.'

Stuart marks up his *A to Z* at the end of each day's walking, drawing black lines through the streets he's covered. Sounds familiar, though unlike me he's obliterating the whole map, rendering it ever more useless. Not that he has much faith in maps to start with. 'Maps are euphemisms,' he writes, 'clean, clear, self-explanatory substitutes for all the mess and mayhem . . . They are fake documents, pathetic simplifications and falsifications.' While Piotr might object to the vehemence of the language, he'd surely agree with the basic point underlying it.

'As soon as you've got a map,' says Geoff, 'you realise that it answers some specific questions but doesn't answer others. San Francisco is the most extraordinary city for that, because of course the map is flat. San Francisco is not. Because large parts of the city are gridded, you think, "I'll just go up here and along there" – then you realise it's not as simple as that. You're confronted with the reality of sweating up a hill. Of course you could have an Ordnance Survey-style map with heights on, and apparently there are now maps of San Francisco with arrows on to indicate steepness. But there'll always be something a map doesn't tell you. Of course the Tube map is the ultimate lie, the way it makes places seem closer or further away than they are. But actually it's not a lie at all, not if you're using it just to get around the Tube. It's the lie that tells the truth, as Jean Cocteau said about camp.'

Geoff's certainly right about San Francisco. I thought I was prepared – I'd seen *Bullitt* and everything – but some of the hills are mind-boggling. You look at the cars parked facing into the kerb (it's illegal not to) and think, 'Someone thought it was a good idea to build houses *here*?' We've picked an appropriate place to talk about it – the Archway Road is really climbing now, through the cutting that was originally a tunnel, until it collapsed, obliging the authorities to build a bridge to carry Hornsey Lane high over the road. In time that height could mean only one thing: this structure is now known as Suicide Bridge. We pause underneath it to gaze up at the leap-inhibiting railings, and I wonder whether Suicide Bridge was the chicken to, or egg of, Archway's reputation as a not-very-nice place. St Etienne's song *Archway People* contains the line 'There are some nice parts of London – you can see them from here'. On another day this might have led our discussion towards the old 'distance/heart of things' debate: whether you want to admire the view of a great city or experience the greatness at first hand. One of us might have mentioned Guy de Maupassant, who lunched every day at the Eiffel Tower, because it was the one place in Paris from which he couldn't see the Eiffel Tower.

On another day. Today our conversation grows darker. Sorry about that. We're two blokes with a joy of melancholy, standing underneath Suicide Bridge in the rain.

'The slog and the weariness of it,' I say.

'Cities wear you out,' replies Geoff. 'Walking in them does anyway, more than walking in the countryside or at the seaside. At the weekend I was staying near Chelmsford, and went walking in the fields there. It was nice, but it didn't feel like *real* walking.' He pauses. 'All the time I lived in London, I was always thinking about moving to another part of it, always wanted to live somewhere else, so I'd walk round places thinking, "Is this somewhere I'd want to be?"' Another pause. 'You know, I reckon writing *Bleeding London* became a repository for everything that had happened to me here. When I come to think about it, immediately after the book was written, before it was published, I struck up the relationship with the woman who became my wife. That began the process – a slow one, of course – of moving to America. That can't be insignificant. It'd be absurd to say I was tired of London, or I'd exhausted its possibilities – but it definitely looks like I needed a new environment.'

In this spirit of 'endings rather than beginnings', I mention Stuart's plan: when he's finished walking the whole city, he's going to kill himself. His attraction to the idea forms much of the book's focus. It's the opposite of my 'each walk is a metaphor for, and a celebration of, life' theory. To me, Stuart embodies the theory that we walk, at least in a city as intimidating as London, as a celebration of death. As the physicist Niels Bohr said, 'The opposite of a great truth is also true.' On a day like today, I want to explore the opposite.

'Do you think we're attracted to London because we know it's going to crush us?' I ask Geoff. 'Because we know we're going to fail the test, because we're never going to leave our mark on it?'

He considers it. 'You're right that we're almost certainly not going to leave any mark on it. Richard Rogers has, and people who have council estates named after them. And whoever had the idea of putting CCTV cameras everywhere, and whoever invented the Congestion Charge Zone – but no, it's true, most of us never do.'

I know that Geoff, being a fan of de Quincey, will have read the chapter entitled 'The Nation of London' from his *Autobiographic Sketches*, in which the writer talks of how 'the immensity which belongs to the coming metropolis forces itself upon the dullest observer, in the growing sense of his own utter insignificance . . . nobody sees you; nobody hears you; nobody regards you; you do not even regard yourself'. Is that what we're after? If there really are two contradictory urges within us – to live and to die – then perhaps London satisfies the latter as well as the former? Henry James called it 'not a pleasant place; it is not agreeable, or cheerful, or easy, or exempt from reproach. It is only magnificent.' Nothing I've achieved career-wise has felt as good as I thought it would. Not that that makes me unhappy any more – once you've realised that's the way of things you can accept it. But perhaps it's why London draws us? Perhaps we want the opposite of the bar in *Cheers*, somewhere where *nobody* knows our name?

'Great cities,' replies Geoff, 'are like great art, they're basically indifferent to the visitor, or viewer, or reader. They're there long after we've gone. They don't need us. They don't try to please us, or ingratiate themselves. So you don't like London? Big fucking deal. So you don't like *Ulysses*? Ditto. You don't judge great works or great cities – they judge you.'

'Makes me feel like a stalker, doing all these walks in a place that doesn't care about me.'

'Maybe not so much a stalker as a hapless suitor.'

As Shelley wrote:

> You are now
> In London, that great sea, whose ebb and flow
> At once is deaf and loud, and on the shore
> Vomits its wrecks, and still howls on for more.
> Yet in its depth what treasures . . .

Perhaps the *real* test, the real bravery, would have been for Geoff and me to stay in Sheffield and the Midlands respectively. See how big a fish we could be in the little pond, rather than content ourselves with being minnows on the basis that everyone in London is a minnow. Is every step I take in this city a step towards what Hamlet called 'that consummation greatly to be wished'? A step in the graveyard not only of my own ambitions but of virtually everyone's who comes here?

\* \* \*

Later that evening I accompany Matt, the friend I'm staying with, to his local pub quiz in Highgate. One of the questions is 'Which London Underground line crosses the river four times?' Everyone on our team looks at me expectantly. After a panicky stab at the District, memories return of looking at the big maps, realising with horror how many times the whole length of the Isle of Dogs will have to be walked because of Canada Water, Canary Wharf and North Greenwich.

'Sorry, it's the Jubilee.'

'You're sure now?' says Matt, pen poised to make the correction.

'Yeah. Positive.' Then, by way of showing *how* positive: 'The Jubilee's also the only line to connect with all the other lines.'

Three 'too much information' stares come back at me. Is this how it feels to be Richard?

Later still, as Matt and I walk back to his house, he remembers the 'connections' fact, and asks if it's true – what about the Circle? Only after a few seconds' thought do we realise the Circle connects with Monument rather than Bank, so missing any rendezvous with the Waterloo and City Line. But talk of the Circle leads to an idea: instead of just walking it normally, why don't I do the Circle Line pub crawl, the established challenge wherein you stop at each station and have a drink at the nearest pub? Except instead of getting the Tube between each stop, I will, of course, walk. It's soon agreed that this is, in every sense of the phrase, a capital plan.

'Except . . .' I say.

'Except what?'

'Bit sad, don't you think? Doing it on my own?'

'How many stops are there?'

'Twenty-odd.'

'Mmm. See what you mean.'

I've been telling Matt how much I enjoyed the walk with Geoff today. In this new spirit of socialised pedestrianism, there seems a logical conclusion. 'Well?'

He stops and thinks. 'Twenty-odd pubs. A drink in each.' More thought. 'How many miles?'

'Somewhere in the teens. Is it the drinks or the miles that are bothering you?'

Soon it's agreed. Matt will be my companion for the Circle Line.

The next day starts outside Highgate station, opposite an RSPCA charity shop proclaiming in huge letters that 'NEUTERING *STOPS* AIDS IN CATS'. Oh-nine-thirty hours, 15.07 miles already on the clock from yesterday. Today will be considerably longer: it's up to High Barnet (doing the Mill Hill East spur on the way), then offline to Edgware, then all the way down to Kennington via the City.

Other parts of London have hairdressers called 'Hair Today' or 'Have It Off'. Highgate has one called 'E. Scissorhands'. It also, to spoil the image this rainy morning, has a man standing at a bus stop guiding an approaching double-decker towards him in the manner of an air-traffic controller on the runway. A subsequent bus stop is marked 'The Bishop's Avenue', as though any resident of London's most expensive street would be getting the 143 home from Tesco. Must be for the help.

East Finchley station stands opposite the UK headquarters of McDonald's,[8] though its other Stateside link, as the birthplace of Jerry Springer, seems to be a mistaken one. Springer himself has always believed he entered the world here, as his mother sheltered from a bombing raid in 1944, but Tube enthusiasts point out that it was probably Highgate; East Finchley is a surface station, so would have offered Jerry precious little protection from Jerry. In fact it's the first surface station after those 17.3 miles of tunnel from Morden, which explains the statue of an archer on the roof, aiming his arrow into the tunnel's entrance. There was a matching arrow at Morden too, until it got nicked shortly after the station opened.

A left turn at the Bald Faced Stag (it's a gastropub) leads me along the East End Road, lined with some very un-East End houses, to Finchley Central, outside which an Irish guy in his fifties is saying to a younger Muslim woman, 'I don't want a political argument, I just think he was a very, very good painter.' Having approached the station along a quiet side street, I'm expecting the left-hand turn at the end to reveal yet more of this morning's terrain: large houses, well-kept gardens, the odd newsagent or restaurant. Yet it turns out to be a busy main road, which an acoustic freak of the city means you can't hear until you're on it. A moment of genuine surprise, as thrilling as stepping out of the wardrobe into Narnia.[9] There are shops and buses and pubs and cafés, and an estate agent's employee

8. A disappointingly anonymous building – I was hoping for a 20-foot-tall Ronald.

9. A fitting simile, Finchley being where said wardrobe resided.

whose thick, dark hair is so spiky, finger-in-the-light-socket spiky, that it has to be a publicity tool. Just before Mill Hill East is a butcher specialising in exotic meats: emu, camel, springbok, python . . . Listed under 'snacks', below chocolate-covered ants, vodka scorpions and Thai green curry crickets, are pork scratchings.

A marginally different route back to Finchley Central leads me under the Dollis Brook Viaduct, the point at which, as Richard reminded us, the Underground is least deserving of its name. Never has a statistic had such bodily splendour. The Victorian bricks are arranged into 13 towering yet graceful arches, each with a missing section so that as you stand directly underneath it you can see through to all the others. In fact height is the overwhelming theme now – the land in this corner of London is continually dipping and soaring. Although the overall trend is upwards (High Barnet itself being the summit), the mini-peaks and valleys along the way are what you notice. On one street my head is lower than the front doorstep of a three-storey house just behind me, yet higher than the roof of a four-storey house further along.

Not only has the rain stopped now, but sunshine is breaking through, illuminating the rich reds and yellows of the leaves covering the pavements. Near West Finchley station two entrepreneurial-looking types pass by. 'There's nothing here at all,' says one. 'I had no intention of moving here.' While it's a fair summary of the area's Reggie Perrin feel, it's not strictly true: there *is* something here. It's attached to 60 Courthouse Road: a blue plaque announcing that from 1936 to 1960 this nondescript suburban semi was home to one

Harry Beck. I stand there for a moment, in silent homage to the man who in 1931 created, to borrow Geoff's phrase, 'the lie that tells the truth'. 'If you hadn't drawn your map, Harry,' I think, 'I wouldn't be here now.'

Woodside Park is pleasant enough, notable for being the Tube network's last station alphabetically.[10] It also feels like the first stop outside London. Something about the old people's homes on the same street, the feeling of comfortably financed dotage, recalls yesterday's thoughts of leaving the city at the end of your life. Totteridge and Whetstone, the next station, reinforces that sense. Out in the open spaces near here are some very big houses, as well as South Hertfordshire Golf Club: this ain't no metropolis now. The sign on a block of flats called Thatcham Court has lost its 'm', prompting thoughts of the ex-Prime Minister going into rap. On the High Road leading to Barnet the houses are numbered in the 1500s – I thought it was only America which had addresses like that?

At 12.27 p.m., nearly 25 miles into the walk, the final climb brings me to High Barnet station, and then, a couple of minutes later, to the top of Barnet Hill itself. I'm now in one of the positions occupied by the Grand Old Duke of York's men – this is said to be the hill he marched them up and down. Whether or not that's true, this is certainly the highest point between here and York, and indeed between here and the Urals, a fact best savoured from the top of St John's Church tower, which dominates the town centre. Although

---

10. The first is Acton Town.

the tower isn't normally open to the public, someone at the church is feeling Christian and kindly allows me to go up, after showing me the piece of wood nailed to the church's side entrance, marking a height equivalent to the top of St Paul's Cathedral. The view is indeed wonderful, London and its environs spread out like a sun-dappled quilt.

But, just as at the top of Tower 42, there's that niggling feeling of dissatisfaction. This doesn't feel *quite* as good as it should do. I can't work out why. I don't know it yet, but it's going to be a while – not, indeed, until my very last walk – before the mystery is solved.

The next stretch, from here offline to Edgware, is powered by momentum. Not just the vertical momentum of going from a high spot to a lower one – much of the next hour and a half is simply a case of relaxing my knees and letting gravity take the strain – but the horizontal momentum of heading back into London. Passing through the greenery I saw from the church tower, I encounter farms, fields full of horses, houses so big (when you can see them past the gates) that most of us couldn't afford the mortgage on the stamp duty. Styles range from mid-Elizabethan to late-*Footballers' Wives*. Then the greenery ends, and a footbridge leads across the M1, just south of London Gateway services.[11]

Years spent staring at the maps on Northern Line trains had conditioned me into thinking that High Barnet and Edgware

---

11. That shows how far out of town this is: the guns of HMS *Belfast*, moored near Tower Bridge, are trained on the services, as they happen to be exactly 12.5 miles away, the guns' range.

were identical places, twins guarding the ends of the route. Well, sorry, Geoff, but in this case the Tube map is the lie that tells the lie. The first clue to Edgware's nature is the pile of washing machines for sale on the pavement outside a shop. Barnet was middle England aiming (as its name would suggest) high; Edgware is Lidl and Poundstretcher and signs on boarded-up pubs saying 'This is a private property, Administration'. A mile or so towards London is Burnt Oak, as starved of vigour as its name suggests. More than the poverty, you notice that nothing's quite *right* here. An undertaking firm is called Sydney Hurry Limited. The predominantly black and Asian people at the Job Centre next to the station are promised that Barnet Council is 'providing customers with a choice of access to services'. That doesn't *mean* anything.

The houses get bigger, but not noticeably better kept, on the approach to Colindale, the station used by T. E. Lawrence when he was stationed at RAF Hendon, hence his pseudonym of 'Colin Dale' when writing for the *Spectator*. This was where my faith in human memory started to die; in the pre-internet era, researching books here for a writer friend, I would find that an article I'd swear blind had been on a left-hand page was on the right, and vice versa. Today I gaze at the enormous building, backlit by the setting sun, and shed an inward tear that its contents are being digitised, then moved to Yorkshire. The library, shrine to nerdish completism that it is, will close in 2012. The whole area feels mothballed in the interwar years: the 1930s library, RAF Hendon now a museum, the most famous firm round here the long-gone Franco Illuminated Signs, which made the neon glories that defined Piccadilly Circus in the 1920s but have long since been replaced. A residential street crosses a stream, and on the bridge a middle-aged woman stares into the water, crying.

The Metropolitan Police training centre feels like the point at which London starts again. I think of the copper I know who told me about doing his marching there, the call coming 'left – left – left right left', and the guy in front of him doing exactly that: three tiny hops with the left foot, then a huge step with the right to compensate. (He didn't last long.) The quiet street leading from Hendon Central to Brent Cross is called Cheyne Walk; nice houses, but not as nice as those on the street's more famous namesake.[12] A Council notice lies on the pavement: 'This bin cannot be emptied for recycling. It has been contaminated with the wrong materials.' Just the other side of the North Circular, Heathfield Gardens is as anonymous as all the other streets round here – apart from a huge modern Tube roundel sign between two houses, atop a 12-foot metal pole, indicating a shortcut to Brent Cross station. It's like a spaceship that's landed in an episode of *Terry and June*.

This, though, is where the walk leaves Residentia. From here on in it's main drags, traffic, shops, London pulling you into its centre as though by rope. Golders Green, where the young curate Desmond Tutu used to ask policemen the time just to hear them call him 'sir', is surely the most uniformly (and obviously) religious area London has to offer: Solly's and Bloom's restaurants, the King Solomon Hotel, bookshops

---

12. Ersatz glamour lurks all over the capital: Park Lane in Hackney, The Mall in Croydon, Bond Street in Stratford. There's even an Eaton Terrace in Mile End.

offering 'Torah for Teens'.[13] After that it's a climb up North End Road, the main route through Hampstead Heath. At the top is Jack Straw's Castle, for centuries a pub but now a Matt Roberts Personal Training Club (his others are in Chelsea, Mayfair and the City – get the picture?), and then Whitestone Pond, the highest point in London.[14] But even if it weren't now completely dark, the trees all around mean there's no real view from here. It doesn't *feel* high.

Heath Street dips sharply down into the centre of Hampstead. Through a window in some mansion flats I see a four-poster bed that's completely white, which seems a strange colour for such a traditional piece of furniture. In a nail clinic a man sits with his hands on the desk, having for some reason crossed them over, a different woman working on each while a third squats to beautify his feet. It's like a slightly seedy game of Twister. Hampstead is as it always is (Nicole Farhi, those beautiful brown street names, expensive cakes at Paul), though not, perhaps, as it always was: photos of the Heath after a Bank Holiday in the 1920s show it ankle deep in litter from picnics. But then behaviour in the 'good' old days never quite lives up to scrutiny. Early Tube maps asked passengers to refrain from spitting in the carriages.

The *Big Issue* seller outside Belsize Park station sits on a chair, which is fair enough, I suppose, but does limit his scope

---

13. Michael Winner says he saw a sign in Camden saying 'Golders Green 3 miles' on which someone had written 'to you, two and a half'.

14. The old county of London, that is. The highest point on the Tube is at Amersham, 490 feet above sea level, 50 feet higher than here.

for salesmanship.[15] Chalk Farm station marks the boundary between wealth and the approaching grunge of Camden. The Monarch pub literally vibrates to live music from We Rock Like Girls Don't, then it's falafel stalls and joss sticks as far as the eye can see. On Eversholt Street, between Camden and Euston, a firm of funeral directors solves the age-old problem of what to put in its window by displaying old maps of London, including possibly the most beautiful of them all, John Rocque's masterpiece from 1746. It's the details that make it, such as the shadows cast by the trees in what's now Hoxton.

Outside King's Cross a family of four down suitcases to examine a map. 'It's *this* way,' insists the wife, pointing towards Euston. The husband, disagreeing, storms back into the station. Twenty seconds later he reappears, sullen but finally co-operative, and they all head west. At the beginning of the Pentonville Road is the greasy spoon where I once saw a vegetarian complain because his egg had been fried in the same fat used for bacon; you could hear the hairs going up on people's necks. A climb up to the Angel, down the City Road to Old Street, passing the Bavarian Beerhouse, outside which two stony-faced men in lederhosen stand smoking. Just after Moorgate my route is made that little bit easier by Tivoli Corner, the north-west corner of the Bank of England (the Bank's architect Sir John Soane took his inspiration from a temple in the Italian town), through which a passageway was cut in 1936 so that pedestrians wouldn't get pushed into the road by the corner's sharp angle.

---

15. It is, though, fitting for an area that takes its name from *bel assis*, the French for 'beautifully situated'.

Even after I've left the Bank behind, and am heading across London Bridge, down past Borough[16] and the Elephant to journey's end at Kennington (9.56 p.m., 45.8 miles), the Old Lady stays in my thoughts. Something about tonight is fixing her there as the centre of London. No, that's not true: as I said before, there is no centre of London. Perhaps it's its balancing point, in the way that Lebanon, Kansas is said to be the balancing point of the USA. Does it feel like that because the north–south Northern Line and the east–west Central meet here? Either way there's weight at the Bank, seriousness, a time-proven fame. A sense of being safe, too, hence the well-known phrase.

Opposite the Bank, hiding an Underground ventilation shaft, is a statue of James Greathead, the man who invented the tunnelling shield which enabled the Northern Line (and all the other deep-level ones) to be built. Unsurprisingly most people notice the more prominent statue of Wellington outside the Royal Exchange, but Greathead is a hero too, and the Bank feels like a place for heroes. A place, moreover, that's always caught the imagination, always had things going on. In 1836 the Bank's directors received an anonymous letter claiming that the author could gain access to the bullion room in the vaults. Ignoring it, they received another, then another, finally agreeing to meet the author in the room itself at, as one history of the Bank puts it, 'some dark and midnight hour . . . A deputation from the board, lantern in hand, repaired to the bullion-room, locked themselves in and

---

16. Even though its famous market is closed until tomorrow, I can sense the trendiness seeping out under the gates.

awaited the arrival . . . Punctual to the hour a noise was heard below. Some boards in the floor were without much trouble displaced, and in a few minutes the Guy Fawkes of the Bank stood in the midst of the astonished directors . . . An old drain ran under the bullion-room, the existence of which had become known to him . . . The directors rewarded the honesty and ingenuity of their anonymous correspondent – a working man, who had been employed in repairing the sewers – by a present of £800.' The equivalent of nearly £70,000 today – but still nowhere near the value of the bullion to which the man could have helped himself.

In 1858, meanwhile, the Bank gets a mention in *Twice Round the Clock*, an account by the journalist George Augustus Sala of 24 hours in the life of London. In the chapter entitled 'Nine a.m.: Clerks on their way to work' he observes that 'the most luxuriant whiskers belong to the Bank of England. I believe that there are even whisker clubs in that great national institution, where prizes are given for the best pair of *favoris* [sideburns] grown without macassar.' The same chapter, in differentiating between those who take the omnibus and those who walk, uses as slang for the latter 'the Marrowbone stage'. By the time I wind up at Kennington, that trusty vehicle has propelled me 220 miles at an average speed (again including breaks, though not overnight stops) of 2.32 m.p.h. Six lines vanquished. Five remain.

Still plenty of wandering to do, then. Plenty of wondering as well: what will X be like, what will I find at Y? That's the joy of this. They don't have to be exciting places, they simply have to be new. I'm genuinely intrigued by the prospect of visiting Chesham. Can it be coincidence that 'wander' and 'wonder' are just one letter apart?[17]

At Kennington I recall last night's pub quiz in Highgate, talking to my team about the project. Matt and Martin discuss it eagerly, asking which lines I've done, swapping pieces of Tube trivia, suggesting historical facts I could throw in.

Then Laura pipes up. 'You're really going to walk it all?' she says. 'The whole network?'

'Yeah.'

'Honestly?'

'Yeah.'

Sip of the vodka and tonic. 'Can't you just take the bus?'

This comment, reminiscent of Jo's 'no one would know if you didn't do it', puts me in mind of the Donald E. Brown List of Human Universals. Compiled by the anthropologist of that name, it itemises characteristics known to be displayed by every human culture ever observed. Not 'most', mind you. Not even 'nearly every'. To get on this list, a characteristic has to be shared by absolutely 100 per cent of cultures. And there, amidst 'affection expressed and felt', 'facial communication', 'right-handedness as population norm' and the like, is the entry I'm thinking of now: 'males, on average, travel greater distances over lifetime'.

---

17. Sadly it can: the derivations of the two words meander through Old Saxon, German and the like but don't seem to meet up anywhere.

# 7
# Circle Line
## Two men walk into 27 bars

A London policeman, out on his beat one day, encountered a figure lying in the gutter. Closer examination revealed it to be the actor Richard Harris, hopelessly drunk. The policeman suggested that Harris might like to get up.

'The world,' replied Harris, 'is constantly spinning.'

'True,' replied the policeman. 'But how is that going to help you?'

'I'm waiting for my house to come round,' replied Harris.

There's something very stylish about drinking in London. Drinking excessively, that is. A certain outré rakishness. Get bladdered in Cleethorpes and you're just bladdered. Get bladdered in London and you're paying tribute to the masters. This was where Churchill was in his cups, where Wilkes hit the wine, where Pepys got pissed. Richard Harris himself ended up living at the Savoy ('it's better than marriage'), and when, hours from death, he was carried out on a stretcher, he lifted himself up and called to the hotel's diners, 'It was the food!' In an Irish pub in Chelsea Harbour George Best would drink white wine and soda in a bigger-than-a-pint glass, with double brandy chasers. At Selhurst Park Kenny Sansom scored a goal for Crystal Palace that he can't remember; the first he knew was lying on the pitch being congratulated by his team-mates. (Nor can he remember getting up that morning, arriving at the ground, the start of the match . . .) From a window at the Ritz Peter Langan pointed across Piccadilly to Stratton Street, telling fellow drinker Michael Caine that this was where their new restaurant would be. By the time Caine looked back Langan had fallen asleep. In Mayfair, at 9 Curzon Place, Keith Moon finally hung up his drumsticks, having overdosed not on booze but on tablets prescribed to help him give up the booze.

Yes, if you're going to have a drink in each of 27 pubs and not feel ashamed of yourself, London's the place to do it.

Having said that, taking your first drink of the day at 10 a.m. is a prospect so out of the ordinary as to be almost sobering. Matt and I therefore choose as the starting place for our Circle Line crawl a pub that serves food, the Hamilton Hall next to Liverpool Street station (the former ballroom of the Great Eastern Hotel). Our fry-ups, it is to be hoped, will soak up the two halves of bitter we order, the weakest on offer. Though given our proximity to Shoreditch, perhaps we should be drinking porter: it was invented there in the eighteenth century, deriving its name from the profession of those who drank it. It allowed them to 'undergo tasks which ten gin drinkers would sink under'.

A sign behind the bar says that the pub starts serving at 7 a.m.

'That's for food, obviously,' I say to the guy serving us. 'What time do you start serving alcohol?'

'The same.'

'Really? Who needs a drink that early in the City?' It's not as though this is Smithfield, famous for its early licensing hours on account of the meat market being open all night.

'You'd be surprised. We have regulars in here every day. Suits.'

'Have they been in the office early to catch the markets in the Far East?'

'No, no, they're on their way to work. They'll get the train in from the suburbs and be in here for seven. Between then and nine they'll have four, five pints.'

'Then they go and do a day's work?'

'Oh, yeah. They don't get drunk. It just puts them in a happy frame of mind. There's one guy who comes in every day, orders a pint of Strongbow and then drinks it as he walks out. He's finished by the time he gets to the door.' I pace it out: five steps. All of a sudden our two halves of bitter (3.6%) seem quite modest. Nonetheless we stay mindful of the need to pace ourselves, so in the next pub (The Globe, next to Moorgate station), we're horrified when the weakest bitter (3.8%) runs out as the barmaid pours it. We're forced up to London Pride, which may have an appropriate name but is still an eye-watering 4.1%. Fitting that one of the pub's bars is called the Keats, after the poet born near here, whose 'Ode to a Nightingale' includes the line 'that I might drink, and leave the world unseen'.

On the way up to the Barbican we pass the plaza in front of the CityPoint building. We've been talking about the

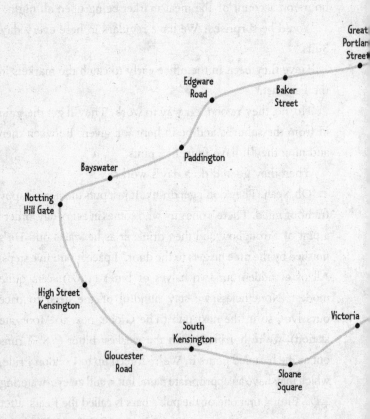

**CIRCLE LINE**

Stations: 27

Line mileage: 14

Price ratio of most expensive to least expensive beer purchased: 5:1

Great
Portland
Street

Edgware
Road

Baker
Street

Bayswater

Paddington

Notting
Hill Gate

High Street
Kensington

Victoria

South
Kensington

Gloucester
Road

Sloane
Square

N

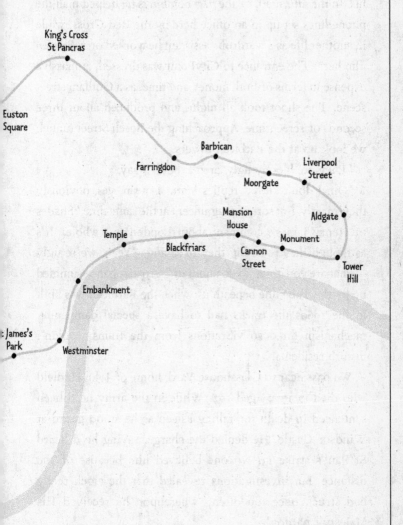

King's Cross
St Pancras

Euston
Square

Barbican

Farringdon

Liverpool
Street

Moorgate

Mansion
House

Aldgate

Temple

Blackfriars

Monument

Cannon
Street

Embankment

Tower
Hill

St James's
Park

Westminster

0    0.25    0.50 mi

0        0.5        1 km

concept of the 'personal Tube line' that occurred to me during the first walk. Matt points out that this would have to be on his. In the aftermath of the 7/7 bombings he helped man the phone lines set up in an office here by the Red Cross, while in another life as a wardrobe assistant he worked on a *Batman* film here. The entrance to CityPoint was dressed, at massive expense in terms of both money and time, as a Gotham street scene. The shoot took all night, and produced about three seconds of screentime. Approaching the Beech Street tunnel, we look up at the Barbican towers.

'They are bloody ugly, aren't they?' I say.

'Oh, I don't know,' replies Matt. 'I mean, yes, obviously they're ugly. But sort of magnificent at the same time.' Shades of Henry James's comment about London as a whole. 'It's as though they're so big they're saying, "Yeah, we're ugly – what are you going to do about it?"' An arrogance summed up by the Tube line beneath us: when the Barbican was built in the 1960s the tracks had to have a special dampening mechanism fitted so vibrations from the trains wouldn't disturb residents.

We pass near to Glasshouse Yard, home of John Hatfield who died in 1770 aged 102. While in the army he'd been sentenced to death for falling asleep as he stood guard at Windsor Castle. He denied the charge, saying he'd heard St Paul's strike 13. No one believed him because of the distance, but investigations revealed that the clock really had struck once too often, 'whereupon he received His Majesty's pardon'.

Round at Farringdon we're aiming for the Castle on

Cowcross Street, the only pub in Britain to have its own pawnbroker's licence.[1] But it doesn't open until midday, which is another hour away, so we repair to the Fox and Anchor, which is run by one of those archetypes among London landlords, the small, smartly dressed Irishman, pub-proud and attentive. 'Yes, gents?' he says as two beermats appear on the pewter bar. The pub's style is hybrid: champagne bottles on the shelves, pickled eggs and pork pies on the bar. Soon we're discussing the challenge.

'You're wise to stick to halves,' says the landlord.

'You mean some people drink pints?'

'Oh, yeah. Mostly the Australians.'

'Twenty-seven pints?'

A nod. 'You want to catch them at the beginning rather than the end.'

This was actually our Barbican pub, so just the other side of Farringdon station we head to the Sir John Oldcastle, named after the one-time local thought to have been the model for Shakespeare's Falstaff.[2] Then it's up to King's Cross St Pancras, where our drinks simply have to be taken at the champagne bar next to the Eurostar tracks: £9 for two bottles of Kasteel Cru lager, plus £1.13 'discretionary service'. This happens to be my round. Matt paid £1.99 at the last place. Hey ho. At the Bree Louise, a serious ale-aficionado's place just north of Euston Square, we opt for Rebellion, though as it's the weakest bitter and we're on halves the name seems rather inappropriate.

---

1. Granted on the spot by George IV, travelling to a nearby cock-fight, so he could pawn his gold pocket-watch for gambling funds.

2. He would surely have approved of today's agenda.

Continuing westward, we pass the point at which perhaps London's most unlikely ever pub crawl collapsed in chaos. There was nothing unlikely about the crawl itself – some friends in the 1850s decided to 'take something' in every saloon between Oxford Street and Hampstead Road, or in other words every pub on the Tottenham Court Road. What made it unlikely was that one of the lads about town was Karl Marx. His friend William Liebknecht wrote later that choosing the 'something' they were to take was 'a very difficult task, even by confining yourself to a minimum, considering the enormous number of saloons in that part of the city.' (Tell us about it, William.) But the group of German comrades 'went to work undaunted and managed to reach the end of Tottenham Court Road without accident'.

In their final saloon, however, they got into a conversation about politics. Never a good idea in a pub, but especially not when one of the people involved is Karl Marx. 'For a while,' reports Liebknecht, 'everything went smoothly.' But then one of Marx's group, 'hurt by some chance remark, turned the tables and ridiculed the English snobs. Marx launched an enthusiastic eulogy on German science and music – no other country, he said, would have been capable of producing such masters of music as Beethoven, Mozart, Handel and Haydn . . . So fluently I have never heard him speak English [though we should remember that by this time Liebknecht was himself hammered] . . . Threatening words were spoken . . . fists were brandished.' The group managed to leave the pub without actual violence, but still needed an outlet for their passions. One of them found some paving stones. '"Hurrah, an idea!" And in memory of mad student pranks he picked up a stone, and Clash! Clatter! a gas lantern went flying into splinters . . . Marx and I did not stay behind, and we broke four or five street lamps.' Despite the fact it was now 2 a.m. the police soon appeared. 'Marx showed an activity that I should not have attributed to him.' In other words, he legged it. Escaping down an alleyway, the friends managed to lose the police.[3]

In the Albany, opposite Great Portland Street station, we make our first switch from bitter, opting for strawberry cider. I enjoy the sweetness after all that ale, but Matt's West Country roots forbid him from enjoying such an abomination. In the Gents I'm reminded of my one and only idea for an invention: a pocket-sized wedge, its diagonal surface covered in a non-slip material, which when placed on those anti-cocaine slopes in the cubicles would produce a horizontal surface on which the forbidden activity could then occur. Can't see it going down too well on *Dragons' Den*, though.

It's between here and Baker Street that the first signs of tension appear. Microscopic signs, admittedly, but signs all the same. Aware of having to dawdle to avoid leaving Matt behind, I gently point out that we don't want to slacken our pace too much. The first seven pubs have taken us just over three hours, and while maintaining that pace would get us over the finishing line somewhere between 10 and 11 p.m., we're surely going to slow down as the day progresses.

---

3. This wasn't the end of Communism's love affair with London pubs. In 1905 the Crown on Clerkenwell Green was the venue for the first-ever meeting between Lenin and Stalin. Of all the pubs in all the world . . .

Matt glances down at my trainers. 'Wish I'd put mine on,' he says.

For the first time I notice he's wearing a pair of suede lace-ups. Beautifully made suede lace-ups, it's true. But not the sort of footwear conducive to a speedy 15 miles.[4] 'Why are you wearing those?' I ask.

He looks down at them. 'God knows.'

'Matt, that's the sort of mistake you should make *after* visiting twenty-seven pubs, not before.'

'Sorry.' He shakes his head. 'It's the Himalayas all over again.'

'Eh?'

'When I went on a mountain hike there. [Doing volunteer work in Mongolia he'd received a message from friends to say they were in Nepal and did he want to meet up?] I had one of those rucksacks with bits of webbing on either side, to store your water bottles in.' He sighs. 'I took two tubes of Pringles.'

Eventually we make it to the Globe opposite Baker Street (Matt: IPA, me: lager), then, after Edgware Road, the Great Western, a small, splendidly unpretentious boozer in which you could imagine a *Sweeney*-era John Thaw being handed the phone with the words 'Call for you, Jack'. The landlord regales us with Circle Line challenge stories. 'There was a load in the other day dressed as *Star Wars* characters. One bloke was done up as Princess Leia. He started heading for the Gents. I said, "You should be using the Ladies." So he did.'

---

4. We're doing the old, proper Circle Line. The westward 'extension' – it doesn't really exist, being simply an increase in the number of trains running on the Hammersmith and City tracks – would make the challenge nigh-on impossible.

After the Pride of Paddington (you can guess which station that's opposite), I deliberately head for Bayswater via Leinster Terrace. I stop Matt outside numbers 22 and 23, and ask if he notices anything unusual about them.

He scans the five-storey frontages, the pillared porches, the black front doors. 'Nope. What is it?'

By way of explanation I lead him round to the parallel street. When we're level with what should be the backs of 22 and 23 Leinster Terrace, Matt sees that the houses do not, in fact, exist. The frontages he was looking at are just Hollywood-style fakes. By clambering on to the gatepost of a neighbouring property, we look over a brick wall at the reason for the trickery. There below us, running at right-angles to the street, is a short open section of the Circle Line. As if on cue, a train rumbles past.

'Leinster Terrace was very posh in the nineteenth century,' I explain. 'The residents only agreed to the Tube line going under them if the company built fake houses to protect the view.'

Matt shakes his head. 'But the *windows* . . . How are they done?'

A sign of how convincingly the trick was pulled off. 'They're painted a light grey, which somehow means you don't even notice them.' As indeed Matt didn't.

Heading round to Bayswater, he decides we've got to eat. 'Don't listen to your stomach,' he keeps saying. Our stomachs are reporting that they've had five pints, thank you very much,[5] there really isn't room for namby-pamby food. But

---

5. We've only just drawn level, it occurs to us, with the Liverpool Street pre-work regulars.

responsible drinkers that we are – all right, as responsible as you can be when you're being this irresponsible – we force ourselves. I just manage a Pret lemon chicken sandwich, while Matt, as would be expected of a man who tackles the Himalayas on Pringles, opts for a sausage roll from Gregg's. Then it's the King's Head on Moscow Road, and (as our Notting Hill pub) the Churchill Arms on Kensington Church Street.

'Real chore now,' I say to Matt, lifting yet another half of lager to my reluctant lips.

He nods.

'It's the *volume*, more than anything. How do they do it? Serious boozers, I mean?'

'The serious ones are on shorts, aren't they?'

'Suppose so.' Not that we can switch to the hard stuff – not yet, anyway. We'd never make the City.

'That's always how it was in the—' Matt names a pub he used to work in near Old Street. It's still there, though under new owners, who have (in our opinion) ruined it. In Matt's day it was another real 'Call for you, Jack' place. And like any great pub it was its own soap opera. Several of the regulars were called Paul: there was Tall Paul (not the DJ), Small Paul, Paul Thumb (tried to fix his motorbike engine while it was still running), Teeth, Barnesy . . . Matt and the other staff did their own music tapes. To this day whenever I hear 'We're Gonna Change the World' by Matt Monro, I see Matt (my one, that is) behind the bar, not just singing but also conducting it. We spend a while reminiscing, and this turns into a moan about the lack of decent London pubs nowadays. The one we're in is good, and the Seven Stars behind the High Court, the Mitre off

Hatton Garden, the Lamb in Covent Garden, the Nag's Head in Belgravia (not natural Nag's Head territory, you'd think).

'No, let's stop it,' I say. 'We're sounding like Jeffrey Bernard.' I look in my notes for the full quote. 'It's from an interview not long before he died. "All pubs are terrible places now. They [the pubs of yore] didn't have fucking music. They didn't have cigarette machines. They didn't sell chemical beer. They were for proper drinkers, not for fucking yobs. I want to go into a pub and meet interesting people." Yeah, fair enough – but then London's never what it was. He goes on here about the old Soho characters. "Genuine bohemians. Now it's full of advertising agency creeps. Bloody Essex man and Soho man – there's very little difference nowadays. But it was like bloody Disneyland." I bet you there were drinkers in his youth moaning that Soho wasn't like it had been thirty years before that.'

We talk about *Jeffrey Bernard is Unwell*, in which Bernard was portrayed by Peter O'Toole, locked in the Coach and Horses overnight. The irony was that O'Toole had long since been compelled to mount the wagon by the time he did the play.[6] 'There was so much laughter when I saw it that I missed half of it,' says Matt. 'Then a few years later I saw the production with Dennis Waterman. I heard every word.'

By the time we pass High Street Kensington it's half-three and we've covered 7.6 miles. Nearly at the halfway point in terms of pubs now (the next will be our thirteenth), but Matt's

---

6. Another teetotaller was Norman Balon, the Coach's landlord. Once famous for his rudeness, towards the end of his reign he was actually disappointingly polite.

footwear mistake is hitting, or rather pinching, home. I can tell this from his muted reaction to the information that we're now over one of only two short sections of track that the Circle Line calls its own. (The other being between Tower Hill and Aldgate.)

At the Builder's Arms, a gastropub in the moneyed Kensington backstreets (crab and wasabi cakes, tomato and olive falafel), we decide the time has come for some Adam Smith-style specialisation. Matt's a quicker drinker than me, I'm a quicker walker than him. Downing his IPA in one, he sets off towards Gloucester Road, leaving me to nurse a cider whose sweetness will hopefully help it slip down. There's still no real drunkenness – the walking seems to be taking care of that – it's simply the volume problem, the feeling of drowning in booze. Not literally, thank God, as happened to several people in 1814. The Meux and Co. Brewery, which stood on the site now occupied by the Dominion Theatre in Tottenham Court Road, stored its porter in huge vats, several of which ruptured, sending nearly a third of a million gallons cascading out into the streets. The noise could be heard five miles away. Apart from demolishing several buildings, the beer also found its way into the St Giles Rookery, a slum area of poor houses and tenements, where it flooded basement rooms, drowning eight people. Meanwhile locals rushed out with pots and pans and glasses, scooping up as much beer as they could. Others shunned such refinement, simply bending down to lap at the boozy tide. Injuries were inevitable, and when people started turning up at the nearby Middlesex Hospital smelling of alcohol, other patients demanded to know why they hadn't been offered a drink too.

En route to Gloucester Road my phone beeps with a text: *Stanhope Arms, opp station*. There I find Matt, finishing his half of Pride, my half of Fosters bubbling ominously on the table. We contemplate conversation, before accepting that neither of us feels up to it, and Matt might as well get on the road.

'Is this what a pub crawl's supposed to be about?' he asks as he stands up.

'Not really. But then this isn't an ordinary pub crawl, is it?'

'Suppose not.'

As he stands up I reflect that our lack of sociability echoes the relationship between Sir Edward Watkin and James Forbes. They were the twin fathers of the Circle Line, being heads respectively of the Metropolitan and the District Lines, which the Circle was designed to link together. Their antagonism delayed the line's completion, and Forbes's claim in a speech at the end of the opening-day banquet that their differences were 'only slight' was belied by the fact that Watkin, sitting next to him, was that very second making notes for his solicitors about the pair's next dispute. Even when services started, the Metropolitan trains running clockwise and the District anti-clockwise, each firm refused to sell tickets for its rival, meaning passengers might have to travel 26 stations in order to travel one. To keep trains running as quickly as possible porters were ordered to push elderly passengers, who sometimes clambered backwards off the train, back into the carriage. If challenged they could say they thought the old dear was trying to get on.

\* \* \*

After lagers in our South Kensington pub (actually a brasserie on the King's Road), we pass (separately) through Sloane Square, next to the Royal Court theatre, in whose private members' club the drinking was once overseen by manager Clement Freud. One night he noticed a diner falsely claiming to be a particular member. Freud said nothing, but added £50 (then a large amount) to the final bill. 'What's this?' queried the diner. 'Oh, that's the money you borrowed last time you were in – remember?' On Eaton Square, after I've caught up with Matt, we see a champagne cork lying in the gutter, and agree that it sums up the general mood. It would make sense to take a break, but we just can't afford the delay – it's 5 p.m. now, giving us serious doubts as to whether we'll make it before closing time.

More beer in the next two venues (a smart bar near Buck House as our Sloane Square boozer, then the Duke of York on Victoria Street) makes up my mind, or rather my stomach. 'Just can't take the volume any more,' I concede. In the Feathers opposite St James's Park station, while Matt sticks with the bitter, I go for a gin and tonic.

'Drunk for a penny, dead drunk for two,' ran the boast seen above many an eighteenth-century pub when London discovered 'Madam Geneva'. Most people had had nothing stronger than beer before, so gin – cheap and potent – seemed a godsend. Even those who couldn't afford a glass of it bought rags soaked in the spirit, and soon the city was reeling towards disaster. Every fourth house in St Giles was a pub, and demands came for the government to end the so-called 'Gin Craze'. But despite increased taxes and a new licensing system, Londoners insisted on following mother to her ruin. Seeking to learn from their mistake, in our Westminster pub (the St Stephen's Tavern opposite Big Ben) I decide against another gin. I have a vodka instead.

The shorts are helping on the volume front, but the general mood refuses to lift. Matt reaches across and writes 'grim, grim, grim' on my notes. In the Gents I stumble over an unseen rise in the floor level (it really isn't drunkenness, even though I know that's what drunks always say), and an American washing his hands says 'Mind the step'. Oh, how I laugh. The barmaid says that because of health and safety legislation she isn't allowed to refill my water bottle[7] in case germs transfer themselves to the tap (do they defy gravity?), but can give me water in a glass which I can then pour into my bottle. The charade is duly performed.

The next stretch – along the Embankment to Blackfriars via Temple – is under a mile and a half, but owing to the three stops (in which Matt joins me on the V&Ts) it takes us nearly two hours. We pass the scene of a 1761 mishap when someone hailing a hackney carriage at Temple Bar failed to spot that the coachman was 'in liquor . . . [he] turned under Blackfriars Gateway in Ludgate Street, drove to the bottom of Water Lane, down the flight of stone steps and on to the causeway; it luckily happened to be quite low water . . . but it was with great difficulty the horses got the coach up again.' Something similar happened to a journalist I once knew, except he didn't need a cabbie to help him. Walking back

---

7. Despite the volume problems I'm making myself sip from this as we walk, an investment in tomorrow morning's well-being.

along the Embankment from Parliament to his office, his bladder unbearably full after a very long lunch, he hopped over the wall on to some of the steps leading down to the river. Wanting to make sure that he was completely out of sight before doing what needed to be done, he descended another step, then another – then on to one that was slippier than it looked . . .

Talking of the fourth estate, Blackfriars puts Matt and me only a short stagger from Fleet Street, which in its old incarnation must rival Soho as the hardest-drinking area of London. During our District Line chat John Pearson recalled his days there. Even though he was on *The Sunday Times* (not a great drinking paper), he socialised with 'absolutely hardened soaks who could produce copy when they were paralytic. George Gale – he was Lunchtime O'Booze in *Private Eye* – and also Patrick O'Donovan, of the *Observer*. Went with him to Jerusalem with the Archbishop of Canterbury, and then to Rome for the Archbishop to see the Pope. We got there, went straight out and started drinking – he was doing six to my one. Eventually we get back to the hotel, and I'm just drifting off when I hear the typewriter rattling in the next room – it was O'Donovan, writing his piece there and then. I had to get up early the next morning to do mine, which was pathetic. O'Donovan's was brilliant. Drink was the great curse of the writing classes.'[8]

Between Blackfriars and Mansion House Matt and I pass St Nicholas Cole Abbey on Queen Victoria Street, which in

---

8. Pearson on his old friend Ian Fleming: 'As he got older the whiskies got darker.'

the early days of the Tube proved very popular with young men: one of the vents in the pavement here lifted girls' skirts whenever a train passed by. Our Mansion House drink is in an Irish pub, our Cannon Street one in El Vino's, sister establishment to the Fleet Street institution, housed in one of the few City buildings to survive the Great Fire. Just the other side of the Monument we've nearly finished our V&Ts in a Balls Brothers wine bar when Matt sniffs the glass suspiciously. 'Are these doubles?' he asks the woman who served us. 'Yes, that's our standard measure,' comes the reply. We've made the task one drink harder than we had to.

Though, truth be told, it doesn't make that much difference. All semblance of enjoyment has long since departed, our lesson not so much driven as poured home: London's 'drinking with the greats' reputation is about as substantial as the froth on a pint of Aussie lager. You can dress up your heavy drinking with anecdotal finery, drape it with actorly bons mots, but in the end an alcoholic is an alcoholic is a pain in the arse, and not just to other people. 'The trouble is,' said Jeffrey Bernard towards the end, 'I bore myself. When even a self-obsessed man is made to yawn by his own daydreams then there's nowhere to go.' Reduced to the withered state where 'my thigh's like the triple twenty on a dart board', and then to the point where the leg had to come off altogether, his final days were spent in a tower block on Berwick Street, where an interviewer once noted that 'the window opposite him was positioned too high for him to enjoy the view over London from where he was sitting. He could see only clouds.'

After the Grange Hotel, our Tower Hill pub, Matt and I

make our way slowly to the beautiful old Hoop and Grapes pub opposite Aldgate station.[9] Here, as we force down our final drinks, I tally up our totals. Him: 12 halves of bitter, 1 of mild, 4 of IPA, 1 of cider, 3 bottles of lager, 1 vodka, lime and soda and 5 vodka and tonics. Me: 4 halves of bitter, 1 of mild, 1 of IPA, 2 of cider, 8 of lager, 3 bottles of lager, 1 gin and tonic, 5 vodka and tonics, 1 vodka, lime and soda, and 1 Pimm's (needed something that tasted vaguely of fruit). On another day this could have entered the lore of our friendship as an adventure of heroic proportions. As it is we glumly note the truth it took Bernard a lifetime to learn, or rather observe without being able to act on: 'Drinking too much,' he once said, 'is just a bloody nuisance.'

Matt points out that Bernard's 'Low Life' column in the *Spectator* was described as 'a suicide note in weekly instalments'.[10] This reminds me that Bertrand Russell called drunkenness 'temporary suicide', and soon I'm remembering the 'Do we want London to kill us?' theme from my conversation with Geoff Nicholson, as well as Peter Rees's 'London as somewhere to run to if you don't fit in' comment. Plenty of people come here to escape their demons. Some of those for whom the attempt fails end up shackled to the demon drink. It seems fitting that this thought occurs to us on the Circle Line, the line that goes nowhere.

---

9. Also pre-Fire – indeed it claims to be the oldest licensed premises in the City.

10. Combining tragedy and farce to the end, the writer was late for his own funeral. Traffic.

# 8

# Piccadilly Line

## Mind the gap

I've now done 235 miles and seven lines. Of the remaining four, the Metropolitan – the oldest Tube line, and very possibly the longest walk – has to be last. The Waterloo and City, a mere bagatelle of less than two miles, can be knocked off on the same day as the Jubilee. So it seems sensible that the next walk should be the only other two-dayer, the Piccadilly.

A member of Charles Yerkes's stable, the Great Northern, Piccadilly and Brompton Railway opened in 1906.[1] The first two words came from the name of the company whose Finsbury Park station gave the line its northern terminus, while in the south it reached Hammersmith. Apart from the Heathrow link, opened in the 1970s, the rest of the Piccadilly Line came on tap in the early thirties – down to Hounslow, and up to the station that was soon featuring in Max Miller's routine. 'I was on the Tube the other day, ladies and gentlemen, it was very crowded, I was pressed up against a very attractive lady. At Turnpike Lane some people got on,

---

1. Sadly Yerkes himself had died the previous year, before any of his lines started running.

she's pressed up against me more tightly. At Arnos Grove some more people got on, she's pressed up against me even *more* tightly. She says, "Is this Cockfosters?" I say, "No, Miller's the name, ma'am, pleased to meet you."'

The cock (or chief) forester was in fact the old head honcho of Enfield Chase, the last remaining bit of which is Trent Park, immediately to the right as I exit the station on a bitterly cold but brilliantly sunny late-November morning. The houses round here mark the limit of the Tube's reach; the inter-war building boom followed the dark blue line northwards, joining Cockfosters up with Barnet, just to the west. (For once the Underground map isn't playing tricks with you – the ends of the Piccadilly and Northern Lines really are that close.) But the Second World War brought an end to house construction, immediately followed by a ban on green-belt development that has kept everything north of here much as nature intended it, starting with Trent Park itself. I've found another point on the boundary where London ends. The countryside, combined with the size of those 1930s houses (the style is sometimes referred to as 'stockbroker Tudor'), explains the prices in the window of Igloo Homes. Given the weather, a fitting name.

Best way to warm up is to get walking. Not that I need any encouragement. Walking all day seems entirely natural now, whereas before the project the idea of traipsing from Cockfosters to Hammersmith (my overnight resting place) would have seemed a real challenge. An exciting one, yes, but a challenge nonetheless. All a question of perspective.

As the American comedian Stephen Wright has pointed out, everywhere is walking distance if you have the time. A rough estimate of tomorrow's itinerary – out to Heathrow, offline to Uxbridge, back into town – shows it could well break my most-miles-in-a-day record (currently 35.5 on the Central Line). Yet this doesn't seem daunting now. The project has altered my perception. Walking as a drug again.

As if to emphasise the affluence of this end of the Piccadilly Line, between here and the next station (Oakwood) I see two of the fattest magpies you could imagine, their feathers sleek and shiny. Just east of Southgate station[2] is the Priory Hospital, where General Pinochet was treated on his controversial 1998 visit to London. The station itself is of the same art-deco design as its predecessors, not *that* beautiful but with a certain retro charm. One feature they all share is the signage, in the Tube-standard Johnston typeface, telling you what everything is, as though you're a visitor from Saturn: 'Public Telephones', 'Newsagent' and so on. At Southgate this even extends to the parade of shops outside, where with Cholmondley-Warner formality you're informed, in capital letters, that the establishment below the sign is a 'FRIED CHICKEN SHOP'.

Arnos Grove – the street, not the station – continues the theme of large houses, some of them behind locked gates. In the park at the end, its white-frosted grass crunching beneath my feet, three dogs walk in obedient single-file behind a well-dressed woman. Strange, I'd always imagined this to

2. Excited message from Richard: the northernmost below-ground station on the network.

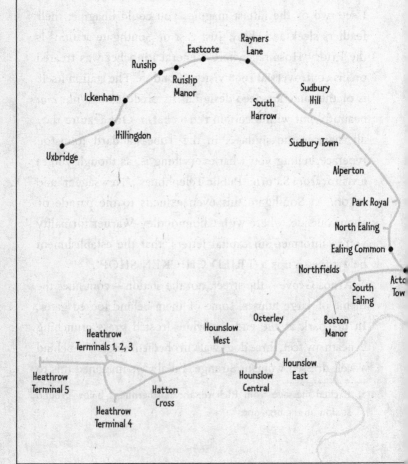

**PICCADILLY LINE**

Stations: 53

Line mileage: 44

Pairs of discarded pink knickers
found on the pavement: 1

Rayners
Lane

Eastcote

Ruislip

Ruislip
Manor

Ickenham

Sudbury
Hill

South
Harrow

Hillingdon

Sudbury Town

Uxbridge

Alperton

Park Royal

North Ealing

Ealing Common

Northfields

Acto
Tow

South
Ealing

Osterley

Boston
Manor

Heathrow
Terminals 1, 2, 3

Hounslow
West

Hounslow
East

Heathrow
Terminal 5

Hatton
Cross

Hounslow
Central

Heathrow
Terminal 4

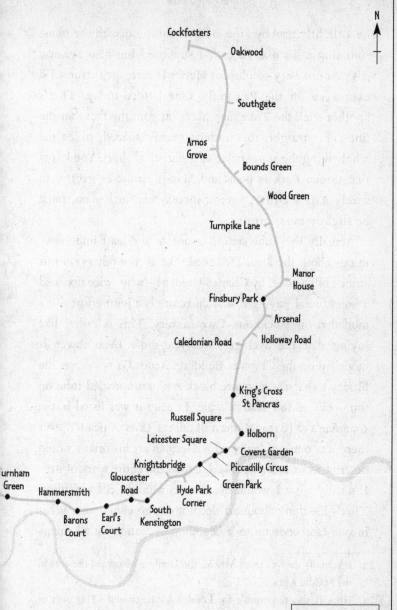

N

Cockfosters
Oakwood
Southgate
Arnos Grove
Bounds Green
Wood Green
Turnpike Lane
Manor House
Finsbury Park
Arsenal
Holloway Road
Caledonian Road
King's Cross St Pancras
Russell Square
Leicester Square
Holborn
Covent Garden
Piccadilly Circus
Knightsbridge
Green Park
Gloucester Road
Hyde Park Corner
urnham Green
Hammersmith
South Kensington
Barons Court
Earl's Court

0    0.5    1 mi

0    1    2 km

be a slightly grubby area. Something to do with the name sounding a bit like 'Argos', I suppose,[3] but also because it's past not-very-salubrious Manor House, the furthest I'd ever been on the Piccadilly Line before today. That's another trick the Tube map plays on you: the fact that the lines are straight, the stations evenly spaced, gives the whole thing the appearance of a statistical chart. You know that Green Park is posh and Manor House is grotty, so surely Arnos Grove, several increments further on, must be slightly more grotty?

Actually the Tube station is one of the least impressive things about the area. Designed, like all the others on this stretch of the line, by Charles Holden[4] – who twice declined a knighthood, saying that architecture is a joint effort – it's modelled on Stockholm City Library. This is rather like saying that the average three-year-old's Lego tower is modelled on the Chrysler Building. Arnos Grove shares the library's shape – a square block with an upended tube on top – but on too small a scale. In 2007 it was listed in the *Guardian*'s 12 'Great Modern Buildings' (kiss of death if ever there was one), as 'truly what German art historians would describe as a *Gesamtkunstwerk*, a total and entire work of art'. It's truly what I would describe as some bricks and glass. That's the thing about art-deco: it can go either way. What in one case ends up as a beguiling evocation of all things

---

3. It actually derives from Arnold, the family who owned the area in the Middle Ages.

4. He was also responsible for London Underground's HQ over St James's Park station.

Poirot, in another becomes a scruffy building from just before the war.[5]

There's a taste of what great modern design can do on the North Circular, where a yet-to-be-opened pedestrian bridge snakes like a twisting rollercoaster over the traffic (its casing, that is – you're not expected to walk upside down), and then the pre-war feel reasserts itself between Bounds Green and Wood Green. It's not an unpleasant feel, just a dated one. Four churches within a few minutes of each other speak of a more 'respectable' age, as does the A4 notice, laminated against the weather and fixed securely to a lamppost with neat plastic ties, announcing Bowes Park Community Association's forth-coming AGM. There will be 'light refreshments' from 7.30 p.m. In the distance, over to the right, is the transmitting tower at Ally Pally, a monument to the days before the BBC let its foul-mouthed presenters taunt elderly actors with explicit boasts involving their granddaughters. Not that the entire area is stuck in the past: St Michael's Church Hall has a large pink banner advertising Zumba classes.

At an internet café next to Wood Green station, checking my emails, I overhear a young couple at the next row of screens talking and laughing with each other in Arabic, their giggling so excited they sometimes begin speaking before the other person has finished. Rising to leave, I see that they're not a

---

5. This will hit home two stations further on at Wood Green. It's the lime-green paint on the metal window frames that does it. Exactly the same shade, I realise, as at the Hoover factory on the Central Line, and a block of flats just off Dorset Square on the Bakerloo. Is it one of the listing regulations that this horrible shade has to be used?

couple at all; in fact they're not even talking to each other. They're both logged on to Skype video connections, wearing headphones and talking to their faraway partners. Heading back out into the cold, which a couple of hours' walking had made me forget about, I re-establish a decent pace for another dose of insulation. Wood Green's shiny Vue cinema and Shopping City arcade soon give way to Turnpike Lane's unbranded retailers offering cheap clothes and discount toys. Then it's Green Lanes, one of London's longest roads with a single name, the ancient route having once linked several greens that no longer exist. The ethnic palette offers up some unusual shades (how many German-Somali doctors can there be in the world?), before the thoroughfare settles down into a succession of predominantly Turkish businesses. In a restaurant window two middle-aged women in traditional headscarves sit making circular *pide* bread, thinning each piece with two different types of rolling pin until you think it must break; it never does. A sign for Harringay Cars has each letter in a different colour, rather like the Gay Pride rainbow flag, leading me to wonder whether they're a specialist taxi business and their name is a pun. In fact they aren't and it isn't; this area really is spelled that way, as opposed to the London Borough of Haringey of which it forms a part. Nice to see ye olde English tradition of inconsistent spelling formalised like this.

On the climb up to Manor House station two men – Middle Eastern, in their twenties, not well-dressed but obviously not sleeping on the streets either – push a supermarket trolley laden with stuff scavenged from bins: a plastic briefcase, a burned-out electric hob, an old saucepan . . . They stop, one preventing the trolley from rolling away as the other spies a discarded vacuum cleaner, which he breaks apart for its motor and plug. London's twenty-first-century Steptoe and Son. Then there's one of those strange moments of silence you sometimes get in big cities, making you feel you're in a film where a dramatic event has been portrayed using freeze-frame. This time it's because of traffic lights a hundred yards back: no cars in my direction, while the ones queuing on the other side coast downhill without needing their engines. Then the lights change, and the movie starts again.

After Finsbury Park it's St Thomas's Road, bookended by the North London Mosque (made infamous by Abu Hamza), and a sports ground that until 1913 was graced by the students of St John's College of Divinity. They leased it to a football team from Woolwich, known as the Arsenal. In 1932 their manager Herbert Chapman got London Underground to change the name of the station opposite to that of his team, otherwise I'd now be heading for Gillespie Road – which is what some Spurs fans still call it. Now the team has moved again, which is why the old Highbury Stadium houses flats and the Kids Unlimited day nursery. Round the corner, heading for Holloway Road, I pass Arsenal's huge new Emirates Stadium. As at Stamford Bridge on the District Line there are tourists taking pictures, but unlike Chelsea's ground this one has real character, a behemoth with beauty.

Drayton Park Primary School has an old boat in the playground, with a proper cabin and everything, but it's a sign of how easily kids get bored with things that none of them are playing in it, preferring instead just to run around yelling a lot. There's a bookbinding business which makes little economic sense until you turn on to the Holloway Road and see the London Metropolitan University; the firm specialises in dissertations. Were I to carry on a little further past the Tube station I'd reach 304 Holloway Road, where legendary 1960s record producer Joe Meek (of 'Telstar' fame) had his home and studio. String sections were recorded in the hallway, backing vocalists in the bathroom, while brass players had to stand on the stairs. This was where Meek tried to kiss a young Tom Jones. Fisticuffs ensued.

But I'm not heading quite that far. A cut-through to the Caledonian Road is to be had, which by happy coincidence leads me past the home of actor Tim Bentinck. For nearly 30 years now he has been the voice of David in *The Archers*, but the reason I've arranged to call in for a cup of tea is his place in Tube history. It was, by another coincidence, a place in the history of the very line on which he lives. For about 15 years from the early nineties onwards, Tim was the Piccadilly Line's 'mind the gap' voice.

Tim's house is a large Victorian semi, with several steps leading up to an imposing white porch. 'It's Mr Pooter's house from *Diary of a Nobody*,' says Tim as he welcomes me in. He's tall and not unstocky, giving him the same reassuringly friendly air as his home. 'In the front of the book is a picture of Pooter's place, and it looks exactly the same as this. His is in Brickfield Terrace, which is a fictional address of course, but it is meant to be around this area. He used to take the tram down the Holloway Road to his job in the City.

That's how Islington started. Somewhere people came to live to get away from the Square Mile.'

We wonder what Pooter would think of his neighbours now, and indeed the buildings in which they live. I noticed the signs on the estate opposite: 'Riding of cycles, go-karts and skateboards is prohibited'; 'Exercising of dogs on this estate is prohibited'. Great, so now we'll have unfit kids and pent-up dogs. Say what you like about the Victorian age, and its self-important characters like Charles Pooter, at least they didn't plaster the whole of London with bright yellow plastic signs telling you what you could and couldn't do.

In Tim's basement kitchen (the stairway to which is lined with maps – I get the feeling I'll like this guy), we discuss his Underground stardom.

'I was the section of the line between King's Cross and Earl's Court,' he says. 'Alternate stations, that is. The other voice was a woman's. Presumably because otherwise you'd go, "Strange, I could swear that man was at Covent Garden and now it's Leicester Square and he's here as well."'

So he was the voice on the platform rather than the train? 'Yes.' He gives an ever-so-'umble sniff. 'I don't aspire to trains.' His announcement in full was: 'This is [e.g.] Green Park. The next station is Hyde Park Corner. Please stand clear of the closing doors.' Except at Russell Square, which was the only station whose ill-fitting platform needed those three legendary words. 'Yes, that one began with "mind the gap". Actually, it was, "Please mind the gap." British politeness, you know.'

If the Tube were a sitcom character (and on a bad day it can be), 'mind the gap' would be its catchphrase. How did

Tim feel, being the one to deliver it? 'Actually, at first I never used to tell anyone, partly because I didn't want it to get out that David Archer was the voice of "mind the gap", but also because my kids were at school. You know what children are like. I could just imagine the bullying: [sneering voice] "Mind the gap . . . your dad's mind the gap." But as they grew up and it gradually got out, it turned out this was actually a bit of kudos for them. Their mates thought it was rather cool.'

Quite right too. The phrase is part of London's aural landscape, as Tim acknowledges. 'It's on T-shirts, mugs, people have done songs called "Mind the Gap", books, movies. There's even a film production company called that. It's in people's consciousness. I did *Through the Keyhole*, and David Frost talked to me about *The Archers*, my other acting, other stuff I've done – no reaction from the audience. Then he got me to do "mind the gap" and they broke out into a huge round of applause.'

A happy accident was that Russell Square was where Tim's wife, Judy, got out for work. 'I found it very comforting,' she says, appearing in the kitchen briefly. 'Whenever he said "Mind the gap", I'd think, "Thank you, darling, I will." The boys said they found it nice too, especially when they were starting to travel on the Tube by themselves. It was good to have their dad looking out for them.'

What about Tim himself? 'It was funny. Sometimes you'd hear people having a laugh about it, sort of taking the piss a bit. I'd be sitting there thinking, "You're having a go at me, and you don't know it's me." Foreigners, too – of course they don't know what it means. "What is this gap? Where is gap?" Part of me did want someone to slip, go down the gap, so I'd be able to say, "I told you.'"

Tim did a one-man show recently, and, needing a recording of his announcement, went down to Holborn. 'At first the guy in the control room looked at me as if I was mad. Then I finally managed to convince him it really was me, but I still had to go and ask someone else, blah blah blah – in the end it was easier for me to come home, record myself saying it again and put some Tube noise on in the background.'

What about the financial rewards? The royalties must have been incredible. 'That's what I thought. Straight after the session, walking away from the studio, I was on the phone to my agent, saying, "How much was that?" She said, "Two hundred pounds." I said, "No, not the session fee: the usage." She said, "There is no usage – it's a flat two hundred pounds."' Tim sighs, but it's clear from the way he talks that whatever the financial regrets, he's also proud of being part of the capital's heritage.[6]

Perversely, Tim's concern for those who *don't* live in the city has backfired. 'When we were doing the Holborn announcements I thought, "They've only read it in their guidebooks, they're not going to know it's pronounced Hoe-bun." So to give them a bit of a chance I added the slightest, faintest hint of an "l" in there, just edging towards

6. I don't think you can truly understand how much the Underground means to Londoners until you've been a Londoner yourself. At university I asked a girl from London whether she ever used the Tube. Her puzzlement at the question was the only answer it needed.

"Hol-bun". The *flak* I got from friends who heard it. "You don't know how to pronounce Holborn, ha ha." It bugged me for fifteen years — wished I'd never done it.'

Then came the day when Tim heard someone else at one of 'his' stations. Then another, and another . . . The lights were going out all over London. Goodbye Piccadilly Circus, farewell Leicester Square. 'It ended up with me just being at Russell Square. That was my last bastion. Which at least meant Judy could hear me. But then even that stopped.' The end of an era, at least for Tim.

The very beginnings of the 'mind the gap' announcement were in the late sixties, when London Underground decided to use recording technology to save their staff's vocal chords. But the actor they used for the session demanded royalties, and, as Tim was to find, London Underground don't do royalties. So they used the version that Peter Lodge, the studio engineer, had recorded for level. 'They still use that one at some stations,' says Tim. 'It's incredibly posh. But then that's what it was like back then. You could [Cockney accent] be a geezer who talked like this, and as soon as they put a microphone in front of you it was, "I say, do mind the gap."'

One of the voices currently gracing the network belongs to my friend Emma Clarke. Unlike Tim she did aspire to trains, and can be heard on several of the lines, the Central, Victoria and Bakerloo among them, though not the Piccadilly and certainly not the Northern, where a woman overdoes the poshness at Highgate, rendering it the old-fashioned 'Highgut'. The fact that I know Emma does take away a fraction of the Tube's mystique when I'm on her lines, though in return I've heard some great stories. There was the recording session where after 'Mary Le Bone', 'Marry Le Bone' and 'Marl Ee Bone', they (in all seriousness) asked her to try 'Mary Lob On'. And there's been the hate mail. Yes, people – very often from Texas, apparently – go to the trouble of searching out Emma's identity, then her website, so that they can communicate their anger at just how much her announcements ruined their Tube journey. One criticised her dentistry. Another called her a 'tacky bitch'.

When it comes to London, Tim's another 'can't live in it, can't live without it' merchant, or rather he can't live in it the whole time. Several years ago he inherited a cottage in Norfolk, where he and his wife now spend weekends. 'I couldn't live in the country all the time – it would drive me round the bend – but equally living in London the whole time would drive me round the bend. We've got used to this peripatetic, half-and-half thing.' He talks about being in the club at the top of Centrepoint, the one that showed me a mixed-up City skyline. 'On a clear day you can see the greenbelt around whole parts of London; it's like the city is ringed by green.' It reminds me of the view from Tower 42, seeing Epping Forest and the countryside beyond Metroland. The memory elicits a feeling of safety, a comforting knowledge that London, enchanting monster that it is, remains under control, securely caged.

Tim's also aware of how people in different professions see London differently. 'Soho is still a village if you're in my job. That's where all the studios are, so because it's a community of voice artists there's not a day goes by that I don't see someone I know and we'll stop and have a chat. We'll have a cigarette, catch up on the gossip. Bruno's Café on Wardour Street [just north of Old Compton Street, a genuine old Italian tea-and-formica place] is a second home for me. Nothing better than having a big breakfast there, do the crossword.'

I mention that I once saw Tom Baker in there, eating egg and chips, obviously between voice sessions. 'Oh, yes, Tom's an aficionado of the Bruno,' says Tim. When I was there some cabbies were sitting with their legs blocking the aisle, prompting an 'Excuse me, gents, could I just get through?' Hearing these mundane words delivered in such recognisable tones was a treat my mental dictaphone replayed for the rest of the day.

Another London trait shared by Tim is that he has stayed living in the area he first got to know. 'When I was a kid we lived near Berkhamsted. My mum died when I was thirteen, so I was sort of home alone and I'd come into town to visit my dad, who worked in Berkeley Square [at J. Walter Thompson, the legendary advertising agency – hence Tim's entry into a branch of the profession]. I always thought that was fantasti-cally exciting. Then my sister married a guy and they moved to Camden Passage in Islington, and I'd visit her. So that was the first bit of London I really got to grips with, and when I got married we sort of gravitated here.' He moved to his current house in 1982, the same year he moved to Ambridge.

'I couldn't possibly go to live anywhere else now. And that north/south divide is absolutely there. If you're North London you can't live south of the river, and vice versa. It would be like living in a foreign country for me.' We mention the recent Underground map that omitted the

Thames. Public reaction was so hostile that the map was instantly withdrawn. Until now I've never really felt the importance of the river to London's identity. Water's never been my thing, be it rivers or the sea, and the Thames is now so easy to get over and under that I never really notice it. The bridges, yes, and the views you get from them, but not the actual wet stuff. Talking with Tim, though, the river's role as a boundary comes to the fore. I'm reminded of that friend of Rachel's grandmother who'd never been 'across the water'. With our modern wealth of crossings we can easily forget that until 1750 there was only one, London Bridge. Opposition from the watermen was a big factor in vetoing plans for new bridges; when the second one (Westminster) opened, it did for the horse ferry that gave the nearby road its name.[7]

'Driving in South London is the worst,' adds Tim. 'When I'm down there I become a bus-route driver. Whereas up here I know all the streets, all the shortcuts.'

Until they change the one-ways, I say. Which they do all the time.

Tim gives a 'tell me about it' grimace. 'They're barking mad, these people in Islington. It's not just one-ways, it's the bloody speed humps too. And the street furniture. Every single junction has got fifteen signs all repeating each other. You think, have you got no aesthetic values at all? Do you

---

7. The boat operators have never really had a good name; to this day the Watermen and Lightermen (passengers and goods respectively) are not a full livery company, an exclusion originally imposed because they charged those fleeing the Great Fire.

not understand what architecture is meant to be? That when this was laid out by the Victorians they meant it to look like this, and you've gone and completely ruined it with these totally pointless signs which nobody ever looks at because there are so bloody *many* of them?'

The nostalgia sensors are bleeping here, but it's a false alarm: Tim's argument is spot on. My agreement, though, is from a pedestrian's point of view, since I very rarely drive in London. It seems a generational thing. People who got their licences before, say, 1985 see it as perfectly natural to drive around London, whereas the rest of us have been conditioned by stricter drink-driving laws and later the Congestion Charge to ask 'What's the point?' We prefer someone else, be they in charge of a bus, a Tube or (if we've recently won the Lottery) a taxi to do the driving for us. The previously quoted volume of Michael Palin's diaries that saw him strolling around Paris covers the 1980s, a decade in which he simultaneously champions public transport yet goes everywhere around London by car. He's regularly tootling into the West End, including one memorable night when he offers George Harrison a lift home but then can't find the car, forcing the attention-hating Beatle to parade up and down a Charlotte Street packed with pavement diners.

Out on the Caledonian Road late-afternoon darkness has descended. The sheets of a Sky Sports billboard have been carelessly pasted, compressing Michael Owen's face so he looks like Les Dawson in the Cissy and Ada sketches. Pentonville Prison looms on the left, the hanging beam from the old Newgate jail bricked up in what is now its synagogue. Across the road is Knowledge Point, the school Rachel mentioned. I pop in and loiter outside the side-by-side entrances to the two practice rooms. Each contains a dozen tables, their tops filled with huge laminated maps of London. Pairs of would-be cabbies face each other across the maps, like combatants over infinitely complex chess boards, except they're trying to help their opponent, naming runs to see if he can correctly call them.[8] 'Comply roundabout, forward Peartree Way, left Parkside . . .' 'Left Formby Avenue, right Kenton Lane, left Ivanhoe Drive . . .' The combined mutterings are hypnotic, like the chanting in a monastery, a respectful hum in worship of the great god Knowledge. Though there can't be many monasteries where you'd hear the sentence, 'As soon as I went Maddox Street I'd fucking had it, hadn't I?'

Halfway down the Cally, after the very smart parlour offering 'Bespoke Tattooing and Piercing', the pavement is graced with a pristine pair of pink knickers. Then it's King's Cross, in Frank Dobson's constituency of Holborn and St Pancras, hence his nickname – coined by the late Tory MP Nicholas Fairbairn – 'the Member for two Tube stations'. The intervening stop is Russell Square, where a tall twenty-something emerges, his trousers slightly too short, reading a book in so self-aware a manner that he surely can't be taking anything in. After Holborn I head down towards Covent Garden, the old area known as Seven Dials to my right, where in 1767 the Annual Register

8. On the day I visit it is exclusively 'he', though the racial mix is wide, conjuring bizarre memories of the classroom in *Mind Your Language*.

recorded a man going home 'in expectation of having his dinner ready, but found his wife on the bed intoxicated with liquor; on which he placed a train of gunpowder, with the diabolical resolution to blow her up, but in setting fire to the flame he was so terribly burnt that he was carried to the hospital with little hopes of recovery. The woman escaped unhurt.'

Then it's Leicester Square, and in the living nightmare that is the junction of Charing Cross Road and Cranbourn Street I for once force myself to find a quiet spot, pause and look up. This is stations at dawn, Tube architecture's very own *X Factor* final: the terracotta building on the north side of the junction is by our old friend Leslie Green, the later grey concrete one on the south side by Charles Holden. As if the materials themselves didn't give you the hands-down winner, the fact that Green's building incorporates three cricket stumps and the words 'J Wisden & Compy' proves the clincher. The first-floor offices were originally occupied by the publishers of the fat yellow book.

On Piccadilly, passing the Burlington Arcade, I stop and ask one of the uniformed beadles (the arcade's private police) exactly why it is you're forbidden from whistling there. I'll admit that an ornate builder's trill can be irritating, but the arcade's ban has always seemed a touch harsh to me. 'It was because these first-floor rooms,' replies the beadle, indicating the spaces above the purveyors of posh ties, shoes and watches, 'used to be occupied by prostitutes, and when they saw guards coming they'd whistle to warn their pickpocket friends down here.' The narrow arcade's other no-nos, such as hurrying, opening umbrellas or pushing prams, still seem reasonable today. Then it's past the hotel opened in 1905 by César Ritz, who ensured his female guests would feel beautiful by using diffused lighting from alabaster bowls, and then, next to Green Park station, the house on the corner of Stratton Street where Queen Victoria used to gaze down from a top-floor window because it was 'the only place where I can go to see the traffic without stopping it'. Outside it today a harassed mother tells her toddler son, 'You're really starting to piss me off.'

Hyde Park Corner, my twentieth station of the day, faces a statue of Achilles just inside the park gates. His skimpy apparel offended public opinion when this tribute to Wellington appeared in 1822. One correspondent informed the *Morning Herald* that if his mother 'who was a Newcastle woman, had caught any of her children looking at such an object, she would have soundly whipped them'. It's prim up North. Around Knightsbridge, the line makes a rare departure from that 'follow the road' rule of early Tube lines: a seventeenth-century plague pit sent it well south of Harrods. I catch a glimpse of the Tea Clipper pub on Montpelier Street, where a friend of mine once had a drink bought for her by Clint Eastwood, whom she'd saved from a pestering colleague. Just before South Kensington station another rightwards glance reveals Exhibition Road, leading up to the Royal Geographical Society's building whose statues of David Livingstone and Ernest Shackleton have earned it the cabbies' nickname 'Hot and Cold Corner'. Next door to that is the Royal Albert Hall, venue in 1909 for an indoor marathon: 524 laps of the arena and only two competitors – one of whom failed to finish, surely owing to dizziness. From a vent in the tunnel between South Ken station and Exhibition Road emerges the sound of a busker's saxophone playing the *Pink Panther* theme. It adds a nice touch of silliness to the museumic grandeur round here.

Past Gloucester Road, and then Earl's Court. On the main Talgarth Road, two Thai men stand smoking outside a grubby B&B, wearing pyjama bottoms and T-shirts; an advertising hoarding nearby announces that the temperature is minus one. A wheelless bicycle frame has been left chained to the railings, the second such sight today, carcasses of the urban jungle. Yet a flyer for a local cleaning company wafting down the street announces that 'you will have the same person each time'; relationships count even here. Approaching Barons Court I fear disappointment – but no, if anything the station is even more attractive than I remember it. Then it's Hammersmith, and at nearly eight o'clock, the welcoming sight of tonight's hotel.

Thinking back on today's 19 miles, the one that stands out (slightly less than one, actually – 0.78) is Piccadilly. It usually does stand out, because of its beauty and history, its quint-essential Englishness, even the name, which derives from those ruffed-up Elizabethan collars called piccadills: a man who'd made his fortune from them built his mansion there. Bertie Wooster lived off it (Half Moon Street), while Lord Peter Wimsey lived on it (110a Piccadilly, chosen in tribute to 221b Baker Street). William Fortnum and Hugh Mason[9] still emerge

---

9. No relation. Sadly.

from the clock outside their store every hour and bow to each other. But none of this is what struck me tonight. What hits home as I think about Piccadilly is how alive it seemed, almost literally alive, like an organic being. Like a person.

You can overdo this sort of thing. If I had to find a piddling fault with the brilliant London writing of Peter Ackroyd, it would be his contention that different parts of the city have different personalities, by which he doesn't just mean character, he actually means *person*alities. Yet tonight even that reservation slips away. London does seem like a person. Whether friend or foe is unclear, but a person nonetheless. That's what sets it apart from other big cities – Manchester, say, or Birmingham – which have got greatness to them, in size if nothing else, but aren't truly great. They may have character, but that character is always the same. Manchester: smirkingly cynical. Birmingham: well, there's a reason for the old joke about a true Brummie being born within the sound of someone moaning. But London has mood swings. The rationalist may contend that these are only mirrors of your own mood at any given time; but at least that capacity is there in London, and that's what shows it's alive. Manchester and Birmingham always bend you to their own mood.

We humans have our tangible physical presence but have never been able to pin down the soul. We debate whether it's in the heart, the brain, the senses or the blood, when of course it's in all of these things and none, hence the age-old mystery of consciousness. I think London's soul evades capture in exactly the same way. It has its buildings, its roads and streets, its rivers and sewers, its inhabitants, its visitors, its vehicles, its power supplies, its signage (sorry, Tim) . . . And yet what is it that brings it to life? All of these things and none.

The next morning starts at eight. As it's a Saturday there are very few people up, only those who have to be, hunched against the cold as they wait for buses to take them to work. My short-term destination, on the other hand, is casting a vaguely bizarre shadow over proceedings. Because today is the day that I'll do something I can't imagine any sane person ever contemplating: walk to Heathrow Airport.

Turnham Green is summed up by the fact that the Low Cost Mini Market has gone bust but the Himalayan Day Spa next door seems to be thriving. A jogger passes on Chiswick Common. Suffolk instincts kick in and I say hello, forcing him to do likewise, wasting breath that's in short supply. I feel guilty. A woman wears black ear muffs, obviously aiming for elegance, but I can't help thinking of Minnie Mouse. The chairs in the Bollo gastropub are all stacked, though a few doors down a team of builders are up and working on a house conversion. A sign announces that the firm's name is Zulu Fish. That's the sort of thing builders are called round here.

Just to the east of Acton Town is a housing estate, one of whose high-rises, Harlech Tower, gained fame as Nelson Mandela House in *Only Fools and Horses* (a long way from Peckham). A sign asks, 'Have you seen this dog? Answers to Zelda. But it's deaf.' Happier news up the road, where someone declares that they've found a cat (picture included), and invites the owner to call. A camper van opposite Gunnersbury Park, its curtains drawn, has the word

'Cockfosters' written on it; is someone else following the Piccadilly Line? On a parallel side street (my route to South Ealing) there's another van labelled 'Sheepshagger', then 'Morning Glory' and 'In and Around the Mouth'. The latter two are marked 'Van Tour 2010'. Who can imagine what the vans' insides are like? Who would want to? On Almond Way an electricity substation hums ominously, while two young Russian men, still drunk from a night out, stagger home, stopping every few steps to argue and/or giggle. All this and the vans before nine o'clock. You think suburbia's a bland place, then it throws you these grenades of strangeness.

The cut-through from Northfields starts with Blondin Avenue, named after adopted local boy Charles, the parallel avenue being Niagara; the fact that his first crossing of the falls ended with him saying 'thank God that's over' didn't stop him repeating it several times (blindfolded, on stilts, stopping halfway to cook an omelette . . .). After the next station, Boston Manor, a combination of the M4 and the Grand Union Canal forces me to go the long way round, down on to the Great West Road. The scale of this – several lanes of roaring A4 – sets the mood for what's at the end of this branch of the line: Heathrow Airport. Although there's heavy cloud this morning, putting the planes out of sight, the sound of them is getting more and more noticeable. Not intimidating yet, just a reminder of who governs this corner of London.

But with its consistent inconsistency, London has one more dose of suburbia for me before the final approach to Heathrow. After Osterley I veer south of the A4, and even further south away from the motorway, into a succession of quiet (if not especially attractive) streets and avenues. At a newsagent's next to Hounslow East station a Montessori school advertises for teachers with a handwritten note on a brown paper bag – surely not the image they want to promote? At one point, near Hounslow Central, the peace is shattered by the sudden flapping of a swan's wings as it passes overhead. Given the size of the bird, its flight seems a far more incredible feat of aeronautics than even the largest jumbo.

Hounslow West is down-to-earth verging on depressing. In a car park next door a market offers cheap cleaning products, cheap furniture, cheap everything. After nearly three hours on the road I've earned a cup of tea in the station café, where miserable-looking people eat fried eggs and chips while a radio DJ asks his caller if she wants to 'shout anyone out' before the next banging record. I distract myself with a 2008 diary retrieved from a patch of grass back in South Ealing (it's taken this long for the frozen pages to thaw). You shouldn't read diaries, of course, but this is a business rather than personal one, and anyway they threw it away, didn't they? It obviously belonged to a builder: January and February are full of quotes for kitchens and bathrooms, payments made to labourers, costs of materials bought. In April he enjoys two weeks in Valencia. July and August start to look quiet. In September there's nothing. Then: '1 Oct – 10 a.m. – Job Centre'.

This is where the airport really starts to dominate. I'm back on to dual carriageways now, lined with warehouses set well back from the road and labelled things like 'British Airways World Cargo'. Outside one of them sits Concorde.

A plane appears from behind a terraced house as though it's taken off in the garden. Hearing one overhead I look up, and when it appears in a gap between the clouds it's at about half the height I'd expected – I physically flinch. But by the time the A4 reaches Hatton Cross I've got used to the idea, and positively relish the noise of the jets still on their climb from the eastward-facing runways. The ponies grazing in the field opposite seem unimpressed, but two middle-aged blokes have brought their sons here, to the strip of grass between the road and the perimeter fence, just to savour the experience. Depending on which runway the plane has used, it can be as low as 300 feet as it banks directly above you, vapour trails shimmering, the roar of its engines drowning out not just conversation but thought itself, leaving only an animal thrill. For anyone with a young child (or who still thinks of themself as one – yes, that means you), there are far worse days out in London than a trip to Hatton Cross Tube station.

It takes another half-hour of hugging the perimeter fence to my right before Heathrow Terminal 4 appears. The curved ramp up to it has a very narrow pavement, but pavement it is nonetheless, and soon I'm standing in the terminal building. It feels strange to be here having used no powered or wheeled form of transport whatsoever. Flying is such an adventure that it's impossible to conceive of arriving at the place that lets you do it simply by walking. You feel that the Heathrow Express, or the Tube, or the cab, or whatever it is that delivers you to the airport is a necessary part of the experience, as though air travel takes place in a separate dimension inaccessible to mere pedestrians. Yet here I am. It's simultaneously enjoyable (a bizarre new experience that would surely never have happened were it not for this project) and disappointing (it's taken some of the mystery away not just from this airport but the very notion of an airport). A lift delivers me to the Tube station, then back up and out into the cold afternoon air. The walk round to Terminal 5, at the very western end of Heathrow, takes another hour. Warehouses and roundabouts pass slowly by. Planes queue to take off, the enormous whines and rumbles and roars as they taxi towards the runway giving the airport the feel of a dinosaur park.

Terminal 5 may be a giant vacuum chute for luggage, but architecturally it's a winner: a huge glass frontage, large and airy inside, with escalators to the Tube taking you down through a cavernous hall. After that, though, working my way round the west and then north of the perimeter, towards Heathrow's third and final Tube station (Terminals 1, 2 and 3), a small cloud of depression descends. Even the American Airlines plane that feels as though it's going to land on my head can't blow that away. For this is the one part of today's journey – the one part of the whole project – that it won't be possible to complete on foot. The tunnel which goes under the runways, connecting the perimeter road with the terminal, used to be open to pedestrians – but no longer. Even the narrow cycle lane, which I was thinking of using, has been opened up to cars, which have to toodle along behind any bikes there might be. Not much fun walking three-quarters of a mile with a Mondeo up your derrière. The gate to the old pedestrian path is locked shut, and while it would just be possible to squeeze round the edge, CCTV cameras dot this whole area like acne; I wouldn't last more than a minute. Everything screams what my advance research has led me to fear: this really is the Land that Feet Forgot.

It's an irritation, but not a huge one, and actually serves as an exception-to-the-rule reminder of how pedestrian-friendly London is. There have been points, mainly up in the north-west of the city, near the M1 on the Northern Line, or the Westway on the Central, where I've worried that whatever the *A to Z* might seem to show, pedestrians wouldn't be welcome. But no, wherever four wheels are allowed, so are two feet. Walking these routes may not be pleasant, or quiet, or anything but calamitous for your lungs – but you can do it. And that's something to be proud of in a city.

Right here, though, all I can do is wait for the free shuttle bus. When it comes I get on board and, determined to stay as true to the project as it's possible to be, insist on standing the whole way to the terminal.

By now it's 2 p.m., so I have a late lunch at Caffè Nero, listening to the delightful tannoy announcements ('this is the last and final call for . . .'), then bus it back to the perimeter road. Somewhere round here, I've read, is a spot that holds a special place in any cartophile's heart: a cannon, buried upright in the ground, marking one end of the first triangulation line on which all the Ordnance Survey's subsequent measurements were based. Laid out in 1784, the distance between here and the other cannon in Hampton (about five miles away) was measured by General William Roy, after men of the 18th Regiment of Foot had levelled the intervening ground. The cannon takes a bit of finding, so much so that a planespotter, standing alone and red-faced in the biting wind, has never noticed it, his expression implying he thinks I'm socially inadequate for even looking. (It's come to this.) Eventually it appears, lurking behind some bushes near the business car park. The plaque reveals that Roy's original measurement was accurate to within three inches.

It's staggering to find that, within minutes of starting the northward offline slog to Uxbridge, I'm in countryside. There are fields, farm buildings, a village(ish) feel to the settlement of Sipson.[10] A bus stop amplifies the impression with its sign 'towards Cranford', though Elizabeth Gaskell's village was (a) in Cheshire and (b) fictional. How can you go from Heathrow to this so quickly? The Homer Simpson 'duh' moment arrives soon enough – where else are you going to build a runway except in a field? – but it reveals the contradiction inherent in any big airport. Heathrow is not just one but several huge buildings, full of flashy computer screens and men with sub-machine guns, which a lot of people reach by its own train service, and where you need all sorts of ID documents. What could be more urban than that? And yet it's also the edge of London, the place where, by definition, you leave the city. Walking its perimeter today, seeing the uncut grass and clumps of mud just inside the fence, demystified Heathrow for me, reduced its capacity to intimidate. It's nothing but a field with attitude.

The less said about West Drayton the better.[11] It takes an

---

10. Which they want to preserve, hence the anti-third runway posters.
11. It has a pub called the De Burgh Arms – you do worry about the music.

hour and a half to reach Uxbridge, which like Oxford took its name from the cattle that used to pass through. There are still olde-worlde streets nestling in the shadow of the modern shopping centre. Both work well in their centuries-distant ways. Sitting in the middle, temperamentally as well as geographically, is the Tube station, another Charles Holden creation (as are several others on this branch). Unlike some of his stations at the northern end of the line, this one is impressive. It's a lot bigger, being incorporated into a parade of shops, and there's something about this scale that allows the design – boxier and less sensuous than Green's terracotta marvels – to work. The stained-glass windows in the ticket hall are beautiful, especially now that winter-afternoon darkness has come and they're illuminated by the modern street lighting.

Saturday's shopping is reaching its pre-conclusion frenzy. Is it illegal to drive a shopmobility vehicle while using a mobile phone? If not it should be, based on the example of the woman who nearly mows me down. Life is safer once the town centre has been negotiated, and the quiet streets of Hillingdon and Ickenham and Ruislip settle down for another cosy night in. A boy dressed as Santa plays on his Wii. I pass the second Acacia Avenue of the project. But as this morning in Acton, suburbia has a store of incongruities up its sleeve: a bus route is called U2 . . . a bare, undecorated front room contains nothing but a freshly pressed naval uniform, still in its dry-cleaning wrapper, hanging from a door . . . a house is called Kenneth Lodge. Perhaps the weirdness is heightened because I'm tired and cold (frost is reappearing on windscreens), but there's another reason too: I'm back in Metroland.

This is the third line that's brought me here, and as Ruislip Manor gives way to Eastcote, I begin to conclude that there's something unreal about this part of London, its residents hung on the Tube lines like so many Christmas cards. Part of you likes it, especially the areas that live up to those beautiful old ads of the early twentieth century: 'Your chance – seize it . . . the district leaves nothing to be desired . . . the Estate is but 20 minutes from Town by the fast and frequent train service . . .' There are some very large houses, in which it can't be anything but a pleasure to live.[12] 'And all that day in murky London Wall,' wrote John Betjeman, 'the thought of Ruislip kept him warm inside.' Perhaps, though, on a night like tonight Rayners Lane's nickname comes to mind more easily; because of its windswept platforms it was known in the 1920s as Pneumonia Junction.[13] Despite the good things about it, the climate of optimism and expansion in which Metroland was built, you can't quite escape the urge to scream and shout and run away, run towards London. As Julian Barnes put it: 'you lived there because it was an area easy to get out of'. The structures that really stick in your mind are the Tube stations themselves. They were here first, waiting

---

12. Though it's disappointing that between South Harrow and Sudbury Hill some of them have seceded to create a private estate, slinging a white gate across the road to bar motorists (not pedestrians, though – I march blithely on). This feels disturbingly American, as well as a rebuttal of everything cities stand for.

13. The station's subsequent passenger numbers tell the story of Metroland's expansion. 1930: 22,000. 1937: 4 million.

for the developers to cluster round. Some are visually appealing too, Sudbury Town being another Holden success. But when the buildings that define an area are the ones that enable you to leave it, what does that tell you?

The final few miles are hard work, harder with every step. Well past 30 miles for the day now. That seems to be the figure at which the endorphin-high begins to wear off, its place taken at first by a neutrally vacant feeling, then actual depression. Everything is viewed through this new prism. The fact that Sudbury has a fast-food outlet called Tennessee Halal Chicken would at any other time have made me laugh; now it leaves me (very) cold. After Alperton, on the Westway, there's Park Royal: it lives up to neither word of its name (which actually derives from the Royal Agricultural Society's Edwardian exhibitions here), and even the thought that local kids use the station's easily accessible roof for summer sunbathing, prompting the tannoy announcement 'please come down, this is not a holiday resort', fails to raise a smile. Between North Ealing and Ealing Common a couple sit on opposite sides of a table in their front room, each staring silently at a laptop. They're probably just catching up on emails, but I insist on seeing an imminent divorce.

Journey's end, however, brings its own relief, when at 9.22 p.m. I collapse through the ticket barriers at Acton Town. Today's mileometer comes to a halt at 39.5 (if I'd been allowed to walk the Heathrow tunnel it would have been 40.8), bringing the total for the line to a shade under 60. All of this inspires a warm fellow feeling with the Ealing fruit pickers who used to walk from near here to Covent Garden in the eighteenth century, a journey of about nine miles, often doing it there and back twice in a day. Changing from the Piccadilly to the Central Line, I get a West Indian driver who completes his 'remember your belongings' announcement with, 'Wherever you go, whatever you do, and whatever the weather, have a lovely weekend. God bless and take care.' He's following in an honourable tradition, so honourable that several websites have been set up to record drivers' gems. They include:

*Ladies and Gentlemen, I do apologise for the delay to your service. I know you're all dying to get home – unless, of course, you happen to be married to my ex-wife, in which case you'll want to cross over to the Westbound and go in the opposite direction.*

*Ladies and gentlemen, we apologise for the delay, but there is a security alert at Victoria station and we are therefore stuck here for the foreseeable future, so let's take our minds off it and pass some time together. All together now: 'Ten green bottles, hanging on a wall . . .'*

*To the gentleman wearing the long grey coat, trying to get on the second carriage: what part of 'Stand clear of the doors' don't you understand?*

You just don't get that sort of thing on the Paris Metro.

# 9
# Waterloo and City
# Line / Jubilee Line

## The dreamlike world of the mad

One night, at 3 a.m., Samuel Johnson heard a knock on his door. It was two of his friends – drink had been taken – urging him to come out for a walk. 'What, is it you, you dogs?' replied Johnson. 'I'll have a frisk with you!' They went to Covent Garden, where they offered to help the greengrocers arrange their stalls (curiously the offer was declined), then to a tavern, then down to the river where they obtained a boat and rowed to Billingsgate. At one point Johnson railed against sleep: 'Short, O short then be thy reign, And give us to the world again!'

London at night is a changed city. The difference is greater than on a Sunday, the version I explored on the District Line walk. While the Sabbath is growing more and more like the rest of the week, night-time is still the right time for getting some kip. I've always enjoyed walking round London during the small hours, usually when insomnia strikes, though occasionally as a pursuit in itself. It's only now, when I decide to do it for the project, that the reason becomes clear: it's because London's guard is down. Whether you're trying to counter the city's bullying quality that Geoff and I discussed, or you simply want to solve the mystery of its appeal, exploring London at night increases your chances. The empty streets give more room for reflection, more space to flex your mental muscles. When the giant is sleeping the odds are evened.

It has to be the Jubilee Line, the one remaining single-dayer that can be converted into a single-nighter. Before heading up to Stanmore, though, I decide to spend the early part of this Thursday evening knocking off the runt of the Underground litter, that mile and a half of tunnel that somehow got itself promoted to parity with the big boys: the Waterloo and City. It only links two stations, Waterloo and Bank, though we shouldn't really criticise it for that as it's the very reason the line was created (in 1898), to let all those Surrey stockbrokers nip straight across to the office. Still, it's not what you'd call a challenge: you could fit the entire line twice over into the gap between Chalfont and Latimer and Chesham on the Metropolitan Line.[1] The route is easy enough – from Waterloo, the line burrows under Stamford Street to just west of Blackfriars Bridge, where it turns left under the river, arriving at the bridge's north end. Then it's right and along Queen Victoria Street all the way to Bank. The descents to get under the riverbed are really quite sharp – ride the line and you'll experience something alarmingly close to freefall. As if that wasn't bad enough, the Waterloo

---

1. The network's longest gap between stations: 3.89 miles.

and City is known to its drivers as the Drain, owing to the leakiness of the tunnels. The water has to be continually pumped out.

Leaving Waterloo station at seven o'clock, against the tide of Home Counties-bound commuters, I descend the steps towards the enormous IMAX cinema. The line runs straight underneath this, only 12 feet below the surface; the building had to be mounted on anti-vibration bearings to prevent any interference with customers' 3D viewing pleasure. Another stunning modern building is the Coin Street Neighbourhood Centre on Stamford Street – it looks like luxury flats. Gives you hope that London council provision doesn't have to be all concrete and worthiness. In a doorway on Hatfields, the street leading up to the Oxo Tower, a woman waits with a vacuum cleaner. As I pass she gives it a concerned glance, as though it's a pet dog.

I pass the art galleries and craft shops on the ground floor of the Oxo Tower. By the 1970s the beef extract itself was no longer made here; the company only used the building for creating 'long eggs', the ones you find in meat pies and which are actually several eggs combined (yolks and whites separated, cooked separately, then put back together to form one enormous egg). Across the water, on the Embankment, two female joggers pass me for the second time in ten minutes – they've obviously looped round over Waterloo Bridge. Heading up Queen Victoria Street I pass a heavyweight four-storey building, constructed in 1866 by the British and Foreign Bible Association, with wooden glass-fronted noticeboards incorporated into the stonework of its ground floor. These

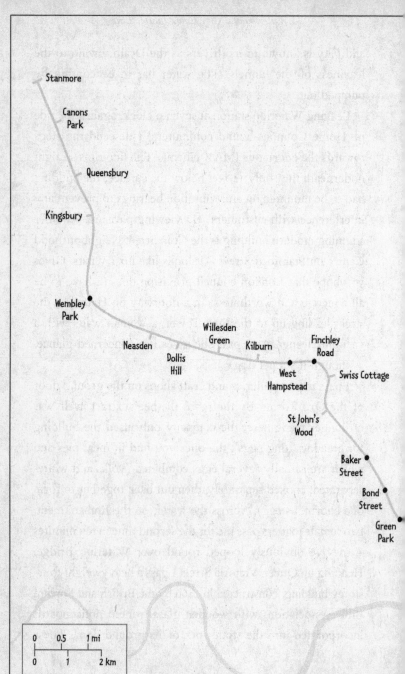

Stanmore

Canons Park

Queensbury

Kingsbury

Wembley Park

Neasden

Dollis Hill

Willesden Green

Kilburn

West Hampstead

Finchley Road

Swiss Cottage

St John's Wood

Baker Street

Bond Street

Green Park

| 0 | 0.5 | 1 mi |
| 0 | 1 | 2 km |

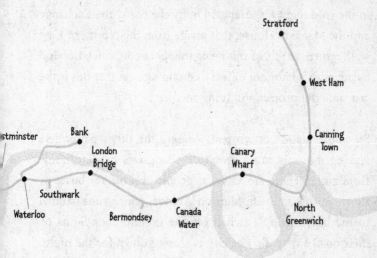

Stratford

West Ham

Canning
Town

Bank

London
Bridge

Canary
Wharf

stminster

Southwark

Waterloo

Bermondsey

Canada
Water

North
Greenwich

N

now house plasma screens playing adverts for the building's new owner, the Church of Scientology.

The rest of the walk is an object lesson in London's juxtaposition of yesterday and tomorrow. Queen Victoria Street is lined alternately with Wren churches and the College of Arms – buildings from the era of the woman after whom the street is named – and glass-and-light twenty-first-century office blocks. Summing up the message of old meets new is the pair of buildings you can see ahead all the way along, drawing you on to the line's terminus: the Royal Exchange lying in the shadow of the Gherkin. Just over half an hour after leaving Waterloo I arrive at that terminus, where the station entrance at the corner of Princes Street and Threadneedle Street is built into the Bank of England itself, making it the Tube's only Grade I-listed structure. Standing in the cold night air, triangled in by the Bank, the Exchange and the Mansion House, that image from the Northern Line walk returns to me, of this being the spot upon which London balances. It's hard not to feel a certain sadness that this is the last time the project will bring me here.

Stanmore station, 11.30 p.m. Among the other passengers leaving the train are a group of youngsters heading home from a gig. There are kisses as people peel off for buses or short walks home. On Merrion Avenue, which runs parallel to the line, a couple switch off the ground-floor lights of their post-war semi. The city is closing down for the night. My walk is only just beginning. There's a certain pleasure in contrariness.

The grass on Howberry Avenue's mini-roundabouts has been neatly mowed. Stanmore's dull respectability is summed up by the fact that until he became Prime Minister this was where Clement Attlee lived. Canons Park, the next station, where two women wait for a car at the minicab office next door, takes its name from the mansion of the Duke of Chandos, built here in 1718, where mealtimes were accompanied by an orchestra playing music specially composed by Handel. The building lasted less than 30 years, but its colonnade survived and is now on the front of the National Gallery. These lost aristocratic roots seem fitting for the Jubilee Line. It had never occurred to me until now to wonder where the name comes from. Only in Richard's latest email have I learned that the Jubilee in question was the Queen's silver one, hence the line's colour on the map. But this was 1970s Britain, remember. The line didn't get up and running[2] until 1979, two years after the street parties had packed away their bunting.

On Honeypot Lane, which used to have clay soil that became sticky during wet weather (hence the name) but is now a dual carriageway with speed cameras, I pass the offices of the local Community Mental Health Team, and am reminded of 'Night Walks'. This is an essay by probably London's most famous pedestrian, the man who said that 'if I could not walk far and fast, I think I should just explode

---

2. Technically most of it already had been up and running – the Jubilee took over what had previously been a branch of the Bakerloo Line. The only new bit was from Baker Street to Charing Cross, where the line terminated until its extension in the late 1990s.

and perish', adding that he must be 'the descendant, at no great distance, of some irreclaimable tramp'. Averaging anywhere between 15 and 20 miles a day, and (according to his friend Marcus Stone) making sure he increased his speed whenever he ascended a hill, Charles Dickens even set out at 2 a.m. once to walk from London to his home in Kent. The episode in 'Night Walks' I'm thinking of now is where Dickens passes Bethlem Hospital, now the Imperial War Museum: 'Are not the sane and the insane equal at night,' he asks, 'as the sane lie a dreaming? . . . Said an afflicted man to me, when I was last in a hospital like this, "Sir, I can frequently fly." I was half ashamed to reflect that so could I – by night. Said a woman to me on the same occasion, "Queen Victoria frequently comes to dine with me, and her Majesty and I dine off peaches and maccaroni in our night-gowns, and his Royal Highness the Prince Consort does us the honour to make a third on horseback in a Field-Marshal's uniform." Could I refrain from reddening with consciousness when I remembered the amazing royal parties I myself had given (at night) . . . ?'

As the 79 bus to Edgware passes me, empty except for a single person on the top deck, the prospect of walking all night suddenly seems mad as well as contrary. Genuine madness, the scary sort, rather than 'what a wacky thing to do' froth. It adds a darker edge to the pleasurable anticipation I'm feeling. As I crest a hill (trying to ape Dickens's increased pace, but with no one else around it's hard to become motivated) the Wembley arch appears in the mid-distance, framed by the streetscape like Godzilla about to demolish New York.

The loneliness continues with Queensbury station's 'the last southbound train has gone' notice, standing like an unsmiling sentry in the locked ticket hall. Queensbury got its name in a competition organised by the Metropolitan Railway company,[3] the winning suggestion inspired by the fact that the area lies next to Kingsbury. Which is the next station. Near it I see the first of several Royal Mail carts which have been chained to lampposts overnight, like camels awaiting the return of their drivers. Wembley's getting very big in the sights now and is only a couple of miles away, so it's a surprise to find the main road passing through Fryent Country Park. Nature comes right up to the roadside, mostly open ground, dotted with bushes and trees, like a links golf course. What lurks in the darkness? A shooting star traces its brief path across the sky to my right, adding to the spookiness.

Suburbia reasserts itself in the form of Wembley Park. Just before the station a large house breaks the project's record for the number of vehicles squeezed on to a forecourt: six cars plus a van. In another house someone is still up watching QVC (it's half-one), though I can't see them because of the room's shape. Then, around a corner, not just Wembley's arch but the whole of the stadium appears. It literally stops you in your tracks. How can something like this exist next to shopping channels and a 24-hour Asda? Talking of which, I can't resist a quick wander inside. Half a dozen customers, three times as

---

3. Before the Bakerloo this stretch was on the Metropolitan Line – Metroland stations have always changed lines with an almost sluttish abandon.

many staff restocking the shelves. Two Asian women, one in a fake-fur coat, cast mistrustful eyes over a tinfoil promotion. The only voices come from the self-service checkout tills. 'Please take your change . . . please take your change . . .'

Outside, the route eastwards towards Neasden leads me right round the stadium. We've never got this monument to the national game right. The old one was dated virtually by the time they'd finished it, while the new one lacks soul. Huge – too huge – and shapeless, you can't even tell from outside which level the pitch is at or which way it faces. It's like a spaceship to which you can't find the entrance. And close up, in the cold of a December night, it's finally time to admit that I just do not get what the arch is all about. Towers, yes; they might have been crumbling but at least they made sense. An *arch*, though? The PA speakers on the approach walkways hiss and gurgle their way through nocturnal pointlessness. Hemmed in by trading estates (Currys, JD Sports, Allied Carpets, Halfords . . .) the stadium feels like a bad joke. The Emirates beats it hollow.

The next hour is spent negotiating more industrial units ('Skip hire' . . . 'Pallets Always Wanted'), a tortuous route under and then along the North Circular. Every other building seems to be offering self-storage; fitting enough, as this whole corner of London feels as though it's been put into storage. What houses there are seem derelict. Looking closer, you realise with a shudder that they aren't. Cold and tiredness are getting me down now, and I find it easy to agree with *Private Eye* – Neasden was their stock home for losers like Sid and Doris Bonkers – and very easy to disagree with

John Betjeman, for his lines: 'Neasden! You won't be sorry that you breezed in.'

Dollis Hill is nicer (how faint can praise get?), though not as nice as it was in 1900 when Mark Twain spent the summer at Dollis Hill House as a guest of Lord Aberdeen.[4] 'From the house,' he wrote, 'you can see little but spacious stretches of hay-fields and green turf . . . Yet the massed, brick blocks of London are reachable in three minutes on a horse.' Nature doesn't hold much sway round here these days, though I do see two foxes in ten minutes, the second one limping badly.[5] Willesden Green – strange this, something about the name had always made me fear the worst – continues the upwardly mobile trend. There is a posh deli, a smart estate agent, and, on the residential street leading to Kilburn, some unbelievably large houses. Some of the detached Edwardian jobs are so big they have what could be not just granny flats but granny annexes.

It's three o'clock now, and while the streets are almost deserted there's the occasional straggler returning home after a night out. Near Kilburn station a besuited office worker lurches outside a kebab shop, while a girl in a floppy red hat and smudged make-up resolutely avoids eye contact with him. A Bounty bar from one of several 24-hour shops helps my blood-sugar levels so much that I instantly have another, and soon my mood is recovering from its wee-hours slump. Spotting from a street sign that this is now Camden Council

---

4. The same summer he popped into town to christen the Central Line.
5. In a few hours' time I'll see another one in Berkeley Square. Obvious jokes about the song aside, this just doesn't seem *right*.

territory helps further – the centre of town is beckoning, and I float on as if in a dream. West Hampstead and then Finchley Road are where things get really upmarket, though this is something I know rather than experience, as the Yummy Mummies who'd normally be swarming round Waitrose are very sensibly under their Hungarian goose-down duvets. The compensations are there, though, many of them auditory, the London sounds that you can only hear at this hour. A bird sings beautifully, despite dawn being so far away. Passing a manhole cover I hear the water rushing through a sewer, something you'd never notice in daytime traffic. It feels as though London is sharing its secrets. The same impression recurs when I pass a building on Broadhurst Gardens labelled 'English National Opera'. Turns out this is their rehearsal studio. Surely the ENO can only mean St Martin's Lane, that flashing electric globe on the top? But no, there's a small satellite of West End glamour out here. Who knew?

When Tube workers were excavating the line near Finchley Road they found evidence that this was where the glacial sheet which nearly covered Britain during the last Ice Age had come to rest. After the thaw trees sprouted, many of those just south of here being owned by the crusading Knights of St John of Jerusalem – hence St John's Wood. They remained part of the royal hunting ground until Charles I's time.[6] Now the area is typified by large blocks

---

6. The intervening station, Swiss Cottage, had its own leaflets printed for air-raid shelterers during the Second World War, with advice that included 'vibration due to heavy gunfire or other causes will be felt much less if you do not lie with your head against the wall'.

of mansion flats. Whenever you see people entering or leaving these you're instantly convinced of two things: (1) the residents, who are always at least 65, have spent a lifetime accruing great wealth in respectable professions; and (2) this achievement has brought them no pleasure whatsoever. You get the feeling they haven't smiled in decades. Sounds from St John's Wood station can be heard at the beginning of 'Down in the Tube Station at Midnight' by The Jam, a song based on a real-life attack suffered by Paul Weller. Surely this station has the most beautiful escalators on the Underground? Those art-deco up-lighters illuminating the bronze metalwork? As if going to Lord's wasn't exciting enough already.[7]

A phone box near Regent's Park contains an ad left by a building firm: 'We our the perfectionist'. Then it's Baker Street, and the spot where 221B would have stood, had that address ever existed. Now it's a block of luxury flats, but until recently was the headquarters of Abbey National. They undertook the job of replying to the hundreds of letters that Sherlock still received every year from misguided readers, regretfully informing them that Mr Holmes had now retired. The new flats received planning permission as long as the Abbey's famous bell tower remained in place, necessitating one of those architectural feats you often see in London where everything but the building's frontage is demolished; a sort of facelift in reverse.

---

7. St John's Wood also holds a place in every pub quizzer's heart for being the only Tube station to share no letters with the word 'mackerel'.

Over the Marylebone Road, into Baker Street's W1 stretch. Two men stand smoking outside a hotel, obviously at the end of a very long night in the bar, arguing about the significance of a long ring finger. Down on Oxford Street the famous stores stand silent, all lit up with no one to welcome. Traffic lights go through their routines despite the lack of vehicles. Outside Bond Street station a coatless Swedish businessman pulls his jacket collar round his neck. 'They wouldn't let me wait inside,' he explains. 'The first train isn't until 5.13.' It's now 5.06. Down in Mayfair, on the way to Green Park, the kerbs are lined with Rollers, Ferraris, Mercs – and, on Davies Street, a tiny blue 1960s Fiat 500. It doesn't even reach my chest level. Anyone over 5'8" would need surgery to get into it. Looking at the number plate, I see it's a diplomatic car. Italian Embassy, surely?

The lights on Claridge's are beautiful, but with no one coming in or out the famous hotel looks like a doll's house. Further along in Cipriani the bar is covered with trays of glasses, the floor with sacks of linen waiting to be laundered. Down on Piccadilly the Ritz and the Wolseley and the Royal Academy are all equally lifeless. I stand for a moment, savouring the unreality of it, remembering Dickens's words about night-time being the period when we inhabit the magical, dreamlike world of the mad. After a few moments, though, I realise he got it the wrong way round: it's daytime when London becomes magical. At the moment these famous buildings on this famous street are just that – buildings on a street. It's only when daylight arrives, and people turn up from all over the world, that the bricks and concrete become invested with meaning. That's when they miraculously come alive. Right now they're just a set of toys with no children to believe in them.

Heading south down St James's Street, towards the same saint's palace – still the official home of the British monarch – I pass Ryder Street. This small turning on the left was the last place the Two Ronnies ever spoke to each other; Corbett had received a message from his sick colleague, and asked his driver to pull over while he returned the call. 'I'm going,' said Ronnie Barker, and several days later he did. Corbett now says he can never pass that street without thinking of his friend. Westminster Abbey has the same effect on me, after learning that at Barker's memorial service there the choir entered behind vergers carrying four candles.

Round into Pall Mall, which in 1807 became London's first gas-lit street. There hasn't been a single moment of the last six hours where my walk hasn't been illuminated to some degree or other, yet for most of London's history things were very different. A law of 1416 obliged every householder to burn a candle in a lantern outside his front door on dark nights, but only from dusk until 11 p.m. Those who could afford it undertook night walks with 'link-boys' carrying burning torches.[8] The early eighteenth century saw the spread of oil lamps, and by 1738 Oxford Street alone had more than

---

8. The telescope-shaped extinguishers can still be seen outside some Georgian front doors.

the whole of Paris.[9] Gas lamps brought more than light; a study of 1835 found that they increased the temperature of the City by three degrees.

The city is showing its first real signs of waking by now. A Chinese man hoovers the marble floor of an office building. He pauses to nod to the driver who arrives in a red Transit van and drops off a string-bound bale of newspapers. In a doorway a tramp sleeps soundly in what looks like an expensive thermal sleeping bag. Ready for a cup of tea, I resign myself to waiting until Westminster, and so am surprised, in clubland, and at not quite six o'clock, to find a café already open at the eastern end of Pall Mall. The small Italian owner and his young female employee prepare for the day's battle, unloading loaves of bread from plastic baskets, laying out trays of sandwich fillings, providing a couple of regulars with takeaway hot drinks. Both words of the owner's cheery 'yes, sir?' have 'a' tacked on the front. The cup of tea is excellent. The café's warmth nearly has me nodding off, things sounding muffled and distant. It's a pleasant feeling, slightly surreal.

In Waterloo Place, outside the Athenaeum Club, are two rectangular stones, one on top of the other to form a platform, placed there at the request of Wellington so he could dismount his horse when visiting. I descend the steps by the (Grand Old) Duke of York column, which was paid for with one day's wages from every soldier in the army. On the Mall I look left through Admiralty Arch, where there's another

---

9. The only remaining trace of them is in Henry Blofeld's cricket commentaries, where batsmen often set off 'like a lamplighter'.

Wellington memorial: a small metal nose attached to the wall of the left-hand archway, at just the right height for a soldier on horseback to rub it for luck.[10] One or two joggers are out now. A man clad entirely in black (including leggings) does stretching exercises by the railings in St James's Park; I half expect to see a box of Milk Tray, or possibly an Uzi, at his feet. Round in Parliament Square they're hosing graffiti off the Treasury; last night a student fees protest produced London's worst riots for 20 years. Zach woz here, apparently. Two red phone boxes have had every pane of glass smashed out.

Just as it did for me and Matt on the Circle Line walk, Big Ben chimes as I pass: quarter to seven. There's steady business at Westminster station: cleaners entering, suits leaving. Out on to the bridge, thinking both of Wordsworth (it was pretty much this time of day, though in summer, when he was inspired to write the famous poem) and of diarist James Boswell, who once picked up 'a strong, jolly young damsel' in the Haymarket and brought her here, where 'in armour complete did I engage her upon this noble edifice. The whim of doing it there with the Thames rolling below us amused me much.' At Waterloo the commuter invasion is gathering strength. Even though it's still dark, London's night is all but defeated. Just east of Southwark station, on Union Street, I glance down into a basement and see a workshop in which a man sits perfectly still, contemplating a trombone. Repairs obviously start early at

---

10. It's thought to be a tribute to Wellington as he was famed for the size of his hooter.

Paxman Limited. A rushing sound from behind just gives me time to get out of the way of six joggers. They stream past in single file.

Breakfast (the full works at a greasy spoon – I think 18 miles merits it) marks the real end of the night; having sat with my back to the window, I emerge into daylight. On to London Bridge. The mainline station was the capital's first, opened in 1836, though Vice Admiral Hardy refused to use it because he saw rail travel as too risky – a disappointing reaction from the man who was there when Nelson bought it. The spot's future fame is guaranteed by the Shard, still unfinished as I pass but already the UK's tallest structure. A builder putting on his boots in Tooley Street shows the obligatory bum cleavage – it really isn't the weather for that.

I have a real sense of the river now. I'm heading due east, a couple of hundred yards away from the south bank, and I know the twists and turns of the Isle of Dogs are waiting to trip me up. This is Bermondsey. 'Owing to the loop of the river,' wrote V. S. Pritchett, who ran errands here as an office boy during the First World War, 'Bermondsey has remained the most clannish and isolated part of London; people there were deeply native for generations. Their manner was unemotional but behind the dryness, there was the suggestion of the Cockney sob.' When he buys a condolence card the woman in the shop asks: 'What'll y'ave? Lovin' mem'ry or deepest sympathy?' I mentioned this to Rachel when we spoke about her home area. 'It's still true even now,' she said. 'I think it's one of the few places you can still get that tribal feeling. It's like the Millwall fans' chant, "Let 'em all come down the Den . . ."[11] My very few previous visits here have always confirmed this,[12] though today the rush-hour drudgery detracts from the menace, the pavements full of resigned pedestrians. That and the bright pink hoarding outside a new flat development called Bermondsey Spa.

Straight ahead is Canary Wharf, the aircraft-warning light on the top of 1 Canada Square flashing away. It's one of my strongest London memories: my first few months spent living here, straight after university, were in Shadwell at a friend's flat. Wherever I walked that light would be there, a thrilling reminder that I really did live in the same city as Britain's tallest building (for a short time it was Europe's too). This morning I grieve for the loss of Canary Wharf's record. Of course the Shard is in London as well. And it's not even as though I don't like the Shard; if anything I prefer it to 1 Canada Square. It's just that *that* London has gone, the London of my twenties. Ask not for whom the skyscraper surges, it surges for thee.

After an annoying half-hour in which the housing estate next to Canada Water station hints at shortcuts that never materialise, I descend into the Rotherhithe Tunnel. 'Exhaust fumes,' says a sign. 'Do not loiter.' Piffle, I'm looking forward

---

11. Talking of Rachel – she's passed. Her first fare was a group of five 30-somethings, Clerkenwell Green to Liverpool Street station. It would have been £7.50. When she told them it was free they gave her a round of applause.

12. But that's the thing: why *would* you come here?

to this, a Heathrow-style assault on the senses, notably the hearing. But within yards it becomes clear the sign wasn't joking. Breathing becomes harder and harder, forcing me to use my scarf as a makeshift mask. At one point the litter includes a pair of stick-on ginger sideburns, but my mind is focused on the score or so of smashed wing mirrors adorning the road and narrow pavement. I'm walking against the flow of traffic; if I am to be clipped, I want to see the car that does it. Eventually the atmosphere gets a little clearer, then daylight appears, and finally I'm up in Limehouse, swigging down the air as though it were purest Alpine oxygen. Down Narrow Street (passing the Grapes I remember John Pearson's tales of Francis Bacon and his gang), and then the riverside walk traces the north bank to Canary Wharf. Smart young professionals queue at the coffee and juice outlets; a man in his fifties stands out, with his moustache and sensible coat and tweed cap. I feel an impostor too, sitting in Starbucks surrounded by a sea of iPads while I consult my paper notes about walking a Tube line.

Canary Wharf derived its name from number 32 berth of the West Wood Quay, where Fruit Lines Ltd imported stock from the Canary Islands. Now a van passes me with 'High Bandwidth Connectivity Solutions' written on its side. Ideally I'd be heading due east as the line does, but there's that unfortunate matter of a quarter-mile-wide river in the way. So it's south towards the Greenwich Foot Tunnel at the tip of the Isle of Dogs. Halfway down, where the multinational banks give way to working-class housing – it's hard to believe Thomas Cubitt built this as well as Belgravia – two signs on the same post point in opposite directions: 'Blackwall

Children's Centre' and 'Millwall Children's Centre'. I know London is all about tribes, but does the segregation have to start this early? Two old Chinese women pass, talking in their native tongue; funny that such a harsh sound can come from such kindly faces.

It's eleven o'clock now, and for the first time real tiredness is making itself felt. There's that 'up all night' taste in my mouth, which even chewing gum can't shift. But there's nothing to be done except plough on in completely the wrong direction. Through the tunnel, where an ominous leak drips from the ceiling (worrying shades of the Waterloo and City Line), and then a footpath kindly lets me trace the river bank rather than having to head into Greenwich itself. Outside the Trafalgar Tavern is a bronze life-sized statue of Nelson. It's interesting to examine his face, which for obvious reasons you never get the chance to do in Trafalgar Square – the eyepatch is indeed a myth – though very quickly my attention is drawn to what can only be described as the admiral's quite astonishing trouser presence. Eventually the footpath comes to an end, forcing a grim inland progress alongside gasworks and the Blackwall Tunnel Southern Approach: just as scenic as the name suggests. The O2 comes into view, still an unlovable structure despite the miracle of its engineering,[13] though at least now its pop concerts give people what they want rather than what Peter Mandelson wants them to want. Even its Tube station, North Greenwich, is unremarkable, not what you expect on the stretch of the Jubilee Line that gave us

---

13. The roof weighs less than the air inside.

Westminster, whose awesome exposed-concrete structure makes every journey a proper subterranean adventure.[14]

A crow's journey between the last two stations would have been just over a mile. Mine has been four and a half. And all but a few hundred yards of that has to be repeated as I make my way back on to the Isle of Dogs – past Nelson, through the dripping tunnel – and up its eastern side. Then there are flyovers and dual carriageways to be skirted. Normally these would be intimidating, but tiredness is now tipping over into shutdown mode, so it's a case of traffic roar and pollution: where is thy sting? At Canning Town, a multi-level chrome and glass interchange-with-the-DLR job (as sometimes happens, this is the area's only notable building), I rest in the adjacent bus station. It's like the café on Pall Mall: conversational snippets arrive as if through a long metal tube, echoey and stripped of meaning, or rather injected with new, deeper, untouchable meanings. An old couple discussing milk sound sinister. A yoof on his mobile might be talking to God.

Come on, Mason, two more minutes of this and you'll be snoring. Up and on the feet, north through industrial estates and waste ground towards West Ham. Thick oil has leaked from every factory on either side, covering the road and pavement; it's six inches deep and every step is a struggle . . . Another dream, of course, though a real sign at the

---

14. The space housing the escalators down to the Jubilee Line was the deepest-ever excavation in Central London. Reinforcement work had to be carried out to safeguard Big Ben's foundations. Even then the famous tower started to lean, though only within acceptable limits: one inch.

half-constructed Star Lane DLR station would be equally at home in Wonderland: 'A tidy site is a safer site'. Do they really think this is the sort of language to make builders take note? West Ham links up with the District and Hammersmith and City Line walks, then Stratford does likewise with the Central. A stab of sadness pierces my somnolent fug; these are two of the last connections the project will make. Only one line left now, only one real bit of virgin territory, up in the Wild North West of Metroland.

Stratford marks the penultimate journey's end. Ten to three, a shade under 35 miles through night and then day. Pre-dawn Piccadilly is the image I will remember of the Jubilee Line walk, and the realisation that London is a place whose dreaming gets done when it's awake. No better example of that than the futuristic structures going up here in Stratford, a javelin's throw from the station: the Olympic stadia. Already they're magnificent shells. In a year and a half the whole world is going to come here, fill those stadia, cheer and shout and clap and cry. And why? Because some people are running and jumping. Because we think it matters how well those people run and jump, just like we think it matters whether or not other people can kick pigs' bladders into nets. Of course it matters. It matters because we suspend our collective disbelief, and do and watch and say all sorts of silly things, and get hung up and happy, triumphant and desolate, have moods and go mad, all in the cause of things that a good night's sleep would tell us were meaningless.

In fact, that's a pretty good definition of London.

# 10

# Metropolitan Line

## Infinitely tall skyscrapers

And so this is Christmas. And what have I done? I've decided to walk the Metropolitan Line in the worst weather London has seen for years, that's what.

No, really. This is *seriously* bad. Christmas Day is Saturday, today is Monday, and already Heathrow is warning that Santa may make it back home before some of its passengers do. It's not just the capital: the whole country has been paralysed by snow. Even the news bulletins are paralysed, whole specials given over to the chaos, Met Office spokesmen turned into household names. The authorities are issuing their time-honoured plea for motorists to remain at home 'unless your journey is absolutely essential'. But I'm not a motorist – or at least not once I've driven to the station I'm not. I'm a train passenger to Liverpool Street, then a Tube passenger to Moor Park, and then, for three whole days,[1] a pedestrian. There was a moment last night, watching the latest reports, when Jo's 'Are you sure about this?' found an echo in my own thoughts.

---

1. It might just have been possible in two, but only by doing much of the walking in the dark. Besides, I'm putting off the moment when the project has to come to an end.

But no, I've got to go for it. This whole thing started on a hot day in June. It has to end on a cold day in December.

Persistence gets rewarded. Friends will tell me some horror stories over the coming days, but I'm one of the lucky ones: apart from a couple of minutes' delay at Chelmsford because the train doors have frozen open, everything goes OK. By 9 a.m. (having started from home at 6) I'm at Moor Park, a small, cheerily unassuming station in Hertfordshire, about to take the project's first steps outside Zone 6.[2] Several of the walks have been challenging to plan, but the Metropolitan, with its branches off branches off branches, has taken the logistical biscuit. Eventually, after long hours with the Stanfords maps, a set of compasses and a steady supply of Aspirin, I've concluded that the quickest way to walk this line, whose north-west section looks like a probability diagram, is as follows:

- *Day 1*: Moor Park to Amersham, offline to Chesham, Chesham to Chalfont and Latimer, offline to Watford (the only day of the project that lies completely outside the *A to Z*);
- *Day 2*: Watford to Harrow-on-the-Hill, Harrow-on-the-Hill to Uxbridge, offline back to Harrow-on-the-Hill;
- *Day 3*: Harrow-on-the-Hill to Aldgate

---

2. This used to be the last proper zone, everything beyond here saying 'special fares apply' or some such cryptic wording. Now the numbers carry on upwards: Moor Park is on the border of 6 and 7, while Amersham and Chesham are in the positively Siberian 9. Given the weather, an apt word.

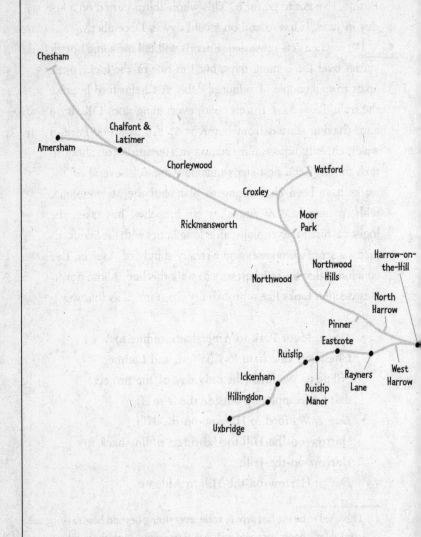

Chesham

Amersham

Chalfont &
Latimer

Chorleywood

Watford

Croxley

Moor
Park

Rickmansworth

Harrow-on-
the-Hill

Northwood
Hills

Northwood

North
Harrow

Pinner

Eastcote

Ruislip

West
Harrow

Ickenham

Rayners
Lane

Ruislip
Manor

Hillingdon

Uxbridge

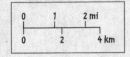

| 0 | 1 | 2 mi |

| 0 | 2 | 4 km |

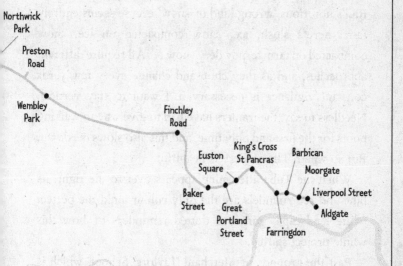

**METROPOLITAN LINE**

Stations: 34

Line mileage: 41

Angle from the vertical of cleverly constructed snowman: 45°

Northwick Park

Preston Road

Wembley Park

Finchley Road

Euston Square

King's Cross St Pancras

Barbican

Moorgate

Baker Street

Great Portland Street

Farringdon

Liverpool Street

Aldgate

N

It's nostril-pinchingly cold, but it isn't actually snowing any more, leaving just the foot or so that's settled in this fairly rural pocket of the world not far inside the M25. Tall trees marshal the tracks as they head north out of the station. It feels like one of those films where there's stillness in the woods, a deer grazing, occasionally looking nervously about, then a shot rings out, shaking snow from the branches, causing the deer to start even though it's not the intended target.

The first couple of roads are lined with large detached houses, most of Metroland vintage but all individually designed; no stockbroker-Tudor by the yard here. The pavements are treacherous, and it's much easier to walk in the road, kindly prepared earlier by the BMWs and Porsche 4x4s. Even here, though, you have to watch out. Suddenly British Rail's notorious 'wrong kind of snow' excuse seems entirely fair: there's slush, ice, snow compacted on ice, snow compacted on tarmac, powdery snow . . . All require different approaches, and as they chop and change every few yards constant vigilance is necessary if I want to stay vertical. Needless to say, the trainers have had to give way to walking boots for the first and only time, and this also slows me down. But so what? The scenery is beautiful.

When the Tube after mine appears over to the right, its blue and red roundels are the only colour amid the perfect white landscape, gorgeous dotted reminders of how this whole project started.

Past the grounds of Merchant Taylors' School, which is up there with Eton and Harrow as one of the nine original public schools, its old boys including the usual great and good, politicians and diplomats and Clive of India, with Boris Karloff thrown in for a bit of colour. The next stop is Rickmansworth, a very small town that still lives up to its name's meaning of 'rich moor-meadow'. There are very few cars that wouldn't attract the maximum emissions tax, and even the horses are well looked after: three of them are tucking into a bale of hay the size of a skip. Whole stretches of the Grand Union Canal, which winds peacefully through the town, are frozen solid. A man in suede loafers outside the station speaks into his mobile: 'Julian, the world has stopped.'

On Valley Road, which will lead under the M25, comes the first properly downhill stretch of the morning. Alarming snatches of the *Ski Sunday* theme music appear in my head, but thankfully the bottom is reached on two limbs rather than four. People are clearing their spacious driveways of snow – each and every one looks up and returns my gaze, smiles, says hello. It seems that British reserve disobeys the laws of physics, thawing when it gets colder.[3] The motorway does its usual trick of hiding away, only appearing round a bend when the houses have stopped, up on 40-foot concrete stilts, the vehicles invisible and barely audible. The Tube track runs at right angles to it at the top of a high bank to my left, so the trains pass just a few feet below the cars. One glides over in the opposite direction, prompting thoughts of Santa's sleigh. Country lanes lead under and then over the track to

---

3. It's still below zero, though because of the walking I've had to remove both scarf and gloves to prevent overheating. Exercise turns you into your own eco-system.

the village of Chorleywood, as though they were threaded needles stitching the project into place.

In a field a mother and daughter are sledging, their Irish wolfhound spraying snow as it runs alongside. The Victorian station has icicles hanging from its canopy, which seems very Dickensian, and automatic ticket barriers, which don't. The electronic departure board announces overground trains as well as Tubes – the Chiltern Railways logo has been tootling past me at intervals, taking away from the Undergroundness of this morning, which in turn detracts from the Londonness. No, that's wrong: there's no Londonness from which to detract. This is Hertfordshire, and in about ten minutes it'll be Buckinghamshire. But that's OK. The Chilterns are pleasant terrain, they've got to be covered – and they give me London to look forward to. That's the real reason for doing the line this way round. The project has to end in London. In fact, it's going to end in the City, the capital's oldest nook. Proto London.

There's a benignly affluent air to things out here. A furniture firm proclaim themselves 'the Innovators of Comfort' (great name for a band), while next door is Rootz, an 'ethical trading store and coffee lounge'. It's always been thus in Metroland. A century ago the Metropolitan Line even had two Pullman carriages specially made, each seating 19 people in single armchairs at tables, with an attendant to bring light refreshments and drinks from the bar. They were attached to morning and evening businessmen's trains into the City, though never showed a profit and were withdrawn in 1939.

Another street of large houses gives way to a footpath through woods, though not Old or New Hanging Wood, both of which stand nearby. Still I'm weaving under and over the line, fields on either side stretching to the horizon in unbroken white. It gets more built up at Little Chalfont, which will shortly merge with Amersham. Chalfont and Latimer station serves not just the Little variety but Chalfont St Peter and Chalfont St Giles too. The latter is where John Milton came to escape the Great Plague and finish *Paradise Lost*, and is also (along with all the territory north to Chesham) part of the Chiltern Hundreds, the stewardship of which is an MP's clever way of resigning, something they're not technically allowed to do[4] – but sadly for its inhabitants Chalfont St Giles is nowadays best-known as rhyming slang for something unpleasant.

Near the centre of Amersham a shopper pulls her groceries home on a sledge. It's a nice little town, its inhabitants and office workers braving the weather to head out in their lunch hours. A noticeboard advertises a meeting of the Chiltern Humanists entitled 'Is Religion Harmful?' Not content to let God monopolise the refreshments, they're offering mince pies and mulled wine to 'celebrate the midwinter solstice'. Indeed Amersham doesn't feel as religious as this sort of town sometimes can, and certainly not as religious as that Bounds Green stretch of the Piccadilly Line did. It's conventional to see cities as the home of reason, while out in the sticks illogical deities rule. But actually there's something calming and measured about the countryside. It's in the

---

4. So they apply for the stewardship, which is an 'office of profit under the Crown' – you're not allowed to hold one of those and remain in the House.

intensity of urban life that crazes usually happen (look at the anti-Catholic Gordon Riots). Not just religion and violence – stock-market bubbles too.

The road up to Chesham (a couple of miles away) is lined with woods, including at one point a Christmas tree farm, thousands of spruces half-buried in the snow. The view through a valley to the east has too much north in it to let me glimpse London's skyscrapers, or even the Wembley arch – the metropolis is hidden from this bit of the Metropolitan. Chesham, it has to be said, is a less than enchanting town. On its outskirts a discarded pair of surgical gloves lie in the gutter, while in the high street you could film a 1970s drama without having to change a thing – the pale blue and orange shop signage is already there. Its one nod to the new millennium is a Starbucks, where I rest over a sandwich and coffee, remembering High Barnet and Edgware, how the Tube map only tells you that they're joint ends of the line but hides the fact that one is much nicer than the other. It's the same with Amersham and Chesham.

Today, though, Chesham has at least one claim – and it's a big one – to a place in my heart. For its Tube station, a humble Victorian grey-brick structure just round the corner from the high street, is the furthest station from Charing Cross anywhere on the network.[5] A straight line from here to the statue of Charles I in Trafalgar Square[6] measures 24.87 miles. This, as the far as the project is concerned, is the edge of London.

---

5. As of 1994 – until then it was Ongar on the Central Line.
6. The measuring point for road distances, so why don't we use it for this as well?

A train pulls in, delivering passengers laden with presents and rolls of shiny paper in which to wrap them. Most head into town. A teenage girl stops and expectantly scans the parking spaces. Her lift hasn't arrived yet. She looks disappointed, but takes the chance to apply more perfume. A man about to board a train uses his phone to check Watford locations with a friend. The friend can't help, so I offer the use of my maps (photocopied from the Stanfords ones). 'How far will that be to walk from the station?' he asks. Surprise surprise, I'm pretty good with this sort of question at the moment. 'About twenty minutes.' 'Really? I'd better book a taxi.' I decline to point out that I'm walking the whole way from here to Watford. Five sheets of A4, mate.

He goes through the ticket barrier, the girl's boyfriend collects her, and once again I'm alone. The furthest station from London. This is my centrifugal moment, the final turn for home. I feel like a swingball at the end of its last trajectory, about to come to rest.

The south-easterly trek back to Chalfont and Latimer is hard work (slopes of varying degrees) but scenic (woods and the River Chess, the latter frozen solid). At a small terraced house a landlady delivers a fan heater to her student tenant. 'That should help, it's very powerful,' she says, 'but if you're still cold do let me know.' 'Thanks very much, this is very good of you.' 'Not at all.' She pretends not to notice his 'I Like Grass' T-shirt. A Tube heads westwards, either to Amersham or Chesham (I'm past the fork now) – there are three people on the whole train. For the first time today this is starting to feel a little tough. I'm 17 miles down, and a sign in Little Chalfont reminds me that there are another nine to Watford. Sustenance, then. In the café that provides chocolate pecan tart and a latte, Brummies at the next table discuss the quality of their previous night's steaks.

So now it's offlining for the rest of the day, but the carefree feel of that word is belied by descending darkness and renewed snow flurries. St Clement Danes School, which like Merchant Taylors' emigrated from Central London, lies on the main road. St Paul's, George Osborne's alma mater, did the same, from the obvious location to Barnes – do these top schools know something we don't? The northern half of Chorleywood (the station this morning lay in the southern half) seems rather well-off; a gastropub offers 'crustacea' rather than just seafood. There are at least three retirement homes, though one euphemistically describes itself as offering 'Senior Living'. The sign also highlights its 'SPECIAL NEIGHBOURHOOD for the MEMORY IMPAIRED', as though capital letters will help them remember. Then, after the project's final crossing of the M25, comes its first use of a torch. For half an hour the countryside north of Rickmansworth and west of Watford is just that: countryside. Pitch black, ponies in fields, lanes with one huge house every few hundred yards, the lot. Finally the outskirts of Watford begin to make themselves felt, the evening rush hour, as much as anything or anyone can rush in these conditions. Pedestrians pick their way along slippy pavements towards the warmth and dryness of home. Outside a terraced house a tanned couple unload suitcases from a minicab (presumably they flew into Luton – it's one of the few airports still open). Their expressions are not far off shell-shocked.

There are snowmen, including one cleverly leaning back at 45 degrees; the slightest rise in temperature and he's history. Several 'Merry Xmas' messages are written in the white blanket. But it's gone seven now, and real tiredness is dogging my spirits. Somehow the map plays a friendly trick on me (probably assisted by the tiredness itself), and only at the last minute do I realise how close journey's end is. Parachutists call it ground rush, the sensation in the final few seconds that the earth is accelerating towards you. Tonight's terra firma is a Premier Inn. Rarely has a hotel reception been so gladly trudged into.

Christmas is a time, at least in a certain Charles Dickens story, for ghosts to make themselves known. The spectre at my project's feast has been dear old Richard, his research suggestions accompanying me on every walk, paragraph after paragraph of Tube history and Underground lore. OK, so the intricacies of route-planning on the 'tragically now-defunct' Northern Heights service[7] weren't what you'd call gripping stuff. But there have been some gems in there. Like, in the notes for this line, Edward Watkin's proposal for a link with Europe. You'll remember that we last encountered Watkin as he bickered with James Forbes over how to run the Circle Line. Wearing his Metropolitan hat, he planned an extension

---

7. A complicated set of extensions to the North London part of the Northern Line, using existing above-ground lines. It never materialised as planned, and was dropped altogether in 1954.

all the way from Baker Street to the Kent coast, where huge lifts would carry the trains down into a tunnel under the Channel – this is 1880 we're talking about – joining up with a French railway on the other side. Victorian adventurers like Watkin trod a narrow ledge between genius and madness. The War Office knew which side they saw him on, replying that such a tunnel would allow foreigners to invade Britain. Watkin countered that, in a worst-case scenario, the whole thing could be blown up at the touch of a button. The War Office saw this as settling Watkin's ledge status once and for all.

Ever since Richard couldn't make it on the Northern Line we've been saying he's got to join me for another of the walks. And so we've arranged that today he will, like Jacob Marley, appear from out of the ether, meeting me for a section of the Harrow-to-Uxbridge branch. That will be this afternoon. This morning it's another chilly promenade to Moor Park, then down through Northwood and Pinner to Harrow. Watford's Tube station, known to the locals as Watford Met to distinguish it from its mainline cousin, lies the other side of the town centre. A businessman stands outside the main shopping centre on his mobile: 'We've been proactive. Did you explain that to Gail?'

At a housing development on the town's outskirts, boards depict artist's impressions of the finished properties. Memories return of Essex on the Central Line: achievement is proven by a private number plate (H1 OSCAR). Croxley station, like Watford, has a pillared portico with lovely blue glass to display its name. Round the corner the lettering is more amateurish, though no less striking: on one of a row of garages someone has sprayed 'Gordon Brown – More Like Fucking Clown'. The common that leads through to Merchant Taylors' School, and then the roads back to Moor Park, are the last rural patch of the project; from here on in it's suburbia and big bad city. I think back on all the green steps I've taken since June, starting with that nature park near Tottenham on the Victoria Line, the point where London unexpectedly ended. There were the fields that came unexpectedly close to the A12, the pastures right opposite Heathrow, the horses near Dagenham. But the thought that keeps crowding all these places out is that one from the Central Line, inspired by Wordsworth: Central London itself seems like a work of nature, as timeless as any field or tree or mountain.

Just to the west of the route as the line heads south to Northwood is Kewferry Road, where at numbers 53 and 55 *The Good Life*, supposedly set in Surbiton, was filmed. Margo would love the area today – there's a *very* nice Waitrose – and would be reassured by the estate agent's window near the station offering a house on her road for £1.2 million. When Tom and Barbara's house sold in 2001, a neighbour reminisced about the filming: 'Goodness, yes,' she said, 'it was all rather exciting.' There were more subversive undertones when Northwood was built in the early 1930s: despite Porridge Pot Hill being renamed Potter Street to seem more sophisticated, one new resident wrote, 'I was to find that residing in a suburb adds a thrill and a zest to life. It is an experience in having no tradition to live up to.' I like the sound of him. In 1933 a second station was opened down the line towards Pinner, and as in Queensbury a competition was held to name it. A lady from North Harrow won £5 for her suggestion of Northwood Hills, despite the area actually being lower than Northwood.

The territory between the two stations marks the border between affluence and something not quite like it. There are still nice houses, but they're terraced rather than large semis. Two men sit in a BMW testing the boot speakers they've just fitted – you fear for surrounding windows. In a café next to the station I break for a warming drink, looking over at the Northwood Hills pub where Potter Street boy Elton John did his first gigs (£1 plus a whip-round). Builders breakfast swearingly as Elvis croons 'The Wonder of You', then as if to match my thoughts the radio DJ plays Elton's 'Step Into Christmas'. Just to repeat the trick his next choice is Johnny Cash's 'Walk the Line'.

Back on the road again, where several people are walking with ski poles. I pass one of those photographic studios whose windows are filled with huge family portraits. As ever – and yes, this is unseasonably morose – I can't help wondering how many of those families are still together. The terrain is definitely more downmarket now, though over to the left is Pinner Hill Golf Course, surrounded by larger houses, including *Sans Souci*, named (after Frederick the Great's palace near Berlin) by the man who had it built, Nazi Germany's Ambassador to Britain Joachim von Ribbentrop. He had bricks imported from Germany, and was rumoured to have incorporated swastikas into the staircase. He passed it to Hermann Goering's sister, but eventually our chaps from the RAF got their hands on it and used it as an officers' mess.

Pinner itself has a pretty little high street with a church at the top, not the sort of place you'd expect to produce actress Jane March, star of various erotically charged films in the 1990s, hence the delight with which the tabloids dubbed her 'the sinner from Pinner'. At the station London Underground continue their tradition of excellent adverts, this one using the Tube's roundel as Rudolph the Reindeer's red nose.[8] North Harrow? The nicest thing I can say about the area is that it contains a 'Dental Practice and Snoring Clinic'.

I have a quick rest at Harrow-on-the-Hill to liaise by phone with Richard. He only just made it into the capital at all, luckily catching the last train before the line was shut down (his version of the final helicopter out of Saigon). Now he's wrestling with the Metropolitan Line, which is in turn wrestling with faulty trains and several million tons of snow. He's stuck somewhere to the east of Finchley Road, so we agree that I'll start walking and he'll join me as soon as possible. My only virgin territory is the first stop, West Harrow, which, apart from a Karma Way, is as unmemorable as North Harrow.

As of Rayners Lane the afternoon is a re-run of the same stretch of the Piccadilly Line, only in reverse. For a good hour the Marrowbone stage outstrips the Metropolitan's A stock, so I pull further away from Richard with every step. To help with the handicapping I stop for a sandwich at a greasy spoon next to Eastcote station. Even by normal standards it offers a bewildering choice of breakfasts (Traditional English, Vegetarian English, Special, Big, Builders, All Day,

---

8. Another, directed at shoppers, features a bar code with lines in the Tube's different colours.

Mega . . .). At the next table a labourer reads a text out loud to his mate: 'You were such a fucking shit dad . . . [waits for the words to scroll up] . . . right from when I was young I . . . don't know how you can fucking . . . look yourself in the mirror the only . . . reason I don't mention it round mum's is . . . I don't want to upset her so if . . .' On and on it goes, each new section producing bronchial chuckles from the man and his colleague. 'She's sort of right,' he adds. 'I was a bit of a shit dad, I've put me hands up to that years ago.'

Down the road at Elm Park Luncheon and Social Club for the Over 60s it's turkey-and-all-the-trimmings time. Several dozen paper-hatted pensioners cheerfully clap along as a female entertainer delivers 'How Do You Do It?' to a karaoke backing. Then finally, at Ruislip Manor, the other side of the ticket barrier, is the unmistakable form of Richard. I feel like Stanley catching sight of Livingstone.

'Sorry about this,' he says, patting his pockets.

'It's all right. The snow isn't your fault.'

'No, I mean . . .' The patting continues. 'Er . . .' Richard has lost his ticket.

Another advantage of walking: not only do you not get delayed, it's also free. Luckily the attendant is in a festive mood, and lets Richard through for nothing.

'Not the only ticket loss I've suffered lately,' he says, as we head out into the snowy wastes of HA4. 'Ali was tidying up the other day. Some of my old ones have gone missing.' I should point out that Richard isn't the sort of bloke who keeps every Tube ticket he's ever bought in specially annotated scrapbooks.[9] He's talking about vintage ones, for which he occasionally dives into the sea of modern temptation known as eBay. 'She's on the case.'

He's trying to appear unconcerned, but there's a definite note of tension.

'Were there many of them?' I ask.

'A few.' To shake himself out of it he adds: 'While we were looking I came across a really old one I'd forgotten about, marked "one dog".'

'You used to have to pay for pets?'

'Yeah. Even now you're limited to two dogs. Take a third and you have to pay.' He's only been here about 90 seconds and already the insights have started.

We trudge the short distance to Ruislip station. The sight of it brings a smile to Richard's face. 'My Auntie Olive,' he says. 'She lived round here; we used to use this station to visit her when I was a kid. That and Ruislip Gardens on the Central Line. Not that I saw many gardens. It was probably only a short walk to her house, but it seemed to take ages.'

The area holds other childhood memories too. 'My dad's Uncle Arthur lived in Uxbridge. That was fantastic. He used to take me along to the local Conservative Club, feed me clandestine shandies as I sat in the corner. Then he'd give me the contents of his coin purse as a reward for not telling Aunt Peggy – he was supposed to have taken me to the park. But I'm sure she knew anyway. He'd done the same to my dad years earlier.'

---

9. Though I am quite nervous that reading that sentence might give him ideas.

Gradually it emerges just how many London relatives Richard has. 'The whole family are Londoners. I'm the odd one out. Dad moved out to Suffolk for work when I was four. Until then I'd lived in Maida Vale.'

'Can you remember it?'

He gives a sad shake of the head. 'Apart from one really bizarre memory of walking out into the traffic to try and follow Dad to work.' For a few seconds there's just the sound of our feet crunching through the snow. 'You know, I think that's where my love of the Tube comes from. There they were, my parents, both London-born and bred, both with their families still scattered all over the city. We spent weekends and holidays visiting them all – and I was an only child. My parents were quite old when they had me, so I had no cousins to speak of, none of my age. Everyone was so much older than me, it was as though I developed a nostalgia for a place I didn't know. For things that happened before I was born.'

As we tick off Ickenham and then Hillingdon, Richard reminisces about his London explorations. His grandfather lived in a high-rise block of flats near Maida Vale, growing vegetables and flowers on his balcony, which Richard blames for his fear of heights. 'I've also got a weird phobia about Routemaster buses – even though I love them – because they always remind me of a story Mum told about seeing one run over a pedestrian's head. She can still remember the cracking sound.' The whole family supported QPR, apart from Grandpa who said he followed Brentford: 'But I think that was just to get a reaction.' His uncle Charlie made replicas of the Crown Jewels for a living. Funny, we say, the jobs that great cities invent for themselves. In nineteenth-century Paris there were professionals called *quatorzièmes*, who in the early evening would get dressed in formal attire, ready to be called into action if a dinner party found itself with an unlucky 13 guests. London's Savoy Grill solved (and still solves) the same problem with Kaspar, an art-deco black wooden cat who gets his own place and is served every course.

'You know,' says Richard, 'it's funny, but London's the only place I can sleep properly. I need the noise. Must be implanted in my genes or something. At home in the country-side I really struggle to drop off. But coming up here to see Auntie Olive I'd sleep like a baby – and she lived on a really busy road. Same when we'd come up to see Ali's best friend. She moved around from Fulham to the Oval to Tooting Bec. I slept next to a Belisha beacon, above a café, above a halal butcher's – out like a light every time.'

Richard's love of the Underground map (and maps of the capital as a whole) is, I'm sensing, much like my own – it's to do with a sense of ownership. London was where I spent my twenties and half my thirties, a place where I changed and grew. Some of the changes would have happened anyway, but the process would have been different, the results, I think, less marked. In Richard's case it's a childhood thing, a relationship with a place that had (almost) never been his home but in which he *felt* at home.[10] For Richard and me the

---

10. This is something he's passed to his two primary-school-age daughters, both of whom – unsurprisingly – feel totally comfortable on the Underground. (Both have 'Mind the Gap' T-shirts, both support QPR.)

Tube map is a passport to the past, a multi-coloured emblem of our younger selves. In fact, maybe those bright colours explain the map's universal appeal – perhaps they remind us all of doodling with crayons?

Let's be honest, this whole thing is about childhood, isn't it? Two men in their thirties walking a particular route from Ruislip to Uxbridge simply because it's the way the London Underground goes. Walking the journey at all. We're playing with the ultimate train set. What's curious, though, is that the more we discuss it, the more the idea of the Tube network as a single entity falls apart.

Richard mentions that he was born in Aylesbury. 'I arrived prematurely; that was where Mum happened to be at the time. But you could say that technically Aylesbury's part of London – the Metropolitan Line used to go there. It stopped thirteen years before I was born, but still.'

'Funny, the Tube's changing all the time, but somehow we think it's set in stone.'

'It's probably the map that does that.'

'You mean because it's so precise?' I ask.

'Yeah. All the nice straight lines, colour-coded. Like it's an architect's plan.'

'The blueprint for something that was built all in one go. Whereas in reality the Tube's just this messy creation that's grown up bit by bit. It was years before all the different companies even agreed to use the single name "Underground".'

Richard nods. '1908.' It's at moments like this that you want to pinch his cheek and ruffle his hair.

This is the thought that stays with me at Uxbridge, where

Richard has to take his leave. Whether it'll be the Piccadilly or Metropolitan Line that conveys him back to town we don't know, but family duties await, and anyway there's little attraction in simply turning round and retracing our steps. I should know, I'm the one that's got to do it. Before setting out, though, I take a pocket-sized Tube map from the rack in the ticket hall and peruse it over a coffee in Pret. Richard's right – it tricks you into believing that there is this eternal, unchanging thing called the London Underground network, whereas some stations, like Aylesbury, have been airbrushed from history (and so from London) as if by Stalin's photography department.[11]

I fold the map back up, and see that the front cover is part of an artwork which, like Simon Patterson's famous The Great Bear, takes the Tube map and replaces the station names with (in this case) emotions and concepts. On the Northern Line, for instance, you pass from Envy to Power to Compassion, where you can change on to the Piccadilly Line and travel through Irony to Awe. Holborn is Joy, Russell Square Doubt. Who knows what Harry Beck would have thought? But today, after my talk with Richard, the work seems to tell a fundamental truth about maps: they can stand for anything you want them to stand for.

Technically the walk back to Harrow, tonight's resting point, is offline. But the quickest way there is actually the way I

---

11. There are the famous disused stations in Central London – Aldwych, Down Street, British Museum and so on – but another one in this corner of the network, beyond Amersham, rejoiced in the name Brill.

came, minus the odd hundred-yard dart to reach a station entrance. Today's milometer already stands at 21, nine of which were the section from Harrow that I'm now repeating. So it's going to be another 30-miler, and night has arrived already: today's the shortest day of the year. At first the going isn't too bad. My mood has been buoyed by the time spent with Richard. The sight, in someone's garden, of a snowman wearing a pork-pie hat, a dinner jacket and a red bow tie makes me smile. Soon, though, as the mercury dips and it starts to snow again, things begin to get difficult. Way more difficult than last night. Passing a house where a couple sit with their dinners on trays watching *The Weakest Link*, I feel horribly excluded from Indoors. The thought of how far there is to go – a couple of hours at least – is daunting. *Don't be stupid*, says my inner resilience, *you've done this journey already, you've got its measure; it won't seem so long this time*. But actually it's the other way round, isn't it? Journeys always seem longer the more you do them – novelty isn't there to take your mind off things.

Eventually the emotional wheel comes full circle, and I start to enjoy it. Not the experience itself – that's still miserable and cold and hungry[12] – but rather observing how my body's reacting. This is as tired and low as I can ever remember being. Even running a marathon was easier – it was during the day, with no snow to negotiate and with people to cheer you on. As things reach what I suspect will be their

---

12. Stopping for something to eat would solve the last one, but only at the price of forcing me back out into the cold again afterwards, doubling the misery after a respite.

nadir, forcing me to rest, something very curious happens. It's sort of like the shutdown mode I experienced at the end of the Jubilee Line, but in a much more physical form. Everything seems to get quieter and darker, almost womb-like. It must just be that I'm not looking around so much, concentrating on my feet, worrying only about my steps rather than the terrain they're carrying me through – but it really does start to feel like my senses are closing down, insulating me from discomfort.

Don't get me wrong: I'm sure this only happens because the situation's temporary, because I know a warm hotel room is waiting up ahead. There are plenty of people in this city tonight who aren't in that lucky position, and I bet they aren't indulging in self-referential wonder at the mysteries of the human psyche. But just for now, in the closing moments of the project's penultimate day, I savour this new experience. An extreme version of the lesson learned from Ealing on the Central Line – walking brings a heightened awareness not just of your surroundings but of yourself. It just so happens that in this case it's a heightened awareness of how awareness can be lowered.

Starting in early 2010, small laminated notices began to appear at seemingly random locations across London, tied to lampposts and bearing the words: 'A cake circle runs through homes adjacent to this notice.' It's the third word, of course, that gives the lie to that 'seemingly'. Should anyone, by a miracle of coincidence, have encountered not just one or two but three of these posters on their travels and been intrigued as to what was going on, they could have returned home, plotted the locations on a map and (assuming they were very good at geometry) worked out the centre of the circle that had all three spots on its circumference. Even if they'd done this, though, there'd be no way they could have known the significance of that centre: it's the home of Bill Drummond.

Drummond, the ex-pop musician best known for his time in the KLF, the band that famously burned their last million pounds as a way of retiring from the music business, now cuts a weird and wonderful path through life as an . . . well, do we use the word 'artist'? And if we do, do we put the even more fraught word 'conceptual' before it? Drummond himself, in the time we'll spend together this morning – I have, for reasons that will become clear, asked him to walk a section of the Metropolitan Line with me – doesn't really bother using the 'A' word to describe his work. He just gets on and does it, an attitude that makes me like the work even more than I already do. The older I get, the more this sort of thing interests me. It links with the 'childish joy' thing I touched on with Richard. The older you get, the more you rediscover the pleasure the six-year-old you took in trying something simply because it's new. Instead of asking 'Why?' you ask 'Why not?'

Drummond's Cake Circle was the thing that first caught my attention about his work. But that, it turned out, was only part of a wider and lifelong fascination he has with maps. The more I read about this, the keener I became to talk the subject over with him. Hoping that the idea of walking a line on a map would appeal to him – as a boy Drummond used to write the word 'Bill' on maps of his native Scotland, then follow the lines of the letters – I emailed an invitation. It was accepted, and so at Harrow-on-the-Hill station on this, the last morning of the project, I'm greeted by a tall, physically imposing but very un-conceptual-artist-looking man of fifty-seven, dressed in jeans and walking boots and wearing a rucksack. With his square jaw, untrendy glasses, thinning hair and down-to-earth manner it's hard to believe that Bill's records filled the nation's dancefloors in the late eighties and early nineties. Or, indeed, that something as off-the-wall as the London Cake Circle could be his creation.

Having said it's off-the-wall, its workings are perfectly simple. With the circle drawn on his Ordnance Survey map – it extends down to Shoreditch and up almost as far as the North Circular – Bill periodically bakes a cake, travels to a house somewhere on the circle, and gives them the cake. End of, as they say. We start by discussing how it's going.

'I've decided to carry it on longer than I'd planned,' says Bill, as we head through the station car park and out on to the main road. Although it's still cold there's been no fresh snow, so today's progress is easier. 'I was just going to do one cake every week this year then stop, but in the end I've only done about fifteen, so I'm going to spread it over all the time I'm living in London. That should be until 2017, when my youngest son will be leaving school.' We'll get on to the reasons for these timings later.

'What do you say to people when they open the door?'

'Something very simple. "Good afternoon, my name is Bill and I've baked you a cake." Of course they say, "Eh? What?" For me that's part of it, the surprise, the confusion. I'll say, "I don't know if you know this, but your house is on a cake circle. You may have seen one of these." And I give them one of the leaflets I've delivered. That's part of the set-up in advance, along with putting the posters on lampposts.'

'And do they accept the cake?'

'Sometimes. You get some refusals, of course, but other people go, "Great, you've baked me a cake, how lovely." If the first person refuses, I take it next door. Sometimes it's taken a few goes, but I've found takers for all the cakes.' It doesn't have to be a residential address. 'I go to offices, estate agents, anywhere. In fact, it's easier when it isn't residential, people are less defensive. The first one was a business, just off the Old Street roundabout, on City Road.' Bill also did a smaller cake circle, over the course of a week, in Gothenburg during the summer of 2010. 'There's a big Middle Eastern community there, they invited me in, gave me tea, the whole works.' He smiles. 'That hasn't happened in London.'

Notwithstanding the 'why-not-rather-than-why' point, the question of purpose does occur. 'I'm not particularly into trying to explain the things I do, all the whys and wherefores,' says Bill. 'Not even to myself. But I guess the Cake Circle has got something to do with trust between strangers, with my love of leaving a layer of meaning on a map. Then there are the stories that might happen and spread after a strange man turns up on your doorstep offering you a cake.'

He means the idea that the circle exists in the memories of the recipients, and indeed in his own memory?

'Yeah, absolutely. I mean, I talk about "constructing" the circle – but there's nothing physical left behind, is there?'

The circle follows on from another of Bill's projects, the Soup Line. Having been involved in arts projects in Belfast and Nottingham, he imagined a straight line running between the two and continuing all the way round the world. As part of a festival in Belfast he visited the homes of people who lived on the line (and who had invited him), to cook them soup. 'I like the fact that that was a straight line and the circle is, obviously, a circle. For me they're the two most powerful marks you can make on a map. One's the ultimate symbol of male, the other the ultimate symbol of female. I guess my Soup Line across the British Isles was the biggest phallic symbol I'll ever need to make. When you've got a Soup Line you don't need an Aston Martin.' It strikes me later that the Tube roundel is a combination of a circle and a straight line. What this says about the Underground's role in sexual politics, I hesitate to conjecture.

To draw the Soup Line Bill ordered all the relevant 1:25000 Ordnance Survey maps from Stanfords, stuck them together on his workshop floor and stretched a piece of string from just north of Formby to Felixstowe. At that scale the distance was over 30 feet. I tell Bill it reminds me of Rachel and her fellow cabbies having to be 'on the cotton'. 'I'd *love* to do the Knowledge,' he says. 'If time was no object, of course. Whenever I pass one of them on their scooters, I think it's fantastic.' Bill and I discover a shared trait: we both hate travelling the same route twice. 'Whenever I visit my girl-friend, I always try and drive a different way. It's the same with walking: you constantly want to find new roads, new ways of going.'

How does Bill find marking a map? Has he ever experienced the timidity I did when first applying that magimarker to Brixton Road?

'Not at all. I'm not precious about that sort of thing – I *enjoy* marking maps. As much as I love them, in all shapes and forms, I've never had a problem with it. So many of my maps have got all soaked and torn, even when I'm out walking in the country and they're in one of those plastic things [this makes me feel better about the 'geography teacher' charge], they end up falling to bits. I kind of like the look of that, the idea that they're lived in and used.' It also strikes me that Bill's treatment of maps is an attempt to personalise them, to let any subsequent viewer know exactly who they were owned by. When he lived in Buckinghamshire, for instance (yes, he was once an habitué of the Metropolitan Line), he started marking up all the damson trees he found in hedgerows. The most literal 'making his mark' move, though, has to be writing 'Bill' on maps. 'I've done that lots of times, not just when I was a kid. I did it in London once, and right at the end of the walk, where the second "l" finished, was a gallery. I went in, and they'd got a work by Richard Long. He's an artist who specialises in walking. For instance, his first work was a photograph of a straight line he'd made in the grass somewhere in the English countryside by walking up and down it again and again. The fact I'd just been doing exactly that – walking – made me think, "Wow, someone's making art out of this."'

Later, reading more about Long – including mentions of him in Geoff Nicholson's *Lost Art of Walking* – I come to realise just how tricky this type of stuff is, how easily the charge of pretentiousness and/or pointlessness gets made. That first work, from 1967, was called *A Line Made by Walking*. If ever there was a good, honest, does-what-it-says-on-the-tin name then this is it, and yet precisely the opposite connotations can surface. The real problem, not just for Long but for Drummond too, comes when people ask that dreaded question: 'But is it *art*?' Surely the best answer is, 'Who gives a toss?' If it's witty, different, engaging, interesting on any level at all, then why do we have to bother with definitions? Looking at Long's line online (as it were), I find it interesting, the notion of someone walking up and down the same stretch of grass, getting nowhere yet still leaving his mark – indeed, leaving his mark precisely *because* he got nowhere. All those thoughts it prompts about the effects we have on our surroundings, the routines of life, the futility of effort . . . and yet as soon as you start to ask any of them, you're trapped inside an earnest BBC2 late-night review programme.

As we're there, though, let's trim the goatee, brush down the black polo-neck and mention Bill's other circular urban work, Surround. This is performed in many cities round the world – he's currently in discussions with the Barbican about doing it in London – and entails him and 99 volunteers standing at 50-metre intervals around a five-kilometre circle he's drawn on the map. The first person shouts 'whey-oh', followed by the second and so on. Once the shout has travelled around the circle five times the performance is deemed complete. 'I can get more pretentious about it,' says Bill with a smile. 'But basically that's it.'

Does he record it? 'No, it's never recorded, that's the whole point. It exists only in your memory. You have to imagine yourself high above the city watching this wave go round five times.'

One of those things that could well elicit a 'So what?' reaction, until you picture yourself doing it. 'I think I'd get quite nervous as the shout got near to me,' I say.

'Oh, you do. Especially when there's someone going past with a buggy at the exact moment you have to do your "whey-oh". Then there's the sense of elation when you've passed it on.'

How far away can you hear the shout coming?

'Depends on the traffic, but about five or six people.'

It sounds fun. Like the Cake Circle its charm lies in the fact that it doesn't exist except as a concept, a set of memories, of stories to be told about the time you shouted 'whey-oh' in a street. Or of the time you were pushing your buggy past someone when they shouted 'whey-oh' for no apparent reason. Except, I decide, the circle *does* exist, and not just on the map Bill has used to plan it. Something about those people turning up, making that effort, sending the shout round not just once but five times – it does amount to something. I couldn't tell you what. But something.

By now Bill and I have reached the next station, Northwick Park. It's tiny, little more than a hole in the wall set back on a residential street, and all the more charming because of that. We pause to pay our respects, then carry on.

Bill has only lived in London for four years. 'The relationship I was in came to an end, and my partner moved with our three children back to London, where she'd grown up. I felt it was my duty to be near them, so I moved here. All my life I've been quite anti-London.' He considers this statement. 'Or maybe not "anti" – just very . . . what's the best way to put it? Suspicious of it?'

Because?

He thinks some more. 'When I was picking which art school to go to in the early seventies, the idea of going to London seemed a very tame and boring one. Even though I knew it was where a lot of stuff happened, going to other parts of the UK seemed a lot more interesting.'

Was this because most people *did* go to London?

'No, it wasn't to be contrary. It was just that London didn't interest me as much as Leeds or Manchester or Liverpool or Newcastle or wherever. I'd been coming down here in my mid-teens to go to Carnaby Street to buy clothes [by this time Bill's family had moved from Scotland to Northamptonshire]. I felt I'd grown out of London by the time I was seventeen. I've got this theory – at least I did in the pre-internet age – that youngsters growing up in London don't develop as strong an imagination as teenagers in the rest of the country. If you're growing up in some far-flung corner of the British Isles, you've got more *time* to dream and make plans and develop ideas. If you're in London there's too much on offer, too much to take up your time just consuming rather than dreaming. There's something deadening about it.'

The area we're walking through is still completely residential, allowing Bill and me to concentrate on our talk. 'There's also the thing,' he continues, 'and this is a thing about capital cities in general – I'd say London's less guilty of it than, say, Paris – of people who grow up here thinking the rest of the country is this place where nothing happens, where people are looking to London the whole time. Most of the people I know who grew up in London don't *know* the rest of the country. They have opinions, based on watching *Coronation Street* or the news, or they might say, "I had really miserable holidays in Bournemouth when I was a kid, why would I want to go there?" But they don't really know what it's like.'

I'm not sure about this. There are certainly Londoners who loudly portray the North as a land of clogs and whippets, but then there are Northerners who make great play of disliking the capital. Both are chippy minorities who, you feel, protest too much. Most people, especially in this age when ease of travel has shrunk the country, are pretty familiar with parts of it that happen not to be their own, and (to varying degrees) comfortable enough when they visit those parts. But sticking to Bill's own experience, moving to London was something he wouldn't have done had circumstances not dictated it. How's he responding?

'I'm making a conscious effort to embrace London,' he says. 'I know it's a finite thing. I've got several things I'm doing. The Cake Circle for one. Another is visiting a different barber every week for a shave – where I live there's a big Turkish community, and barbers are a big part of their culture. I've always had a thing about barbers, always clock them whichever city I go to – there was one at Harrow station, I noticed. I like the fact that whatever technology we get, there's still this basic need. Bill Gates has to go to the barber's. Anyway, I go to these places and talk to the Turkish people about their lives, where they've come from and so on.'

Bill's also visiting different places of worship, attending their services. 'Once I started living here I noticed the incredible amount of religious culture there is. I thought while I'm in the city I might as well embrace some of it. The nearest one to me is a small Turkish mosque, then there's an Afro-Caribbean evangelical church, then a Jewish synagogue a few streets away, then a Methodist place where it turns out Mary Wollstonecraft started out . . .' As we talk about religion I mention the Rabbi Lionel Blue joke I used in the introduction to this book, about the Jewish guy needing a synagogue he doesn't go to. 'There's a guy who lives up my road, a Hasidic Jew. I'd assumed everyone who dresses like that, has that beard and so on, was Hasidic and that was that. But he said, no way, there are all these different groups within that and they hate each other more than they hate any outsiders.'

Yet another way Bill's embracing the capital is with sparrows. 'I've always loved birds. When I moved to my flat there was a squabble of sparrows – that's my made-up collective noun for them – in the hawthorn trees opposite. They were always there making a noise, then one day they weren't. Whenever I've come across a group, I've marked them on my map.'

Yes, as you'd expect, all Bill's projects have been documented on his London map: the Cake Circle, every barber visited, every place of worship, every squabble. I like the thought of this, a man's map as the clue to his personal identity. I ask Bill whether even though he didn't like London as a place, he'd ever loved maps of the place.

'Not really, no. Except the Tube map, that is. I've always loved that, ever since I first saw it as a child in Scotland, just from an aesthetic point of view. I always love it when I go to another city that's got an Underground system, comparing their map to London's. Most of them are nowhere near as attractive. Moscow's is good. It's got that thing of a circular line and then all the straight ones cutting across it, just like the London system.'

We round the corner on to Preston Road, an uninspiring line of cheap supermarkets, newsagents and fried-food outlets clustered around the station of the same name. Grimy and dismal its surroundings may be, but this morning, for me, Preston Road holds a deep significance. Deeper even than its historical role – in a slightly different location and called Preston Road 'Halt' (a request stop) – as the station opened specifically to serve the 1908 Olympics clay pigeon shooting site. Because even though the project still has several hours to go, Preston Road marks the beginning of the end. After six months, 11 lines and hundreds of miles, Preston Road is the 269th station to which my trusty old feet have delivered me. The 269th and *final*. That's it, I've ticked them all off. Every station from here on in has been visited on other lines.

I mention this to Bill, who offers his congratulations. I experience a certain pride, tinged with last-chocolate-in-the-Advent-calendar disappointment.

We head on towards Wembley Park. Another exception to Bill's 'not bothered about London maps' rule, it turns out, is the *A to Z*. 'I love the cover,' he says, borrowing mine for a moment, 'the lumpiness of these bits [the serifs, or end-bars, on the A and the Z]. No modern designer would do that, it's not aesthetically pleasing, but I love it.' He turns back to the page that's guiding us south-eastwards. 'The look of the pages too, I'm not traditionalist about it, I love the fact they've gone colour.' We discuss the merits of spiral-bound (as mine is) versus normal. You don't get the cracking, is the consensus, but there is that annoying gap when you're travelling over the spine – and with repeated use (as I've found) the spiral pages do tend to come out anyway. On balance, normal wins.

'As much as I love OS maps,' says Bill, 'and have plotted my Cake Circle and the barbers and everything on an OS map, I'd rather be looking at an *A to Z* map of London. Yes, the OS is more realistic, but for finding your way round it's not much use. No street names, of course.'

It is, indeed, a bizarre experience, consulting an Ordnance Survey map of Central London. The modern ones take a step towards *A to Z*-level usability by marking Tube stations, highlighting the major streets in a different colour and so on. But those older ones Piotr showed me in Stanfords where, for instance, Oxford Street was given its proper billing, no wider than many of the surrounding streets – it was very hard to work out where was where.

You can get the same sort of effect now from Google Maps – select the satellite view, take off all the labels, and you're confronted with the reality of how this familiar landscape actually looks from on high. Not that familiar at all. Zoom around and you'll eventually find a railway station, one of the big parks, a uniquely shaped road layout (such as Regent Street heading into Piccadilly Circus) – but huge swathes of the West End take real effort to figure out. It reminds me of looking down once from a plane that was stacking over Central London. For a while I couldn't even work out if we were flying east or west, so didn't know whether what was above the river in my field of vision was North or South London. Eventually Tower Bridge solved the mystery. A thrilling experience, being surprised by an old friend. Looking down from on high, I tell Bill, made me feel like I was visiting London for the first time.

'I think that's what makes maps so exciting,' he replies. 'They let you look down from the vantage point of God. The first map I can ever remember was the one hanging in our house when I was a young child, of Wigtownshire, the county where we lived. I just assumed that God had made the map. Probably that was because ours was a religious house. I just thought, "God's the only one who can look down and see the world like that, know what it looks like." And even though I now know that maps are made by men, that sense of wonder has stayed with me.'

I laugh.

'What is it?' asks Bill.

'You've just solved a mystery,' I reply, giving him a brief account of my trips to the top of Tower 42 and Barnet church. 'I haven't been able to work out why they weren't quite satisfying enough. But that's it – it's because I was still getting mankind's view. No matter how tall a building is, you're still looking down at an angle, you're still rooted to the ground. But a map frees you from that. A map is an infinitely tall skyscraper.'

Bill nods. 'I guess so.'

We crunch along in silence for a moment or two. 'Is that what this is all about?' I ask. 'Our love of maps, the things we do with them, your Cake Circle, me walking the Tube system? Do we want to be God?'

Bill considers it. 'It's got to be, hasn't it? It's a very male thing – and I say this even though it was my sister rather than me who grew up to actually be a cartographer – it's a male thing to say, "I can survey all this, I'm higher even than the Tower of Babel, which is higher even than Tower 42." Man's always wanted to build towers, but even the tallest one isn't as good as the "up here" feeling you get from a map.'

So that's it. That's where the niggling dissatisfaction came from. You could say that as Tower 42 was built by a bank it's a victory for God over Mammon, but then again the other tall building was a church. We're both reminded of the ceiling in Grand Central station in New York, the famous map of the constellations, how they're actually the wrong way round because it was copied from a medieval 'celestial' map that pictured the stars as seen by God, looking down from above.

We're at Wembley Park now, with a view of the top of the stadium's arch lost in mist, and Bill has to head off. He wishes me luck for the rest of the walk, I thank him for his time and insights. Particularly the last one. How healthy it is to have a God complex I'm not sure, but if you *do* have one it's probably best that you know about it.

\* \* \*

This is it, then. The final leg of the final leg. No more company, no new stations, no more dots to join. Just tracing over some dots that have already been joined on other lines. What novelty there is this afternoon will come from the fact that Wembley Park to Finchley Road on the Jubilee Line included a load of stops that the Met doesn't bother with, meaning I can walk a quicker route.

This leads initially through the Chalkhill Estate, where outside a small care home for the elderly a man in his fifties brushes his hair before pressing the bell; half a century on and his mum's lessons hold firm even as he visits her. Further along the road a funeral cortège gathers outside a very modest block of flats. Hard to avoid the thought that this is the only time the deceased will ever travel in a Rolls-Royce – why don't we book them as a last treat instead? On Neasden Lane I stop at McDonald's, something I can't remember doing as an adult, but this last day seems a good time to challenge prejudices. It's one of those trendy ones: retro sixties decor, lime-green chat-show chairs and so on. My cup of tea tastes great, the staff are friendly, the other customers largely middle-aged and lively. Prejudice duly dispatched.

Under the North Circular for the last time, then along the south side of Gladstone Park, not far from Brook Road, home of 'Paddock', the bunker to which Churchill would have fled if we'd lost the Battle of Britain and Adolf was closing in on Whitehall. Paddock was so secret that even in his memoirs Churchill only described it as 'near Hampstead'. It's still there, open to the public twice a year. The trees in the park are being used, a notice tells us, to help dogs 'strengthen their jaws and sharpen their teeth' prior to illegal fights. Information is requested. Further along, Neasden comes to an end, one of those times when 'the other side of the tracks' means just that – a pedestrian footbridge over a mainline track marks the beginning of pastel front doors with frosted glass. I'm getting into Cricklewood now, a place Alan Coren joked about for so long that I'd never really believed it actually exists. Then West Hampstead: stressed pine tables for sale, a very chic veterinary practice, Bake-a-Boo Cupcakes. Lunch is taken at the Wetfish Café (formerly a fishmonger's), where twenty-somethings work on laptops and the liquid soap in the Gents is in an optic-mounted whisky bottle.

Swiss Cottage gives way to St John's Wood, and before I know it darkness has fallen and I'm at Baker Street, where this whole thing started. Not long now before it'll all be over. To delay that moment as long as possible I call into Starbucks just over the road, which would have to be a stop on my personal Tube line as I wrote much of my first novel here. Over a coffee I read the *Standard*, and learn that the Beatles' zebra crossing (which I came within a Rickenbacker's throw of less than a hour ago) has today been granted Grade II-listed status, the first piece of 'road furniture' to be so honoured. No harm in that, though thankfully London's real icons get decided by popular will rather than committees, as the regularly whitewashed graffiti outside Abbey Road studios shows. Number 3 Savile Row, the office building famous for hosting the Fab Four's last rooftop gig, is already getting the same treatment, having recently become empty.

More footdragging. Along the main road, at St Marylebone

Parish Church, a man comes out of a side door, carrying a stack of papers and looking hassled and miserable. The staff at London's churches always look like this. Why? It can't be the impression they're after. At St Pancras the interminable Eurostar queues have finally died down now that some sort of service has resumed. As I'm heading down Farringdon Road the Shard rises up, dwarfing the much-nearer St Paul's. I realise this building, which has really taken shape during the project, will always remind me of the months I spent walking the lines. Between Farringdon and Barbican I pass the 70-mile mark, happy that the last walk really has turned out to be the longest. It feels as if that's how it should be.

I'm really dawdling now. Watching people, taking in the Christmas scenes, the end of the working year coinciding with the end of my journey. At a nail bar in the ground floor of CityPoint a woman sways slightly as an assistant works on her Santa-red nails; the partying started at lunchtime, it seems. Near Liverpool Street a group of men leave their office dressed in black tie, laughing and joshing. The heaving pubs are tinselled and baubled to the max, while the reception areas of office blocks compete to see who can have the largest and most elaborate tree, a fitting way to joust in the skyscraper-obsessed Square Mile.

And then, east of Bishopsgate, away from the buzz around Liverpool Street, things get quieter, as if to let me contemplate the walk to my final station. Houndsditch is a darker street with few pedestrians, a last reminder of how London's past lives on in its street names.[13] St Botolph's, the church standing in the middle of the one-way system that marks the last road I have to cross, nails home the message of the capital as a city of opposites. It is positioned, its website tells you, near the border of 'the poorest Borough in London [Tower Hamlets] and one of the world's leading financial centres'. Outside its front door I pause, and look down the road to that familiar sight, a Victorian building with a blue canopy, this time bearing the words 'Aldgate Station'. That first step outside Brixton has been followed by over 900,000 others. Now another 50 will take me to the end.

Before I move, though, I think back on all those miles, that gigantic squiggle of a love-letter to the city I adore. What has it taught me, what have I learned from the slog and the weariness of it, what lessons were there to be learned in the shadow of Wembley, under Suicide Bridge with Geoff, in the pubs with Matt? The memory that comes first is of that pre-dawn Piccadilly on the Jubilee Line walk, London as a toy set waiting to be played with. Then I remember Sir William Peyton's grave in Brompton Cemetery on the District Line: it bore the epitaph 'To live in the hearts of those we love is not to die'. The idea that we exist in other people's thoughts of us somehow feels newly relevant now. The next thing that comes to mind is yesterday, with Richard, the notion that the Tube system isn't real but rather a construct our minds put together from a hotchpotch of unrelated lines and tracks. Bill's in there as well, with his circles that don't

---

13. This is where dead dogs used to be dumped in the days when it was just outside London Wall.

exist but somehow do, made real by the memories of cakes and shouts of 'whey-oh'. The Olympic stadium, too, and our eager anticipation of what is essentially just running and jumping. As I'm thinking this a woman passes on her way to the station, carrying a bag of unwrapped presents that in three days' time somebody will believe came from Father Christmas. And that's when I see it: London isn't real.

It isn't a city, it's an idea. London has such magic simply because we *believe* it has such magic. Take away that belief and it's just a collection of buildings and roads and parks and Tube stations linked by colourful lines that aren't really there, just as the dreams and ambitions of all the people who come to London, who have ever come to London, only amount to anything if you imagine them into a unified whole. Yet still people come. If you build it, that's what they'll do. And the real beauty is that even knowing this thing called 'London' isn't real doesn't stop it feeling real. Somehow the fizzing energy – other people's and your own – gets you every time, tricks you, draws you in and draws you back. 'I always think something wonderful is going to happen,' John Pearson told me. 'And it never does.' Who cares? It's the thinking that counts.

Gertrude Stein said of her native Oakland that there was no 'there' there. As I walk the final few steps, stand outside Aldgate station and watch the ticket barriers opening and closing, people heading home for Christmases that will get them just as excited as their kids, I know there's no 'here' here. London is in our minds. But then our minds are all we have, and all we need.

# *Postscript*

O n trips to London in the weeks and months that
follow, I realise that walking the lines has changed
my view of the city forever. There is an overarching
sense of overarching, of knowing that wherever I go I've been
further, that no trip within the capital can intimidate me. The
city seems to have shrunk, become more manageable, and this
has opened it up. Sights that lay just out of the project's reach
tempt me to visit them. Harrow School, ten minutes' walk off
the last morning's route, gets a visit one day when I have some
time to kill. I'd never known that its buildings lie either side
of the road rather than behind a high wall, making it feel
surprisingly democratic. This is the highest point for a long
way in any direction (the church above the school has red
aircraft warning lights on its steeple), and in the gap between
two of the school's structures you can gaze down on London,
Wembley in the foreground, the City in the distance. I pick
out Tower 42, and some magical sense of time travel lets me
see myself on top of it, looking back over here to Harrow.

Catching sight of the Tube map – as you so often do in
London – I now see simultaneously an enemy that's been beaten

and a friend who showed me around. Names that once were as mythical as Greek gods now elicit fond memories: the security guard in Tottenham Hale, the vodka scorpions at Mill Hill East, the roaring jets at Hatton Cross. And there's the occasional practical benefit. Visiting Matt in Highgate, for instance, I know without having to check the map that I need a High Barnet rather than an Edgware train, something I could previously never get my head round no matter how many times I did the journey. That's because the journey was underground; I didn't need to know where Highgate actually is. Now I've walked the walk.

The project might be over, but the mathematics linger on. The sums aren't a chore, they're a way of reliving the experience. It's a pleasure to work out that I walked 403.2 miles over 174 hours and 50 minutes (or, if you prefer, and I think I do prefer it because it makes it sound more of an achievement: one week, six hours and 50 minutes). That I therefore averaged 2.31 m.p.h. That of the 269 stations, I visited 50 twice (including multiple visits on the same line, such as Euston on the Northern), 16 three times, 6 four times, and 2 five times. These were Baker Street (5 different lines) and Liverpool Street (4 different lines, twice on the Circle). The daddy of them all, though, with six visits on six different lines, was King's Cross.

And of course I'll always have London, because I'll always have the maps. Only one wall in my house is big enough to Blu-tack them all to (seven rather than all nine – the south-west and south-east sheets were never needed). It takes a bit of effort to get them lined up, but that's part of the pleasure. The black magimarker routes come together, the Gospel according to

Stanfords. Standing back I squint, trying to make out the Tube map in the peripatetic spider trail. It isn't there, of course, Harry Beck's kindly con trick being pulled one last time. The only bit that jumps out is the Hainault loop on the Central Line. Concentrating harder, I decipher the District Line, then the branches of the Northern, the way the Victoria and Piccadilly diverge at Manor House . . . Just enough to be able to tie what I've done to the Tube system itself, the foothold needed to root the project in something pre-existing, give it worth and weight. But sufficiently different to make it an achievement in itself.

Jo comes in, unaware that the maps have gone up. 'Oh my God,' she says.

'That's the whole thing,' I say. 'All four hundred miles. Well, apart from a couple up there near Chesham.'

She ponders the sight.

'What do you think?' I ask.

'It doesn't look that much, to be honest.'

'*What?*'

We step up to the maps. 'Just that little bit,' I say, 'from . . . there to . . . there – that's Oxford Street. Imagine walking the whole length of Oxford Street. Then . . .' I wave my arm to communicate the immensity of the maps.

She nods. 'Actually, yeah, you're right.' Her gaze moves from Upminster over to Heathrow. 'Bloody hell.'

I make an 'mmm' sound, the sound of injured pride being restored.

Jo keeps looking. 'It's incredible how much green there is, isn't it?'

'That's what I thought on the top of Tower 42.'

She moves in closer still, peers at individual places. 'What's Chigwell like?' When I've answered, she says: 'Epping Forest. I've never been. We should go.'

And for a moment or two, it all comes alive. Gone are Jo's 'Tube-nerd' jibes, her good-natured teasing about needing to get out more. (What the hell does she think I've been doing?) Just for a while the project draws her in, the maps cast their spell, and together we wander around London, discussing points on my walk, as well as others that weren't. The beauty of the black lines, I can tell, is getting to her.

Then she looks down, notices the length of skirting board revealed by me moving the sofa. 'While it's like this,' she says, 'could you do some hoovering?'

It's hard to accept that it's all over, that this is the maps' last outing. I'll keep them, of course, in their Jackalesque tube, but all the trouble of shifting the furniture and lining them up means I'm very unlikely to display them like this again. So as an easily accessible substitute, a memento of this time that's meant so much to me, I take a photo of the maps and download it to my computer. The camera's a pretty good one, with a tripod to keep it steady, but even so there's a limit to the detail that stays visible as you zoom in on the picture. The black lines themselves are fine, and you can make out stuff at the level of, say, Regent's Park. Even the boating lake in Regent's Park. But go any further than that and it all gets hazy. You can see where the main roads run, but not their actual names. The closer you look, the less real London seems.

And that strikes me as just how it should be.

# Acknowledgements

Huge thanks to Silvia Crompton for editing this book with not just skill and humour but also a genuine love of London. Her revisions, suggestions and nuggets of historical interest have improved the book massively. Thanks, too, while we're in Random House Towers, to Nigel Wilcockson, Amelia Harvell, Gemma Wain and Simon Wilkes, and to Jason Smith for the jacket and Darren Bennett for the maps.

For his endless store of knowledge about the capital I'm grateful to Kieran Meeke; anyone with an interest in the city should check out his excellent website secret-london.co.uk (While you're surfing, visit londonpeculiar.com for great memorabilia, and timbryars.co.uk for some stunning maps.) Thanks to the staff at the Guildhall Library, Andrew Buckingham at the City of London Corporation, Claire Wylie at the Museum of London, Wendy Neville and Robert Excell at the London Transport Museum, Jenna Oxley at TFL and Michelle Goodman at City of Westminster Archives, all of whom knew their stuff inside out. Also to Barry Le Jeune, Adrian Willats and Harry Parker, suppliers of valuable information.

Many thanks to Richard for Tiggerish research and company in the snow, and to Matt for the Alka-Seltzer. I owe a big debt of gratitude to Stanfords, not just for the maps themselves but for insights into what maps mean to us. Thanks to Hannah and everyone at Premier Inn for roofs over the head, and to Rae, Gill and everyone at ASICS for cushioning beneath the feet. Pia and the staff at Tower 42 were very hospitable in showing me London from 600 feet. I'm also indebted as ever to Charlie Viney, Regius Professor of Spinal Tap.

The biggest thanks, though, go to Jo and, for the first time, Barney. Travel's all very well, but it's what you come home to that counts.

# *Index*